MznLnx

Missing Links Exam Preps

Exam Prep for

FINANCE: Comprehensive Exam Preparation

Cram101, 1st Edition

The MznLnx Exam Prep is your link from the texbook and lecture to your exams.
The MznLnx Exam Preps are unauthorized and comprehensive reviews of your textbooks.

All material provided by MznLnx and Rico Publications (c) 2010
Textbook publishers and textbook authors do not particpate in or contribute to these reviews.

MznLnx

Rico Publications

Exam Prep for FINANCE: Comprehensive Exam Preparation
1st Edition
Cram101

Publisher: Raymond Houge
Assistant Editor: Michael Rouger
Text and Cover Designer: Lisa Buckner
Marketing Manager: Sara Swagger
Project Manager, Editorial Production: Jerry Emerson
Art Director: Vernon Lowerui

Product Manager: Dave Mason
Editorial Asittant: Rachel Guzmanji
Pedagogy: Debra Long
Cover Image: Jim Reed/Getty Images
Text and Cover Printer: City Printing, Inc.
Compositor: Media Mix, Inc.

(c) 2010 Rico Publications
ALL RIGHTS RESERVED. No part of this work covered by the copyright may be reproduced or used in any form or by an means--graphic, electronic, or mechanical, including photocopying, recording, taping, Web distribution, information storage, and retrieval systems, or in any other manner--without the written permission of the publisher.

Printed in the United States
ISBN:

For more information about our products, contact us at:
Dave.Mason@RicoPublications.com

For permission to use material from this text or product, submit a request online to:
Dave.Mason@RicoPublications.com

Contents

CHAPTER 1
Test Preparation Part 1 — 1
CHAPTER 2
Test Preparation Part 2 — 26
CHAPTER 3
Test Preparation Part 3 — 55
CHAPTER 4
Test Preparation Part 4 — 76
CHAPTER 5
Test Preparation Part 5 — 95
CHAPTER 6
Test Preparation Part 6 — 103
CHAPTER 7
Test Preparation Part 7 — 116
CHAPTER 8
Test Preparation Part 8 — 140
CHAPTER 9
Test Preparation Part 9 — 163
CHAPTER 10
Test Preparation Part 10 — 178
CHAPTER 11
Test Preparation Part 11 — 203
ANSWER KEY — 205

TO THE STUDENT

COMPREHENSIVE

The *MznLnx* Exam Prep series is designed to help you pass your exams. Editors at MznLnx review your textbooks and then prepare these practice exams to help you master the textbook material. Unlike study guides, workbooks, and practice tests provided by the texbook publisher and textbook authors, *MznLnx* gives you **all** of the material in each chapter in exam form, not just samples, so you can be sure to nail your exam.

MECHANICAL

The MznLnx Exam Prep series creates exams that will help you learn the subject matter as well as test you on your understanding. Each question is designed to help you master the concept. Just working through the exams, you gain an understanding of the subject--its a simple mechanical process that produces success.

INTEGRATED STUDY GUIDE AND REVIEW

MznLnx is not just a set of exams designed to test you, its also a comprehensive review of the subject content. Each exam question is also a review of the concept, making sure that you will get the answer correct without having to go to other sources of material. You learn as you go! Its the easiest way to pass an exam.

HUMOR

Studying can be tedious and dry. MznLnx's instructional design includes moderate humor within the exam questions on occassion, to break the tedium and revitalize the brain

Chapter 1. Test Preparation Part 1

1. A _____ is a debit card that is not issued by, and not tied to, a particular retail financial institution, such as a bank or credit union. In May 2007, Capital One began a one year _____ experiment. This card is novel in that prior to this launch, a debit card was always tied to a traditional financial institution.

   a. 529 plan
   b. 4-4-5 Calendar
   c. Decoupled debit card
   d. Money illusion

2. _____ is a term coined by the media to refer to the current global financial crisis. It's been used by various news sources, and usually refers to a negative turn in the financial well-being of the world.

   One of the first references to this term was used by the BBC in early August 2008 .

   a. Payback period
   b. Forward price
   c. Dow Jones Indexes
   d. Global Squeeze

3. _____ refers to any one of several methods by which a company, for 'financial accounting' and/or tax purposes, depreciates a fixed asset in such a way that the amount of depreciation taken each year is higher during the earlier years of an asset's life. For financial accounting purposes, _____ is generally used when an asset is expected to be much more productive during its early years, so that depreciation expense will more accurately represent how much of an asset's usefulness is being used up each year. For tax purposes, _____ provides a way of deferring corporate income taxes by reducing taxable income in current years, in exchange for increased taxable income in future years.

   a. A Random Walk Down Wall Street
   b. AAB
   c. ABN Amro
   d. Accelerated depreciation

4. _____ is a term used in accounting, economics and finance to spread the cost of an asset over the span of several years.

   In simple words we can say that _____ is the reduction in the value of an asset due to usage, passage of time, wear and tear, technological outdating or obsolescence, depletion or other such factors.

   In accounting, _____ is a term used to describe any method of attributing the historical or purchase cost of an asset across its useful life, roughly corresponding to normal wear and tear.

   a. Deferred financing costs
   b. Matching principle
   c. Bottom line
   d. Depreciation

5. An _____ is a type of letter of credit that is paid by a time draft authorizing payment on or after a specific date, if the terms of the letter of credit have been complied with. There are two types of _____, confirmed and unconfirmed. Unconfirmed _____ means that the seller takes the risk that payment will not be made, due to any number of contingencies such as shipment nondelivery, confiscation by customs authorities, or any other problems.

   a. Americans for Fairness in Lending
   b. Associate company
   c. Acceptance credit
   d. ASCOT

6. _____ is the provision of resources (such as granting a loan) by one party to another party where that second party does not reimburse the first party immediately, thereby generating a debt, and instead arranges either to repay or return those resources (or material(s) of equal value) at a later date. The first party is called a creditor, also known as a lender, while the second party is called a debtor, also known as a borrower.

Movements of financial capital are normally dependent on either _____ or equity transfers.

a. Warrant
b. Credit
c. Comparable
d. Clearing house

7. The _____ is a liquid index that was created to ensure that there exists credible data on the Nigerian sovereign bond market which will help the investors and other stakeholders to make informed investment decisions while providing a benchmark for measuring the performance of the rapidly developing local currency bond markets. This is particularly important as the bonds market is becoming redefined from a primarily sovereign fiscal deficit process to a sound investment option.

The index was introduced on December 29, 2006 and consists of local currency denominated fixed rate Federal Government of Nigeria Bonds.

a. Access Bank Nigerian Government Bond Index
b. AAB
c. ABN Amro
d. A Random Walk Down Wall Street

8. In finance, a _____ is a debt security, in which the authorized issuer owes the holders a debt and, depending on the terms of the _____, is obliged to pay interest (the coupon) and/or to repay the principal at a later date, termed maturity.

Thus a _____ is a loan: the issuer is the borrower, the _____ holder is the lender, and the coupon is the interest. _____s provide the borrower with external funds to finance long-term investments, or, in the case of government _____s, to finance current expenditure.

a. Puttable bond
b. Convertible bond
c. Catastrophe bonds
d. Bond

9. A _____ is a bond issued by a national government denominated in the country's own currency. Bonds issued by national governments in foreign currencies are normally referred to as sovereign bonds. The first ever _____ was issued by the British government in 1693 to raise money to fund a war against France.

a. Zero-coupon bond
b. Government Bond
c. Municipal bond
d. Collateralized debt obligations

10. _____ is a microfinance organization that offers microloans and other financial services to low- and moderate-income entrepreneurs in the United States who are unable to access bank credit for their small businesses. _____ is part of Accion International, a U.S.-based nonprofit organization operating globally, with the mission of giving people the financial tools they need to work their way out of poverty.

_____'s parent organization, ACCION International, began its work in economic development in 1961.

a. Association of Chartered Certified Accountants
b. International Accounting Standards Committee
c. Accion USA
d. IAESB

Chapter 1. Test Preparation Part 1

11. _____ is a contract law concept about the purchase of the release from a debt obligation. The payment is typically less than what is owed and is not paid by the actual performance of the original obligation. The accord is the agreement to discharge the obligation and the satisfaction is the legal 'consideration' which binds the parties to the agreement.
- a. Accord and satisfaction
- b. Operating ratio
- c. Internal financing
- d. Employee stock option

12. _____, in bookkeeping, refers to assets, liabilities, income, and expenses recorded on individual pages of the so called book of final entry or ledger. Changes in _____ value are made by chronologically posting debit (DR) and credit (CR) entries to its page. Examples of _____s are cash, _____s receivable, mortgages, loans, land and buildings, common stock, sales, services provided, wages, and payroll overhead.
- a. Alpha
- b. Option
- c. Accretion
- d. Account

13. Under United States law, _____ is a statement between a creditor (the person to whom money is owed) and a debtor (the person who owes) that a particular amount is owed to the creditor as of a certain date. Often the _____ is a bill, invoice or a summary of invoices, signed by the customer or sent to the customer who pays part or all of it without protest. An _____ may also be established when the debtor retains the statement of account (for example the bill or invoice) without objecting, for an unreasonable length of time.
- a. Assumption of risk
- b. Economic depreciation
- c. Account stated
- d. Employee Retirement Income Security Act

14. _____ or accounting is the system of recording, verifying, and reporting of the value of assets, liabilities, income, and expenses in the books of account (ledger) to which debit and credit entries (recognizing transactions) are chronologically posted to record changes in value Such financial information is primarily used by lenders, managers, investors, tax authorities and other decision makers to make resource allocation decisions between and within companies, organizations, and public agencies. Accounting has been defined by the AICPA as ' The art of recording, classifying, and summarizing in a significant manner and in terms of money, transactions and events which are, in part at least, of financial character, and interpreting the results thereof.'

Financial accounting is one branch of accounting and historically has involved processes by which financial information about a business is recorded, classified, summarised, interpreted, and communicated; for public companies, this information is generally publicly-accessible.

- a. AAB
- b. Accountancy
- c. A Random Walk Down Wall Street
- d. ABN Amro

15. _____ means regulating, adapting or settling in a variety of contexts:

In commercial law, _____ means the settlement of a loss incurred on insured goods. The calculation of the amounts of compensation to be paid by or to the several interests is a complicated matter. It involves much detail and arithmetic, and requires a full and accurate knowledge of the principles of the subject.

- a. Equity method
- b. Adjustment
- c. Asset recovery
- d. Intelligent investor

16. _____ is a procedure in the United Kingdom whereby a creditor can enforce security against a company's assets in an effort to obtain repayment of the secured debt. It used to be the most popular method of enforcement by secured creditors, but recent legislative reform in many jurisdictions has reduced its significance considerably in certain countries.

_____ differs from simple receivership in that an administrative receiver is appointed over all of the assets and undertaking of the company.

a. AAB
b. ABN Amro
c. A Random Walk Down Wall Street
d. Administrative receivership

17. An _____ is the part of a contractually due sum that is paid in advance for goods or services, while the balance included in the invoice will only follow the delivery. It is called a prepaid expense in accrual accounting.

- Advance against royalties
- Pay or play contract
- Signing bonus
- Prepaid expense

a. AAB
b. ABN Amro
c. A Random Walk Down Wall Street
d. Advance payment

18. _____ is an investment of experience, expertise, social capital, and public authority into a company in return for some form of equity in the company. The first known use of the term is in a blog post by Stowe Boyd on February 20, 2006.

a. Intelligent investor
b. Adjustment
c. Inflation derivatives
d. Advisory capital

19. _____ is a risk-adjusted measure of the so-called active return on an investment. It is the return in excess of the compensation for the risk borne, and thus commonly used to assess active managers' performances. Often, the return of a benchmark is subtracted in order to consider relative performance, which yields Jensen's _____.

a. Annuity
b. Amortization
c. Option
d. Alpha

20. An _____ is a technology solution used by quantitative analysts (quants) to develop financial models and create consistent alpha i.e., the process of alpha generation refers to generating excess return. _____s support quants in the creation of efficient and productive alpha generating processes.

_____s are used by quantitative analysts to locate excess return in the capital market.

a. Alpha generation platform
b. Initial margin
c. Efficient-market hypothesis
d. Arbitrage

21. An _____ is the combination of a reverse merger with a simultaneous Private Investment of Public Equity (PIPE.) It allows companies an alternative to the IPO as a means of going public while raising capital.

There are two parts that comprise an _____; the reverse merger and the PIPE.

a. AAB
b. ABN Amro
c. Alternative Public Offering
d. A Random Walk Down Wall Street

22. _____, is when a company issues common stock or shares to the public for the first time. They are often issued by smaller, younger companies seeking capital to expand, but can also be done by large privately-owned companies looking to become publicly traded.

In an _____ the issuer may obtain the assistance of an underwriting firm, which helps it determine what type of security to issue (common or preferred), best offering price and time to bring it to market.

a. Insolvency
b. Asian Financial Crisis
c. Interest
d. Initial public offering

23. An _____ is an asset that is typically not found in an investment portfolio. Examples include rare coins and stamps, artwork, sports cards, and hedge funds. Due to the nature of these assets, an accurate valuation is sometimes difficult to accomplish.

a. Alternative asset
b. Americans for Fairness in Lending
c. Amortising swap
d. Advisory capital

24. In business and accounting, _____s are everything of value that is owned by a person or company. The balance sheet of a firm records the monetary value of the _____s owned by the firm. The two major _____ classes are tangible _____s and intangible _____s.

a. EBITDA
b. Income
c. Accounts payable
d. Asset

25. _____ is an equity trading facility created in the United States by FINRA, a self-regulatory organization (SRO.) The _____ is an alternative to the exchange for publishing quotations and for comparing and reporting trades. This differs from a trading facility with execution capabilities (stock exchange) in that the exchange would simply send back to the owner of the displayed order a notice of execution.

a. Asset-backed commercial paper
b. Asset-liability mismatch
c. Equity method
d. Alternative display facility

26. _____ is a non-profit organization designed to draw national attention to the unregulated lending industry in America. _____'s ultimate goal is government regulation of the lending industry to protect American consumers from financial products which deplete assets and can lead to bankruptcy and foreclosure.

_____ is an umbrella organization for groups working on lending and asset-building issues.

a. ASCOT
b. Americans for Fairness in Lending
c. Experimental finance
d. Asset-liability mismatch

27. _____ is usually an interest rate swap in which the notional principal for the interest payments declines during the life of the swap, perhaps at a rate tied to the prepayment of a mortgage or to an interest rate benchmark such as the London interbank offer rate (Libor.) If the swap allows for uncertain contingent ups and downs in the notional principal, it is called a 'roller-coaster swap'. The opposite of the accreting swap.

a. Ownership equity
b. Experimental finance
c. Asset-liability mismatch
d. Amortising swap

28. In finance, a _____ is a derivative in which two counterparties agree to exchange one stream of cash flows against another stream. These streams are called the legs of the _____.

The cash flows are calculated over a notional principal amount, which is usually not exchanged between counterparties.

a. Local volatility
b. Volatility arbitrage
c. Volatility swap
d. Swap

29. In banking and finance, an _____ is a loan where the principal of the loan is paid down over the life of the loan, according to some amortization schedule, typically through equal payments.

Similarly, an amortizing bond is a bond that repays part of the principal (face value) along with the coupon payments. Compare with a sinking fund, which amortizes the total debt outstanding by repurchasing some bonds.

a. Ownership equity
b. Amortizing loan
c. Annuity
d. Advisory capital

30. An _____ can be defined as a contract which provides an income stream in return for an initial payment.

An immediate _____ is an _____ for which the time between the contract date and the date of the first payment is not longer than the time interval between payments. A common use for an immediate _____ is to provide a pension to a retired person or persons.

a. Annuity
b. Intrinsic value
c. AT'T Inc.
d. Amortization

31. An _____ is an option on a convertible bond used to separate the cash flows of the underlying bond from the equity option embedded in the convert. Buyers of _____ s include fixed income portfolio managers and other investors that want exposure to the rate and credit risks of the convert issuer; cashflows from the convert would be passed through to these buyers. Sellers of _____ s typically include trading desks that want to retain exposure to the potentially lucrative equity optionality.

a. Earnings growth
b. Adjustment
c. Ascot
d. Alternative display facility

32. In finance, an _____ occurs when the financial terms of the assets and liabilities do not correspond. For example, a bank that chose to borrow entirely in U.S. dollars and lend in Russian rubles would have a significant (currency) mismatch: if the value of the ruble were to fall dramatically, the bank would lose money. In extreme cases, such movements in the value of the assets and liabilities could lead to bankruptcy, liquidity problems and wealth transfer.

a. Inflation derivatives
b. ASCOT
c. Intelligent investor
d. Asset-liability mismatch

33. In the most general sense, a _____ is anything that is a hindrance, or puts individuals at a disadvantage.

Chapter 1. Test Preparation Part 1 7

Before we discuss the financial terms, we should note that a _____ can also have a much more important slang meaning.

This is best described in an example.

a. Covenant
b. Limited liability
c. Liability
d. McFadden Act

34. _____ is the process of maximizing the value of unused or end of life assets through effective reuse or divestment. Both large and small organizations practice _____ at some level with the end goal of obtaining the greatest possible return from the asset. While sometimes referred to in the context of a company that is being liquidated, _____ is also used to describe the process of liquidating excess inventory of healthy companies, refurbished items and equipment returned at the end of a lease.

a. Equity in income of affiliates
b. Asset-liability mismatch
c. Asset-backed commercial paper
d. Asset recovery

35. _____ is a form of commercial paper that is collateralised by other financial assets. ABCPs are typically short-term investments that mature between 90 and 180 days and are typically issued by a bank or other financial institution. They are designed to be used for short-term financing needs.

a. Amortizing loan
b. Earmark
c. Asset-backed commercial paper
d. Asset-liability mismatch

36. In the global money market, _____ is an unsecured promissory note with a fixed maturity of one to 270 days. _____ is a money-market security issued (sold) by large banks and corporations to get money to meet short term debt obligations (for example, payroll), and is only backed by an issuing bank or corporation's promise to pay the face amount on the maturity date specified on the note. Since it is not backed by collateral, only firms with excellent credit ratings from a recognized rating agency will be able to sell their _____ at a reasonable price.

a. Book building
b. Trade-off theory
c. Financial distress
d. Commercial paper

37. An _____ is a loan, often for a short term, secured by a company's assets. Real estate, A/R, inventory, and equipment are typical assets used to back the loan. The loan may be backed by a single category of assets or some combination of assets, for instance, a combination of A/R and equipment.

a. Amortizing loan
b. ASCOT
c. External financing
d. Asset-based loan

38. An _____ in accounting and business valuation is a company in which another company owns a significant portion of voting shares, usually 20-50%. In this case, an owner does not consolidate the associate's financial statements. Ownership of over 50% creates a subsidiary, with its financial statements being consolidated into the parent's books.

a. Asset recovery
b. Associate company
c. Amortizing loan
d. Adjustment

39. The _____ is a British chartered accountancy body with a global presence that offers the Chartered Certified Accountant (Designatory letters ACCA or FCCA) qualification worldwide. It is one of the world's largest and fastest-growing accountancy bodies with 122,426 members and 325,606 affiliates and students in 170 countries. The Institute's headquarters are in London with the principal administrative office being based in Glasgow.

   a. International Association of Business Communicators
   b. Institute of Financial Accountants
   c. Association of Chartered Certified Accountants
   d. Accion USA

40. _____ (Designatory letters A_____ or F_____) is a British qualified accountant designation awarded by the Association of _____s (A_____)

The term _____ was introduced in 1996. Prior to that date, A_____ members were known as Certified Accountant. It is still permissible for an A_____ member to use this term. Fellow members of A_____ use the designatory letters F_____ in place of A_____.

   a. Chartered Certified Accountant
   b. Certified General Accountant
   c. Chartered Accountant
   d. Certified Public Accountant

41. An _____ typically refers to a debt instrument (corporate or municipal bonds) with a long-term nominal maturity for which the interest rate is regularly reset through a dutch auction. Since February 2008, most such auctions have failed, and the auction market has been frozen.

The first _____ for the tax-exempt market was introduced by Goldman Sachs in 1988.

   a. Associate company
   b. Alternative display facility
   c. Equity method
   d. Auction rate security

42. A _____ is a fungible, negotiable instrument representing financial value. They are broadly categorized into debt securities (such as banknotes, bonds and debentures), and equity securities; e.g., common stocks. The company or other entity issuing the _____ is called the issuer.

   a. Securities lending
   b. Security
   c. Book entry
   d. Tracking stock

43. The _____ of a company (sometimes referred to as the authorised share capital or the nominal capital, particularly in the United States) is the maximum amount of share capital that the company is authorised by its constitutional documents to issue to shareholders. Part of the _____ can (and frequently does) remain unissued.

The part of the _____ which has been issued to shareholders is referred to as the issued share capital of the company.

   a. Eurobond
   b. Interest rate option
   c. Education production function
   d. Authorised capital

44. _____ is an emerging energy market advisor and fund manager, which operates the ALTEX Indices, including the ALTEXAustralia and ALTEXGlobal, and the Climate Impact Indices. These indices track the financial performance of sectors including low-emission utilities, renewables, uranium, natural gas, environmental technology and hydrogen, as well as monitoring the financial affect of climate change on investment markets.

_____ was founded in April 2006 by the Managing Directors, Mr. Jeremy Baker and Dr. Ross Paul.

a. FIDC
b. Consumer debt
c. Decision process tool
d. Bakers Investment Group

45. _____ was the name given by the Italian press to the finance and banking scandals that played out in the public eye in Italy between July 2005 and January 2006. The main story was that the Italian Banca Popolare Italiana (BPI), in competing with Dutch ABN AMRO for control of Banca Antoniana Popolare Veneta (known as Antonveneta), was given an unfair advantage by Banca d'Italia Governor Antonio Fazio (Banca d'Italia is Italy's central bank.) Fazio was forced to resign, and BPI Managing Director Gianpiero Fiorani was accused of using several illegal tactics and was arrested on a number of charges in connection with the attempted takeover.

a. Time deposit
b. Basel Accord
c. Credit bureau
d. Bancopoli

46. A _____ is the life office of a bank offering life assurance and pensions products to retail customers.

a. Cash equivalents
b. Prepayment
c. Debt cash flow
d. Bankassurer

47. _____ is a legally declared inability or impairment of ability of an individual or organization to pay their creditors. Creditors may file a _____ petition against a debtor ('involuntary _____') in an effort to recoup a portion of what they are owed or initiate a restructuring. In the majority of cases, however, _____ is initiated by the debtor (a 'voluntary _____' that is filed by the bankrupt individual or organization.)

a. Debt settlement
b. 4-4-5 Calendar
c. 529 plan
d. Bankruptcy

48. A company within a corporate group is said to be _____ when the insolvency of that company does not affect any other company in the group, particularly any holding company or subsidiary company of the _____ vehicle. If the company goes into bankruptcy, no other company in the same group would be affected.

In practice, due to the concept of limited liability, most companies in developed legal systems will be de facto _____ from other members of the group (except in limited circumstances where creditors are permitted to pierce the corporate veil.)

a. FIDC
b. Payback period
c. Bankruptcy remote
d. Moneylender

49. _____ is an ongoing series of unconferences about innovation in the financial world. This subset of the software-oriented BarCamp grew out of BarCampParis4, on September 16, 2006 in Paris at Mandriva. The first _____ in North America was held at the office of Evri.com in Seattle in July 2007 and was spearheaded by Jesse Robbins at the request of Frederic Baud, who was instrumental in the creation of the first _____ in Paris.

a. Risk-return spectrum
c. Financial Gerontology
b. Shares authorized
d. Barcampbank

50. In the context of financial futures, _____ can be defined as the spot price minus the futures price. There will be a different basis for each delivery month for each contract. In a normal market, basis will be negative.
- a. Basis of futures
- b. Municipal Okrug #7
- c. Controlled foreign corporations
- d. Legal and regulatory risk

51. A _____ is a type of stock market strategy, where a trader (or group of traders) attempts to force down the price of a stock to cover a short position. This can be done by spreading negative rumors about the target firm, which puts downward pressure on the share price. This may be a form of securities fraud.
- a. Risk-return spectrum
- b. Senior stretch loan
- c. Pattern day trader
- d. Bear raid

52. _____ and behavioral finance are closely related fields that have evolved to be a separate branch of economic and financial analysis which applies scientific research on human and social, cognitive and emotional factors to better understand economic decisions by, say, consumers, borrowers, investors, and how they affect market prices, returns and the allocation of resources.

The field is primarily concerned with the bounds of rationality (selfishness, self-control) of economic agents. Behavioral models typically integrate insights from psychology with neo-classical economic theory.

- a. Deflation
- b. Human capital
- c. Behavioral economics
- d. Recession

53. A _____ is a payment plan where the borrower makes payments toward his principal and interest every two weeks instead of once monthly. The Biweekly payment is exactly one half of the amount a monthly payment would be. The savings a _____ payment plan creates are often astounding, though they can be misleading.
- a. Duration gap
- b. Consumer basket
- c. Biweekly Mortgage
- d. Commuted cash value

54. The _____ (BSTDB) is an international financial institution that supports economic development and regional cooperation by providing trade and project financing, guarantees, and equity for development projects supporting both public and private enterprises in its member countries. Objectives of the bank include promoting regional trade links, cross country projects, foreign direct investment, supporting activities that contribute to sustainable development, with an emphasis on the generation of employment in the member countries, ensuring that each operation is economically and financially sound and contributes to the development of a market orientation. The organization has an authorized capital of $1.325 billion.
- a. Shelf registration
- b. 4-4-5 Calendar
- c. Black Sea Trade and Development Bank
- d. Bought deal

55. _____ of a financial instrument such as a check is only a signature, not indicating the payee. The effect of this is that it is payable only to the bearer.

It is 'an endorsement consisting of nothing but a signature and allowing any party in possession of the endorsed item to execute a claim.'

A _____ is commonly known and accepted in the legal and business worlds.

a. Cramdown
c. Consumer debt
b. Day trading
d. Blank endorsement

56. In investment, the _____ assesses the credit worthiness of a corporation's debt issues. It is analogous to credit ratings for individuals and countries. The credit rating is a financial indicator to potential investors of debt securities such as bonds.
a. Biweekly Mortgage
c. Bond credit rating
b. Reinvestment risk
d. Floating charge

57. A _____ assesses the credit worthiness of an individual, corporation, or even a country. _____s are calculated from financial history and current assets and liabilities. Typically, a _____ tells a lender or investor the probability of the subject being able to pay back a loan.
a. Credit report monitoring
c. Credit cycle
b. Debenture
d. Credit rating

58. A _____ is a collective investment scheme that invests in bonds and other debt securities. _____s yield monthly dividends that include interest payments on the fund's underlying securities plus any capital appreciation in the prices of the portfolio's bonds. _____s tend to pay higher dividends than CDs and money market accounts, and they generally pay out dividends more frequently and regularly than individual bonds.
a. Premium bond
c. Gilts
b. Private activity bond
d. Bond fund

59. The _____ is a financial market where participants buy and sell debt securities, usually in the form of bonds. As of 2006, the size of the international _____ is an estimated $45 trillion, of which the size of the outstanding U.S. _____ debt was $25.2 trillion.

Nearly all of the $923 billion average daily trading volume in the U.S. _____ takes place between broker-dealers and large institutions in a decentralized, over-the-counter market.

a. 529 plan
c. Bond market
b. 4-4-5 Calendar
d. Fixed income

60. A _____ is a listing of bonds or fixed income instruments and a statistic reflecting the composite value of its components. It is used as a tool to represent the characteristics of its component fixed income instruments. They differ from stock market indices in their complexity.
a. 529 plan
c. 4-4-5 Calendar
b. 7-Eleven
d. Bond market index

61. In finance, a _____ is an OTC-traded financial instrument that facilitates an option to buy or sell a particular bond at a certain date for a particular price. It is similar to a stock option with the difference that the underlying asset is a bond. _____s can be valued using the Black model.

a. Dirty price
c. Bond option
b. Nominal yield
d. Municipal bond

62. An _____ is a contract written by a seller that conveys to the buyer the right -- but not the obligation -- to buy (in the case of a call _____) or to sell (in the case of a put _____) a particular asset, such as a piece of property such as, among others, a futures contract. In return for granting the _____, the seller collects a payment (the premium) from the buyer.

For example, buying a call _____ provides the right to buy a specified quantity of a security at a set strike price at some time on or before expiration, while buying a put _____ provides the right to sell.

a. Amortization
c. AT'T Mobility LLC
b. Annuity
d. Option

63. _____ is the process of determining the fair price of a bond. As with any security or capital investment, the fair value of a bond is the present value of the stream of cash flows it is expected to generate. Hence, the price or value of a bond is determined by discounting the bond's expected cash flows to the present using the appropriate discount rate.
a. Catastrophe bonds
c. Collateralized debt obligations
b. Bond fund
d. Bond valuation

64. In finance, _____ is the process of estimating the potential market value of a financial asset or liability. they can be done on assets (for example, investments in marketable securities such as stocks, options, business enterprises, or intangible assets such as patents and trademarks) or on liabilities (e.g., Bonds issued by a company.) _____s are required in many contexts including investment analysis, capital budgeting, merger and acquisition transactions, financial reporting, taxable events to determine the proper tax liability, and in litigation.
a. Procter ' Gamble
c. Valuation
b. Share
d. Margin

65. The term _____ means an extra dividend paid to shareholders in a joint stock company from surplus profits in the form of a share. When a company has accumulated a large fund out of profits - much beyond its needs, the directors may decide to distribute a part of it amongst the shareholders in the form of bonus. Bonus can be paid either in cash or in the form of shares.
a. Cash on delivery
c. Revaluation
b. January effect
d. Bonus share

66. In business and finance, a _____ (also referred to as equity _____) of stock means a _____ of ownership in a corporation (company.) In the plural, stocks is often used as a synonym for _____s especially in the United States, but it is less commonly used that way outside of North America.

In the United Kingdom, South Africa, and Australia, stock can also refer to completely different financial instruments such as government bonds or, less commonly, to all kinds of marketable securities.

a. Share
c. Bucket shop
b. Procter ' Gamble
d. Margin

67. When a joint stock company declares dividends or bonus issues, there has to be a cut-off date for such benefits to be transferred to the shareholders. This date is termed as '_____' date or 'Record Date'. It is the date after which the company will not handle any transfer of shares requests until the benefits are transferred. Only shareholders marked in the company's register at the _____ Date or the Record Date would be entitled to receive these benefits. If a company announces _____ as 1 January, shareholders who as on that day own the stock will be entitled to the dividend/bonus/split benefit.

   a. Financial Gerontology
   b. Cross-border leasing
   c. Book closure
   d. Certified International Investment Analyst

68. _____ is a term used to cover different methods for avoiding using the financial resources of external investors. Bootstrapping can be defined as 'a collection of methods used to minimize the amount of outside debt and equity financing needed from banks and investors' (Ebben and Johnsen, 2006:853.) The use of private credit cards is the most known form of bootstrapping, but a wide variety of methods are available for entrepreneurs.

   a. Financial endowment
   b. Pension fund
   c. Financial bootstrapping
   d. Leveraged buyout

69. _____ or financing is to provide capital (funds), which means money for a project, a person, a business or any other private or public institutions.

   Those funds can be allocated for either short term or long term purposes. The health fund is a new way of _____ private healthcare centers.

   a. Product life cycle
   b. Proxy fight
   c. Funding
   d. Synthetic CDO

70. _____ is a method for constructing a (zero-coupon) fixed-income yield curve from the prices of a set of coupon-bearing products by forward substitution.

   Using these zero-coupon products it becomes possible to derive par swap rates (forward and spot) for all maturities by making a few assumptions (including linear interpolation.) The term structure of spot returns is recovered from the bond yields by solving for them recursively, this iterative process is called the BootStrap Method.

   a. Bootstrapping
   b. Probability of default
   c. Reserve requirement
   d. Bullet loan

71. _____ is a form of project financing, wherein a private entity receives a concession from the private or public sector to finance, design, construct, and operate a facility for a specified period, often as long as 20 or 30 years. After the concession period ends, ownership is transferred back to the granting entity.

   During the concession the project proponent is allowed to charge the users of the facility appropriate tolls, fees, rentals, and charges stated in the concession contract.

   a. 7-Eleven
   b. 529 plan
   c. 4-4-5 Calendar
   d. Build-Operate-Transfer

72. In banking and finance, a _____ is a loan where a payment of the entire principal of the loan, and sometimes the principal and interest, is due at the end of the loan term. Likewise for bullet bond. A _____ can be a mortgage, bond, note or any other type of credit.
    a. Bear raid
    b. Bankruptcy remote
    c. Modern portfolio theory
    d. Bullet loan

73. _____ is mathematics used by commercial enterprises to record and manage business operations. Mathematics typically used in commerce includes elementary arithmetic, such as fractions, decimals, and percentages, elementary algebra, statistics and probability. Business management can be made more effective in some cases by use of more advanced mathematics such as calculus, matrix algebra and linear programming.
    a. 7-Eleven
    b. 529 plan
    c. 4-4-5 Calendar
    d. Business mathematics

74. _____ is a process and a set of procedures used to estimate the economic value of an owner's interest in a business. Valuation is used by financial market participants to determine the price they are willing to pay or receive to consummate a sale of a business. In addition to estimating the selling price of a business, the same valuation tools are often used by business appraisers to resolve disputes related to estate and gift taxation, divorce litigation, allocate business purchase price among business assets, establish a formula for estimating the value of partners' ownership interest for buy-sell agreements, and many other business and legal purposes.
    a. Family and Medical Leave Act
    b. Business valuation
    c. Covenant
    d. Federal Deposit Insurance Corporation Improvement Act

75. _____ are codes of practice that are used in business valuation. Each of the three major United States valuation societies -- the American Society of Appraisers (ASA), the Institute of Business Appraisers (IBA), and the National Association of Certified Valuation Analysts (NACVA) -- has its own set of _____, which it requires all of its accredited members to adhere to. The ASA's standards are published, for example, as the ASA _____.
    a. Selling short
    b. The Security Industry Association
    c. Business valuation standards
    d. Taylor series

76. The _____ is headquartered in the United States of America at Charlottesville, Virginia with offices in Hong Kong and London. Formerly known as the Association for Investment Management and Research (AIMR), the Institute awards the Chartered Financial Analyst (CFA) designation.

In 1925, an organization of investment analysts founded the Investment Analyst Society of Chicago.

    a. Payback period
    b. Credit card balance transfer
    c. Financial rand
    d. CFA Institute

77. _____ are a type of bond commonly issued in American security markets. They are a type of mortgage-backed security backed by mortgages on commercial rather than residential real estate. CMBS issues are usually structured as multiple tranches, similar to CMOs, rather than typical residential 'passthroughs.'

Many American CMBSs carry less prepayment risk than other MBS types, thanks to the structure of commercial mortgages.

a. Stop order
b. Contract for difference
c. Stock market index
d. Commercial mortgage-backed securities

78. _____ is early repayment of a loan by a borrower.

In the case of a mortgage-backed security (MBS), _____ is perceived as a risk, because mortgage debts are often paid off early in order to incur lower total interest payments through cheaper refinancing. The new financing may be cheaper because the borrower's credit rating has improved or because interest rates are lower, but in either case, the payments that would have been made to the MBS investor would be above market rates.

a. Bankruptcy remote
b. Prepayment
c. Disposal tax effect
d. Retention ratio

79. The _____ Ltd. (CDS Limited) is the holding company for three operating subsidiaries: CDS Clearing and Depository Services Inc. CDS INC. CDS Innovations Inc.

CDS Clearing and Depository Services Inc.

a. 7-Eleven
b. Canadian Depository for Securities
c. 4-4-5 Calendar
d. 529 plan

80. _____ is a measure of the ratio between the net operating income produced by an asset (usually real estate) and its capital cost (the original price paid to buy the asset) or alternatively its current market value. The rate is calculated in a simple fashion as follows:

- annual net operating income / cost (or value) = _____

For example, if a building is purchased for $1,000,000 sale price and it produces $100,000 in positive net operating income (the amount left over after fixed costs and variable costs are subtracted from gross lease income) during one year, then:

- $100,000 / $1,000,000 = 0.10 = 10\%$

The asset's _____ is ten percent.

_____s are an indirect measure of how fast an investment will pay for itself. In the example above, the purchased building will be fully capitalized (pay for itself) after ten years (100% divided by 10%.)

a. Cash concentration
b. Conditional prepayment rate
c. Profitability index
d. Capitalization rate

81. The _____ of an asset is the return obtained from holding it (if positive), or the cost of holding it (if negative)

For instance, commodities are usually negative _____ assets, as they incur storage costs, but in some circumstances, commodities can be positive _____ assets as the market is willing to pay a premium for availability.

This can also refer to a trade with more than one leg, where you earn the spread between borrowing a low _____ asset and lending a high _____ one.

   a. Bankruptcy remote   b. Financial assistance
   c. Carry   d. Cramdown

82. A _____ is the cost of storing a physical commodity, such as grain or metals, over a period of time. The _____ includes insurance, storage and interest on the invested funds as well as other incidental costs. In interest rate futures markets, it refers to the differential between the yield on a cash instrument and the cost of the funds necessary to buy the instrument.
   a. Carrying charge   b. Coupon leverage
   c. Securities offering   d. Commercial finance

83. The _____ are quarterly nominal house price indices for the United States.

The indices are calculated from data on repeat sales of single family homes, an approach, developed by economists Chip Case, Robert Shiller and Allan Weiss. The indices are normalized to have a value of 100 in the first quarter of 2000.

   a. Case-Shiller Home Price Indices   b. Mitigating Control
   c. Flow to Equity-Approach   d. The Goodyear Tire ' Rubber Company

84. Cash and _____ are the most liquid assets found within the asset portion of a company's balance sheet. _____ are assets that are readily convertible into cash, such as money market holdings, short-term government bonds or Treasury bills, marketable securities and commercial paper. _____ are distinguished from other investments through their short-term existence; they mature within 3 months whereas short-term investments are 12 months or less, and long-term investments are any investments that mature in excess of 12 months.
   a. Par value   b. Secured debt
   c. Tick size   d. Cash equivalents

85. _____ is the balance of the amounts of cash being received and paid by a business during a defined period of time, sometimes tied to a specific project. Measurement of _____ can be used

- to evaluate the state or performance of a business or project.
- to determine problems with liquidity. Being profitable does not necessarily mean being liquid. A company can fail because of a shortage of cash, even while profitable.
- to generate project rate of returns. The time of _____s into and out of projects are used as inputs to financial models such as internal rate of return, and net present value.
- to examine income or growth of a business when it is believed that accrual accounting concepts do not represent economic realities. Alternately, _____ can be used to 'validate' the net income generated by accrual accounting.

_____ as a generic term may be used differently depending on context, and certain _____ definitions may be adapted by analysts and users for their own uses. Common terms include operating _____ and free _____.

_____s can be classified into:

1. Operational _____s: Cash received or expended as a result of the company's core business activities.
2. Investment _____s: Cash received or expended through capital expenditure, investments or acquisitions.
3. Financing _____s: Cash received or expended as a result of financial activities, such as interests and dividends.

All three together - the net _____ - are necessary to reconcile the beginning cash balance to the ending cash balance. Loan draw downs or equity injections, that is just shifting of capital but no expenditure as such, are not considered in the net _____.

a. Cash flow
b. Corporate finance
c. Shareholder value
d. Real option

86. _____ is a sort of debt financing, in which a bank lends funds against cash flows that a borrowing company generates. To secure repayment, the bank covenants a borrower on such levels and ratios as enterprise value, EBITDA, total interest coverage ratio, Total debt/EBITDA, and so on. In contrast, an asset-based loan is lent against company's assets.
a. Death spiral financing
b. Cash flow loan
c. Treynor ratio
d. Specific risk

87. A _____ is an organization holding securities either in certificated or uncertificated (dematerialized) form, to enable book entry transfer of securities. In some cases these organizations also carry out centralized comparison, and transaction processing such as clearing and settlement of securities. The physical securities may be immobilised by the depository, or securities may be dematerialised (so that they exist only as electronic records.)
a. Central Securities Depository
b. Market price
c. Market portfolio
d. Cost of carry

88. _____. is a professional acceditation in the field of investment performance analysis. It is offered by the CIPM Association, a body associated with the CFA Institute.
a. Security market line
b. Portable alpha
c. Late trading
d. Certificate in Investment Performance Measurement

89. _____ is the return on an investment portfolio. The investment portfolio can contain a single asset or multiple assets. The _____ is measured over a specific period of time and in a specific currency.
a. Alternative investment
b. Asset allocation
c. Investment decisions
d. Investment Performance

90. _____ is the process whereby an organization establishes the parameters within which programs, investments, and acquisitions are reaching the desired results. Performance Reference Model of the Federal Enterprise Architecture, 2005.

This process of measuring performance ofter requires the use of statistical evidence to determine progress toward specific defined organizational objectives.

There are many types of measurements.

a. Decentralization
b. Cash cow
c. Corporate Transparency
d. Performance Measurement

91. _____ is a designation offered by the Association of _____s (A_____) to financial professionals; candidates may be financial analysts, portfolio managers and / or investment advisors. The A_____ is recognised and promoted by both ASAF and EFFAS representing financial analyst federations in Asia and Europe.

The uniqueness of the _____ designation is that it tests members both at the local level from the countries they are appearing and having cleared those country specific exams can only appear for A_____ common international level exams.

a. Certified International Investment Analyst
b. Restructuring
c. Cost of living
d. Cross-border leasing

92. A _____, securities analyst, research analyst, equity analyst, or investment analyst is a person who performs financial analysis for external or internal clients as a core part of the job.

An analyst studies companies and other entities to arrive at the estimate of their financial value. It is normally done by analyzing financial reports, aided by follow-up interviews with company representatives and industry experts.

a. Stockbroker
b. Portfolio manager
c. Purchasing manager
d. Financial analyst

93. _____ is a term used to describe knowledge-based products or services that improve operational performance, productivity inputs, energy consumption, waste regulatory and industry interest in clean forms of energy generation--specifically, perhaps, the rise in awareness of global warming and the impact on the natural environment from the burning of fossil fuels. The term _____ is often associated with venture capital funds.

a. 529 plan
b. 4-4-5 Calendar
c. Cleantech
d. 7-Eleven

94. A _____ is a contractual provision in a loan agreement which provides that all loans must be repaid within a specified period, after which no further loans will be made available to the debtor for a specified 'cleanup' period.

It may also refer to revolving line of credit. Lender may require a cleanup period annually, like borrower may have to pay down the balance to zero for 30 days.

a. Market neutral
b. Package loan
c. Holding period return
d. Cleanup clause

95. _____s (_____s) are a form of securitization where payments from multiple middle sized and large business loans are pooled together and passed on to different classes of owners in various tranches.

Each class of owner may receive larger payments in exchange for being the first in line to lose money if the businesses fail to repay the loans. The actual loans used are generally multi-million dollar loans known as syndicated loans, usually originally lent by a bank with the intention of the loans being immediately paid off by the _____ owners.

   a. Fiscal sponsorship
   c. Financial rand
   b. Tick size
   d. Collateralized loan obligation

96. In the United States, _____ is the function of offering loans to businesses. Commercial financing is generally offered by a bank or other lender. Most commercial banks offer commercial financing, and the loans are either secured by business assets or alternatively can be unsecured, where the lender relies of the cash flows of the business to repay the facility.
   a. Commercial finance
   c. Volatility clustering
   b. Normative economics
   d. Bonus share

97. A _____ is a loan made using real estate as collateral to secure repayment.

A _____ is similar to a residential mortgage, except the collateral is a commercial building or other business real estate, not residential property.

In addition, _____s are typically taken on by businesses instead of individual borrowers.

   a. Shared appreciation mortgage
   c. Chain of Blame
   b. Fixed rate mortgage
   d. Commercial mortgage

98. _____ refers to the present value of an annuity after annuitization. This differs from typical cash value; if a _____ is stipulated in an annuity contract, this allows the owner of the annuity to cash the contract in, even after annuitization. .
   a. FIDC
   c. Bear raid
   b. Bond credit rating
   d. Commuted cash value

99. _____ (or the law of business associations) is the field of law concerning business and other organizations. This includes corporations, partnerships and other associations which usually carry on some form of economic or charitable activity. The most prominent kind of company, usually referred to as a 'corporation', is a 'juristic person', i.e. it has separate legal personality, and those who invest money into the business have limited liability for any losses the company makes, governed by corporate law.
   a. Companies law
   c. Federal Trade Commission Act
   b. Business valuation
   d. Legal tender

100. _____ is an equity making up a substantial part (usually, more than 30%) of the investor's portfolio. The major risk associated with such a portfolio is a lack of diversification; _____ makes a large portion of the investor's wealth dependent on the performance of one particular stock. The reasons for keeping a _____ may be restrictions for sale , emotional attachment, donation, inheritance, stock options, and the selling of businesses.

a. Forecast period
b. Consumer debt
c. Concentrated stock
d. Credit card balance transfer

101. _____ is the act of consigning, which is placing a person or thing in the hand of another, but retaining ownership until the goods are sold or person is transferred. This may be done for shipping, transfer of prisoners, or for sale in a store (i.e. a _____ shop.)

Features of _____ are as follows: 1)The Relation between the two parties is that of consignor and consignee and not that of buyer and seller 2)The consignor is entitled to receive all the expenses in connection with _____ 3)The consignee is not responsible for damage of goods during transport or any other procedure.

a. 4-4-5 Calendar
b. 7-Eleven
c. 529 plan
d. Consignment

102. _____ is stock legally owned by one party, but held by another.

Ownership of _____ is passed only when the stock is used (issued.) Unused stock in a warehouse may be returned to the manufacturer.

a. Consignment stock
b. Covestor
c. Blank endorsement
d. Concentrated stock

103. In the broadest sense of the term, a _____ is any loan where the proceeds are used to finance construction of some kind. In the United States Financial Services industry however, the term is used to describe a genre of loans designed for construction and containing features such as interest reserves, where repayment ability may be based on something that can only occour when the project is built. Thus the defining features of these loans are special monitoring and guidelines above normal loan guidelines to ensure that the project is completed so that repayment can begin to take place.

a. Conforming loan
b. Construction loan
c. Blanket mortgage
d. HELOC

104. The basket of consumer goods or _____ is the market basket intended for tracking the prices of consumer goods and services, i.e., it is a sample of goods and services, offered at the consumer market. The _____ is the base for the definition of the Consumer Price Index (CPI.)

The list used for such an analysis would contain a number of the most commonly bought food and household items.

a. Money market
b. Covestor
c. Consumer basket
d. Modern portfolio theory

105. _____ is consumer credit which is outstanding. In macroeconomic terms, it is debt which is used to fund consumption rather than investment.

Some consider all debt incurred for anything else other than investments unwise or detrimental to the economy, while others believe that consumer credit is beneficial to the economy.

a. Consumer debt
b. Reinvestment risk
c. Retention ratio
d. Foreign exchange hedge

106. _____ is that which is owed; usually referencing assets owed, but the term can cover other obligations. In the case of assets, _____ is a means of using future purchasing power in the present before a summation has been earned. Some companies and corporations use _____ as a part of their overall corporate finance strategy.
   a. Credit cycle
   b. Partial Payment
   c. Cross-collateralization
   d. Debt

107. _____ refers to making a wide range of secured and unsecured loans to consumers for consumable items such as a car, boat, manufactured home, home equity loan, home equity line of credit, signature loan, signature line of credit, recreational vehicle, or share or certificate of deposit or Stocks and Mutual Funds secured loans.

_____ does not include mortgage loans, typically used for home purchases, which follow some different regulations than consumer loans. Also, consumer loans are different from commercial loans, which can be calculated on a daily basis, rather than 12 monthly payments, and include interest for leap day, such as in Actual/366 loan calculations.

   a. Sogflation
   b. Coupon leverage
   c. Primary market
   d. Consumer lending

108. In finance, a _____ is one who attempts to profit by investing in a manner that differs from the conventional wisdom, when the consensus opinion appears to be wrong.

A _____ believes that certain crowd behavior among investors can lead to exploitable mispricings in securities markets. For example, widespread pessimism about a stock can drive a price so low that it overstates the company's risks, and understates its prospects for returning to profitability.

   a. Day trading
   b. Direct access trading
   c. Secured debt
   d. Contrarian

109. In business, investment, and accounting, the principle or convention of _____ has at least two meanings.

In investment and finance, it is a strategy which aims at long-term capital appreciation with low risk. It can be characterized as moderate or cautious and is the opposite of aggressive behavior.

   a. Duration gap
   b. Debt-snowball method
   c. Conservatism
   d. Barcampbank

110. _____ is a general term used to describe the services provided by a group of networked bank branches. Bank customers may access their funds and other simple transactions from any of the member branch offices.

_____ is normally defined as the business conducted by a banking institution with its retail and small business customers.

a. 7-Eleven
c. 4-4-5 Calendar
b. 529 plan
d. Core banking

111. In economics, business, and accounting, a _____ is the value of money that has been used up to produce something, and hence is not available for use anymore. In business, the _____ may be one of acquisition, in which case the amount of money expended to acquire it is counted as _____. In this case, money is the input that is gone in order to acquire the thing.
   a. Marginal cost
   c. Sliding scale fees
   b. Fixed costs
   d. Cost

112. _____ is the cost of maintaining a certain standard of living. Changes in the _____ over time are often operationalized in a _____ index. _____ calculations are also used to compare the cost of maintaining a certain standard of living in different geographic areas.
   a. Debt restructuring
   c. Cost of living
   b. Cramdown
   d. Consumer debt

113. _____ is an online real-trade sharing service to enable self-directed investors to compete with professional fund managers. Launched in June 2007, and founded on the belief that successful investment strategy is not the sole province of money management firms, _____ enables investors to share real investment decisions, gain recognition and earn fees by helping others.

_____ raised $6.5m in April 2008, in a round led by Union Square Ventures and Spark Capital who were also joined by Amadeus Capital Partners.

   a. Senior stretch loan
   c. Retention ratio
   b. Consumer debt
   d. Covestor

114. _____ is a term used widely amongst real estate investors to refer to non-traditional means of real estate financing, or financing techniques not commonly used. The goal of _____ is generally to purchase, or finance a property, with the buyer/investor using as little of his own money as possible. Otherwise known as leveraging, OPM (Other People's Money.)
   a. Creative financing
   c. 4-4-5 Calendar
   b. Government National Mortgage Association
   d. Jumbo mortgage

115. The phrase _____ (or sometimes creative economy) refers to a set of interlocking industry sectors, and are often cited as being a growing part of the global economy. The _____ are often defined as those that focus on creating and exploiting intellectual property products; such as music, books, film, and games, or providing business-to-business creative services such as advertising, public relations and direct marketing. Aesthetic live performance experiences are also generally included, contributing to an overlap with definitions of art and culture, and sometimes extending to include aspects of tourism and sport.
   a. Creative industries
   c. 4-4-5 Calendar
   b. 529 plan
   d. 7-Eleven

116. _____ is the method by which one calculates the creditworthiness of a business or organization. The audited financial statements of a large company might be analyzed when it issues or has issued bonds. Or, a bank may analyze the financial statements of a small business before making or renewing a commercial loan.

a. Capital note
b. Credit report monitoring
c. Credit crunch
d. Credit analysis

117. A _____ allows a credit card user to transfer the balance on their accounts to a new credit card. This is a process which is actively encouraged by almost all credit card issuers as a means to attract new customers. Such an arrangement is attractive to the consumer because the new bank or credit card issuer will offer incentives such as a low interest or interest-free period, loyalty points or some such other device or combination of incentives.
   a. Financial Gerontology
   b. Credit card balance transfer
   c. Par value
   d. Cramdown

118. A _____ is a monetary instrument issued by a seller that allows a buyer to purchase an item or service from that seller on a future date. _____s may be issued by a seller as a goodwill gesture to a buyer who wishes to return previously purchased merchandise (instead of cash repayment) in circumstances where the original sales agreement did not include an explicit refund policy for returned items. In such circumstances, a _____ of value equal to the price of the returned item is usually issued allowing the buyer to exchange his purchase for other items available with the sale.
   a. Medical debt
   b. Partial Payment
   c. Hard money loan
   d. Credit note

119. A _____ is a party (e.g. person, organization, company, or government) that has a claim to the services of a second party. The first party, in general, has provided some property or service to the second party under the assumption (usually enforced by contract) that the second party will return an equivalent property or service. The second party is frequently called a debtor or borrower.
   a. False billing
   b. NOPLAT
   c. Redemption value
   d. Creditor

120. _____ is a leasing arrangement where lessor and lessee are situated in different countries. This presents significant additional issues related to tax avoidance and tax shelters.

_____ has been widely used in some European countries, to arbitrage the difference in the tax laws of different jurisdictions, usually between a European country and the United States.

   a. Par value
   b. Cross-border leasing
   c. Netting
   d. Sinking fund

121. _____ is a process by which a firm can obtain the use of a certain fixed assets for which it must pay a series of contractual, periodic, tax deductable payments. The lessee is the receiver of the services or the assets under the lease contract and the lessor is the owner of the assets. The relationship between the tenant and the landlord is called a tenancy, and can be for a fixed or an indefinite period of time (called the term of the lease).
   a. Leasing
   b. Foreign Corrupt Practices Act
   c. Royalties
   d. Quiet period

122. _____ is a global payments company based in Victoria, BC, Canada. Operating more than 80 offices in 7 countries, _____ has grown to become North America's largest independent foreign exchange dealer, handling more than $15 billion in transactions each year for more than 50,000 clients worldwide. _____ provides a variety of foreign exchange services for businesses and individuals, including wire transfers, foreign currency drafts, and forward exchange contracts.

a. Pretax Group
c. Certified Public Accountant
b. Prosper Marketplace
d. Custom House

123. A _____ is a trader who buys and sells financial instruments (eg stocks, options, futures, derivatives, currencies) within the same trading day such that all positions will usually be closed before the market close of the trading day. This trading style is called day trading. Depending on one's trading strategy, it may range from several to hundreds of orders a day.

a. Financial analyst
c. Day trader
b. Stockbroker
d. Portfolio manager

124. _____ refers to the practice of buying and selling financial instruments within the same trading day such that all positions are usually closed before the market close of the trading day. Traders that participate in _____ are called day traders.

Some of the more commonly day-traded financial instruments are stocks, stock options, currencies, and a host of futures contracts such as equity index futures, interest rate futures, and commodity futures.

a. Tick size
c. Risk-return spectrum
b. Day trading
d. Bankruptcy remote

125. _____ is a process where convertible financing used to fund primarily small cap companies can be used against it in the marketplace to cause the company's stock to fall dramatically and can lead to the company's ultimate downfall.

Many small companies rely on selling convertible debt to large private investors to fund their operations and growth. This convertible debt, often convertible preferred stock or convertible debentures, can be converted to the common stock of the issuing company often at steep discounts to the market value of the common stock.

a. Cleanup clause
c. Refunding
b. Death spiral financing
d. Liquidating dividend

126. In finance, a _____, AKA net _____, results when an investor simultaneously buys an option with a higher premium and sells an option with a lower premium. The investor is said to be a net buyer and expects the premiums of the two options (the spread) to widen.

Investors want _____s to widen for profit.

a. Debit spread
c. Pin risk
b. Moneyness
d. Swaption

127. A _____ is a term used to describe a company that purchases delinquent debts from a creditor for a fraction of the face value of the debt. The _____ then either attempts to collect the debt on its own or uses the services of a collection agency. It is distinguished from a collection agency because it owns the underlying debt, whereas a collection agency collects the debt on behalf of another.

a. Hard money loan
b. Credit crunch
c. Debt buyer
d. Paydex

128. _____ is the capital that a business raises by taking out a loan. It is a loan made to a company that is normally repaid at some future date. _____ differs from equity or share capital because subscribers to _____ do not become part owners of the business, but are merely creditors, and the suppliers of _____ usually receive a contractually fixed annual percentage return on their loan, and this is known as the coupon rate.
a. Risk-return spectrum
b. Debt capital
c. Financial assistance
d. Floating charge

129. _____ is a finance term describing a firm's non-Equity cash flows. Theoretically, adding the discounted _____ to the discounted Flows to equity (also known as Equity Cash Flows) will give the firm's Enterprise Value. The Enterprise value is the valuation obtained by calculating the Discounted Cash Flow.
a. Par value
b. Foreign exchange hedge
c. Debt cash flow
d. Consignment stock

Chapter 2. Test Preparation Part 2

1. _____ is that which is owed; usually referencing assets owed, but the term can cover other obligations. In the case of assets, _____ is a means of using future purchasing power in the present before a summation has been earned. Some companies and corporations use _____ as a part of their overall corporate finance strategy.
   a. Cross-collateralization
   b. Credit cycle
   c. Partial Payment
   d. Debt

2. _____ is a situation in which a firm's debt is so large that any earnings generated by new investment projects are entirely appropriated by existing debt holders, and hence even projects with a positive net present value cannot reduce the firm's stock of debt or increase the value of the firm (Myers, 1977.) The concept has been applied to sovereign governments, predominantly in developing countries (Krugman, 1988.) It describes a situation where the debt of a country exceeds its future capacity to pay it.
   a. 529 plan
   b. 7-Eleven
   c. 4-4-5 Calendar
   d. Debt overhang

3. _____ is a process that allows a private or public company - or a sovereign entity - facing cash flow problems and financial distress, to reduce and renegotiate its delinquent debts in order to improve or restore liquidity and rehabilitate so that it can continue its operations.

Out-of court restructurings, also known as workouts, are increasingly becoming a global reality. A _____ is usually less expensive and a preferable alternative to bankruptcy.

   a. Commuted cash value
   b. Cost of living
   c. Prepayment
   d. Debt restructuring

4. _____ is the corporate management term for the act of reorganizing the legal, ownership, operational, or other structures of a company for the purpose of making it more profitable or better organized for its present needs. Alternate reasons for restructing include a change of ownership or ownership structure, demerger repositioning debt _____ and financial _____.
   a. Day trading
   b. Restructuring
   c. Cross-border leasing
   d. Concentrated stock

5. _____ is an approach to debt reduction in which the debtor and creditor agree on a reduced balance that will be regarded as payment in full.

As long as consumers continue to make minimum monthly payments, creditors will not negotiate a reduced balance. However, when payments stop, balances continue to grow because of late fees and ongoing interest.

   a. Liquidation
   b. 529 plan
   c. 4-4-5 Calendar
   d. Debt settlement

6. _____s are financial transactions in which a portion of a developing nation's foreign debt is forgiven in exchange for local investments in conservation measures. The concept of _____s was first conceived by Thomas Lovejoy of the World Wildlife Fund in 1984 as an opportunity to deal with the problems of developing-nation indebtedness and its consequent deleterious effect on the environment. In the wake of the Latin American debt crisis that resulted in steep reductions to the environmental conservation ability of highly-indebted nations, Lovejoy suggested that ameliorating debt and promoting conservation could be done at the same time.

a. 4-4-5 Calendar   b. 529 plan
c. 7-Eleven   d. Debt-for-Nature Swap

7. In finance, a _____ is a derivative in which two counterparties agree to exchange one stream of cash flows against another stream. These streams are called the legs of the _____.

The cash flows are calculated over a notional principal amount, which is usually not exchanged between counterparties.

a. Swap   b. Volatility arbitrage
c. Local volatility   d. Volatility swap

8. The _____ of debt repayment is a form of debt management that is most often applied to repaying revolving credit -- such as credit cards.

Under the method, extra cash is dedicated to paying debts with the smallest amount owed.

This method has gained more recognition recently due to the fact that it is the primary debt-reduction method taught by many financial and wealth experts.

a. Line of credit   b. Debt management plan
c. Debt-snowball method   d. Default Notice

9. In economics a _____ is simply an entity that owes a debt to someone else, the entity could be an individual, a firm, a government, or an organization. The counterparty of this arrangement is called a creditor. When the counterparty of this debt arrangement is a bank, the _____ is more often referred to as a borrower.

a. Tick size   b. Debtor
c. Biweekly Mortgage   d. Financial rand

10. A _____ is designed to support an investment management firm that is constructing an investment portfolio of multiple assets. Every investment manager goes through a similar process of finding potential ideas to add to their portfolio, putting them through their own proprietary analytical process and finally constructing a portfolio based on their analysis. A _____ helps bridge the transition from analysis to portfolio construction.

a. Monetary system   b. Duration gap
c. Standard of deferred payment   d. Decision process tool

11. In finance, _____ occurs when a debtor has not met its legal obligations according to the debt contract, e.g. it has not made a scheduled payment, or has violated a loan covenant (condition) of the debt contract. _____ may occur if the debtor is either unwilling or unable to pay their debt. This can occur with all debt obligations including bonds, mortgages, loans, and promissory notes.

a. Credit crunch   b. Vendor finance
c. Default   d. Debt validation

12. _____, in accrual accounting, is any account where the asset or liability is not realized until a future date, e.g. annuities, charges, taxes, income, etc. The _____ item may be carried, dependent on type of deferral, as either an asset or liability. See also: accrual

_____ is also used in the university admissions process. It is the action by which a school rejects a student for early admission but still opts to review that student in the general admissions pool.

a. Current asset
c. Net profit
b. Revenue
d. Deferred

13. _____ is an accounting concept meaning costs associated with issuing debt (loans and bonds), such as various fees and commissions paid to investment banks, law firms, auditors, and so on. Since these payments generate future benefits, they are treated as an asset. The costs are capitalised, reflected in the balance sheet as an asset, and amortised over the finite life of the underlying debt instrument.

a. Furniture, Fixtures and Equipment
c. Net income
b. Gross sales
d. Deferred financing costs

14. In economics, business, and accounting, a _____ is the value of money that has been used up to produce something, and hence is not available for use anymore. In business, the _____ may be one of acquisition, in which case the amount of money expended to acquire it is counted as _____. In this case, money is the input that is gone in order to acquire the thing.

a. Cost
c. Marginal cost
b. Fixed costs
d. Sliding scale fees

15. _____ or financing is to provide capital (funds), which means money for a project, a person, a business or any other private or public institutions.

Those funds can be allocated for either short term or long term purposes. The health fund is a new way of _____ private healthcare centers.

a. Proxy fight
c. Product life cycle
b. Synthetic CDO
d. Funding

16. _____ is an accounting concept, meaning a future tax liability or asset, resulting from temporary differences between book (accounting) value of assets and liabilities and their tax value, or timing differences between the recognition of gains and losses in financial statements and their recognition in a tax computation.

Temporary differences are differences between the carrying amount of an asset or liability recognised in the balance sheet and the amount attributed to that asset or liability for tax purposes (the tax base.)

Temporary differences may be either:

- taxable temporary differences, which are temporary differences that will result in taxable amounts in determining taxable profit (tax loss) of future periods when the carrying amount of the asset or liability is recovered or settled; or
- deductible temporary differences, which are temporary differences that will result in deductible amounts in determining taxable profit (tax loss) of future periods when the carrying amount of the asset or liability is recovered or settled.

The tax base of an asset or liability is the amount attributed to that asset or liability for tax purposes:

- the tax base of an asset is the amount that will be deductible for tax purposes against any taxable economic benefits that will flow to an entity when it recovers the carrying amount of the asset.

- the tax base of a liability is its carrying amount, less any amount that will be deductible for tax purposes in respect of that liability in future periods.

The basic principle of accounting for _____ under a temporary difference approach can be illustrated using a common example in which a company has fixed assets which qualify for tax depreciation.

a. Tax exemption
b. Monetary policy
c. Qualified residence interest
d. Deferred tax

17. _____ is an accounting concept used most often in mining, timber, petroluem, or other similar industries. The _____ deduction allows an owner or operator to account for the reduction of a product's reserves. _____ is similar to depreciation in that, it is a cost recovery system for accounting and tax reporting.
a. Depletion
b. Current liabilities
c. Deferred income
d. Net profit

18. _____

Management Accounting is used primarily by those WITHIN a company or organization. Reports can be generated for any period of time such as daily, weekly or monthly. Reports are considered to be 'future looking' and have forecasting value to those within the company.

a. Composiition of Creditors
b. Linear regression
c. The Hong Kong Securities Institute
d. Managerial Accounting Vs Financial Accounting

19. _____ is the field of accountancy concerned with the preparation of financial statements for decision makers, such as stockholders, suppliers, banks, employees, government agencies, owners, and other stakeholders. The fundamental need for _____ is to reduce principal-agent problem by measuring and monitoring agents' performance and reporting the results to interested users.

_____ is used to prepare accounting information for people outside the organization or not involved in the day to day running of the company.

a. 4-4-5 Calendar
c. 7-Eleven
b. Financial accounting
d. 529 plan

20. _____ is concerned with the provisions and use of accounting information to managers within organizations, to provide them with the basis to make informed business decisions that will allow them to be better equipped in their management and control functions.

In contrast to financial accountancy information, _____ information is:

- usually confidential and used by management, instead of publicly reported;
- forward-looking, instead of historical;
- pragmatically computed using extensive management information systems and internal controls, instead of complying with accounting standards.

This is because of the different emphasis: _____ information is used within an organization, typically for decision-making.

According to the Chartered Institute of Management Accountants, _____ is 'the process of identification, measurement, accumulation, analysis, preparation, interpretation and communication of information used by management to plan, evaluate and control within an entity and to assure appropriate use of and accountability for its Resource (economics)resources. _____ also comprises the preparation of financial reports for non-management groups such as shareholders, creditors, regulatory agencies and tax authorities'.

a. Management accounting
c. Governmental accounting
b. Nonassurance services
d. Grenzplankostenrechnung

21. _____ is a technology which allows stock traders to trade directly with market makers or specialists, rather than trading through stock brokers.

_____ systems use front-end trading software and high-speed computer links to stock exchanges such as NASDAQ, NYSE and the various Electronic Communications Networks. _____ system transactions are executed in a fraction of a second and their confirmations are instantly displayed on the trader's computer screen.

a. Payback period
c. Direct access trading
b. Standard of deferred payment
d. Day trading

22. In finance, the _____ approach describes a method of valuing a project, company, or asset using the concepts of the time value of money. All future cash flows are estimated and discounted to give their present values. The discount rate used is generally the appropriate cost of capital and may incorporate judgments of the uncertainty (riskiness) of the future cash flows.

a. Future-oriented
b. Net present value
c. Present value of benefits
d. Discounted cash flow

23. _____ is the balance of the amounts of cash being received and paid by a business during a defined period of time, sometimes tied to a specific project. Measurement of _____ can be used

- to evaluate the state or performance of a business or project.
- to determine problems with liquidity. Being profitable does not necessarily mean being liquid. A company can fail because of a shortage of cash, even while profitable.
- to generate project rate of returns. The time of _____s into and out of projects are used as inputs to financial models such as internal rate of return, and net present value.
- to examine income or growth of a business when it is believed that accrual accounting concepts do not represent economic realities. Alternately, _____ can be used to 'validate' the net income generated by accrual accounting.

_____ as a generic term may be used differently depending on context, and certain _____ definitions may be adapted by analysts and users for their own uses. Common terms include operating _____ and free _____.

_____s can be classified into:

1. Operational _____s: Cash received or expended as a result of the company's core business activities.
2. Investment _____s: Cash received or expended through capital expenditure, investments or acquisitions.
3. Financing _____s: Cash received or expended as a result of financial activities, such as interests and dividends.

All three together - the net _____ - are necessary to reconcile the beginning cash balance to the ending cash balance. Loan draw downs or equity injections, that is just shifting of capital but no expenditure as such, are not considered in the net _____.

a. Corporate finance
b. Shareholder value
c. Real option
d. Cash flow

24. _____ is a finance term originating from Engineering Economics. When selling the last item of a specific class, the difference between the undepreciated capital cost (UCC) of an object and its salvage value (S) is the disposable tax effect (H.)

In the case of S > UCC, then there has been a relative gain in the sale of the item, which gets taxed.

a. Disposal tax effect
b. Senior stretch loan
c. Fiscal sponsorship
d. Financial Gerontology

25. _____ in finance is a risk management technique, related to hedging, that mixes a wide variety of investments within a portfolio. Because the fluctuations of a single security have less impact on a diverse portfolio, _____ minimizes the risk from any one investment.

A simple example of _____ is the following: On a particular island the entire economy consists of two companies: one that sells umbrellas and another that sells sunscreen.

a. Diversification
c. 529 plan
b. 7-Eleven
d. 4-4-5 Calendar

26. A _____ is a payment made by a corporation to its shareholder members. When a corporation earns a profit or surplus, that money can be put to two uses: it can either be re-invested in the business (called retained earnings), or it can be paid to the shareholders as a _____. Many corporations retain a portion of their earnings and pay the remainder as a _____.

a. Dividend
c. Dividend puzzle
b. Dividend yield
d. Special dividend

27. _____ is the fraction of net income a firm pays to its stockholders in dividends:

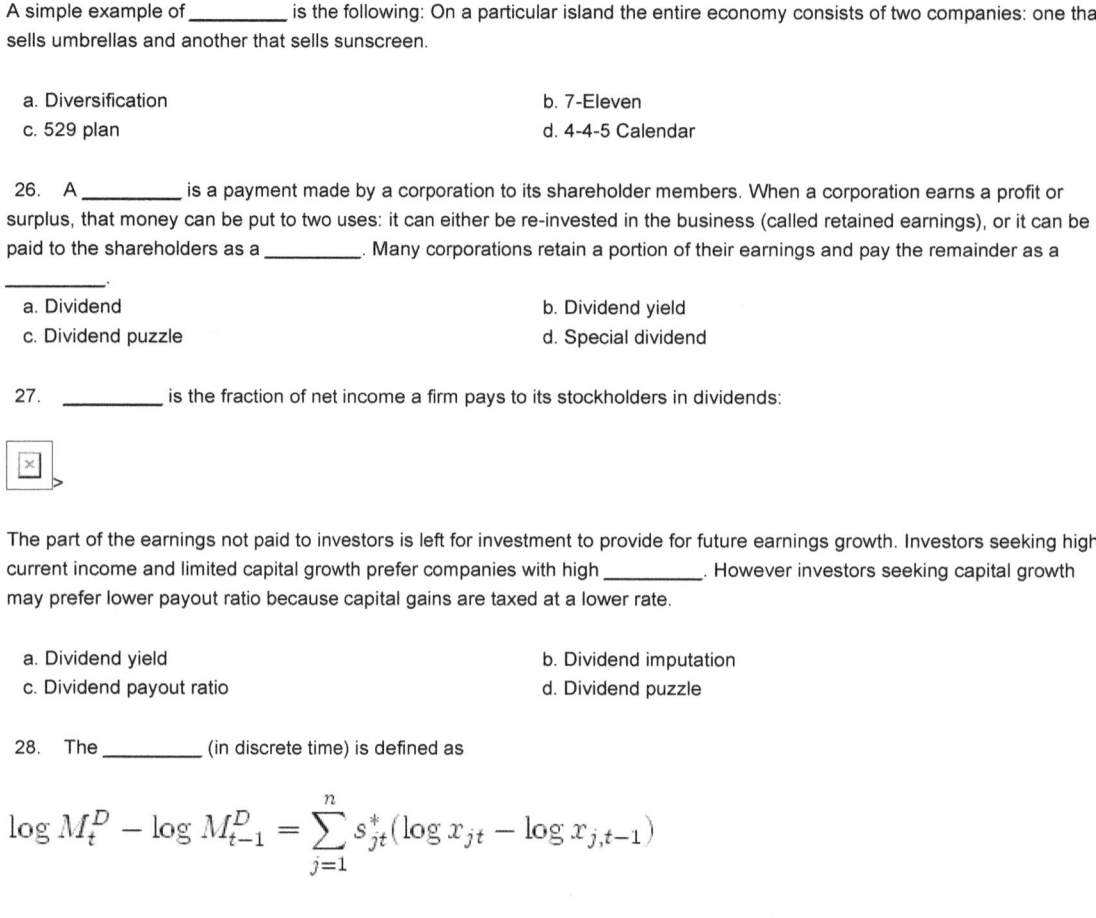

The part of the earnings not paid to investors is left for investment to provide for future earnings growth. Investors seeking high current income and limited capital growth prefer companies with high _____. However investors seeking capital growth may prefer lower payout ratio because capital gains are taxed at a lower rate.

a. Dividend yield
c. Dividend payout ratio
b. Dividend imputation
d. Dividend puzzle

28. The _____ (in discrete time) is defined as

$$\log M_t^D - \log M_{t-1}^D = \sum_{j=1}^{n} s_{jt}^*(\log x_{jt} - \log x_{j,t-1})$$

according to which the growth rate of the aggregate is the weighted average of the growth rates of the component quantities. The original continuous time _____ was derived by Francois Divisia in his classic paper published in French in 1925 in the Revue d'Economie Politique. The discrete time Divisia weights are defined as the expenditure shares averaged over the two periods of the change

$$s_{jt}^* = \frac{1}{2}(s_{jt} + s_{j,t-1})$$

for j = 1,...,n, where

$$s_{jt} = \frac{\pi_{jt} x_{jt}}{\sum_{k=1}^{n} \pi_{kt} x_{kt}}$$

is the expenditure share of asset j during period t, and π_{jt} is the user cost of asset j, derived in Banett (1978),

$$\pi_{jt} = \frac{(R_t - r_{jt})}{(1 + R_t)}$$

which is just the opportunity cost of holding a dollar's worth of the jth asset.

a. Consumer price index
b. 4-4-5 Calendar
c. 529 plan
d. Divisia index

29. The _____ is one of several stock market indices, created by nineteenth-century Wall Street Journal editor and Dow Jones ' Company co-founder Charles Dow. Dow compiled the index to gauge the performance of the industrial sector of the American stock market. It is the second-oldest U.S. market index, after the Dow Jones Transportation Average, which Dow also created.

a. Dow Jones Industrial Average
b. 4-4-5 Calendar
c. 7-Eleven
d. 529 plan

30. _____ is an American publishing and financial information firm.

The company was founded in 1882 by three reporters: Charles Dow, Edward Jones, and Charles Bergstresser. Like The New York Times and the Washington Post, the company was in recent years publicly traded but privately controlled.

a. Holding company
b. The Dun ' Bradstreet Corporation
c. Federal National Mortgage Association
d. Dow Jones ' Company

31. _____ was formed in 1997 as an entity within Dow Jones ' Co. It produces, maintains, licenses and markets indexes as benchmarks and as the basis of investible products such as exchange traded funds (ETFs), mutual funds and structured products. The company currently has employees in 18 cities worldwide, including Princeton, NJ, New York, Boston, Chicago, Los Angeles, London, Frankfurt, Zurich, Paris, Madrid, Stockholm, Singapore, Hong Kong, Beijing, Mexico City, Sao Paolo, Santiago and Dubai (its latest office.)

a. Pattern day trader
b. Dow Jones Indexes
c. Payback period
d. Tick size

32. _____ is a term used for a number of concepts involving either the performance of an investigation of a business or person, or the performance of an act with a certain standard of care. It can be a legal obligation, but the term will more commonly apply to voluntary investigations. A common example of _____ in various industries is the process through which a potential acquirer evaluates a target company or its assets for acquisition.

a. Bond indenture
b. Due diligence
c. Down payment
d. Quiet period

33. In finance, the _____ of a financial asset measures the sensitivity of the asset's price to interest rate movements, expressed as a number of years. The reason for expressing this sensitivity in years is that the time that will elapse until a cash flow is received allows more interest to accumulate. Therefore the price of an asset with long term cashflows has more interest rate sensitivity than an asset with cashflows in the near future.

a. Yield to maturity
c. Duration
b. 4-4-5 Calendar
d. Macaulay duration

34. The _____ is a financial and accounting term for the difference between the duration of assets and liabilities, and is typically used by banks, pension funds, or other financial institutions to measure their risk due to changes in the interest rate. This is one of the mismatches that can occur and are known as asset liability mismatches. Another way to define _____ is : it is the difference in the sensitivity of interest-yielding assets and the sensitivity of liabilities (of the organization) to a change in market interest rates (yields.)

a. Modern portfolio theory
c. Debt cash flow
b. Net worth
d. Duration gap

35. In public finance, an _____ is a requirement that all or a portion of a certain source of revenue, such as a particular tax, be devoted to a specific public expenditure. For example, in the United Kingdom a tax on televisions (known as the television licence) is directly allocated to the British Broadcasting Corporation (BBC.)

Earmarking bypasses the normal procedure by which tax revenue is pooled with all other revenue in a general fund and then allocated among various government spending programs.

a. Asset-liability mismatch
c. Intelligent investor
b. Amortizing loan
d. Earmark

36. In investments, _____ refers to the annual rate of growth of earnings. When the dividend payout ratio is the same, the dividend growth rate is equal to the _____ rate.

_____ rate is a key value that is needed when the DCF model, or the Gordon's model is used for stock valuation.

a. Alternative asset
c. Annuity
b. Alternative display facility
d. Earnings growth

37. _____ is a type of decision method applied to a project, programme or policy that takes into account a wide range of costs and benefits, denominated in monetary terms or for which a monetary equivalent can be estimated. _____ is a key tool for achieving value for money and satisfying requirements for decision accountability. It is a systematic process for examining alternative uses of resources, focusing on assessment of needs, objectives, options, costs, benefits, risks, funding, affordability and other factors relevant to decisions.

a. ABN Amro
c. Economic appraisal
b. A Random Walk Down Wall Street
d. AAB

38. _____ is an interdisciplinary research field, applying theories and methods originally developed by physicists in order to solve problems in economics, usually those including uncertainty or stochastic elements and nonlinear dynamics. Its application to the study of financial markets has also been termed statistical finance referring to its roots in statistical physics.

The correct name from an etymological viewpoint should be economophysics since economics is a Greek word formed from oikos, meaning home and transformed into eco, and nomos, meaning law and transformed into nomy.

a. AAB	b. Econophysics
c. ABN Amro	d. A Random Walk Down Wall Street

39. _____, refers to consumption opportunity gained by an entity within a specified time frame, which is generally expressed in monetary terms. However, for households and individuals, '_____ is the sum of all the wages, salaries, profits, interests payments, rents and other forms of earnings received... in a given period of time.' For firms, _____ generally refers to net-profit: what remains of revenue after expenses have been subtracted.

a. OIBDA	b. Accrual
c. Annual report	d. Income

40. _____ in accounting is the process of treating equity investments, usually 20-50%, in associate companies. The investor keeps such equities as an asset. Proportional share of associate company's net income increases the investment, and proportional payment of dividends decreases it.

a. Equity method	b. Earnings growth
c. Ownership equity	d. Annuity

41. In finance the _____ is the cost per year of owning and operating an asset over its entire lifespan.

_____ is often used as a decision making tool in capital budgeting when comparing investment projects of unequal lifespans. For example if project A has an expected lifetime of 7 years, and project B has an expected lifetime of 11 years it would be improper to simply compare the net present values (NPVs) of the two projects, unless neither project could be repeated.

a. Indirect costs	b. AAB
c. Equivalent annual cost	d. A Random Walk Down Wall Street

42. A _____ is an international bond that is denominated in a currency not native to the country where it is issued. It can be categorised according to the currency in which it is issued. London is one of the centers of the _____ market, but _____s may be traded throughout the world - for example in Singapore or Tokyo.

a. Education production function	b. Economic entity
c. Interest rate option	d. Eurobond

43. _____ N.V. is a pan-European stock exchange based in Paris and with subsidiaries in Belgium, France, Netherlands, Luxembourg, Portugal and the United Kingdom. In addition to equities and derivatives markets, the _____ group provides clearing and information services. As of 31 January 2006, markets run by _____ had a market capitalization of US$2.9 trillion, making it the 5th largest exchange on the planet.

a. Euronext	b. ABN Amro
c. A Random Walk Down Wall Street	d. AAB

44. An expert system for mortgages is a computer program that contains the knowledge and analytical skills of human experts, related to mortgage banking. Loan departments are interested in _____ because of the growing cost of labor which makes the handling and acceptance of relatively small loans less profitable. They also see in the application of expert systems a possibility for standardized, efficient handling of mortgage loans, and appreciate that for the acceptance of mortgages there are hard and fast rules which do not always exist with other types of loans.

a. ABN Amro
b. A Random Walk Down Wall Street
c. AAB
d. Expert systems for mortgages

45. The goals of _____ are to establish different market settings and environments to observe experimentally and analyze agents' behavior and the resulting characteristics of trading flows, information diffusion and aggregation, price setting mechanism and returns processes. This can happen for instance by conducting trading simulations or establishing and studying the behaviour of people in artificial competitive market-like settings.

Researchers in _____ can study to what extent existing financial economics theory makes valid predictions and attempt to discover new principles on which theory can be extended.

a. Experimental finance
b. Earnings growth
c. Alternative display facility
d. Intelligent investor

46. In the theory of capital structure, _____ is the phrase used to describe funds that firms obtain from outside of the firm. It is contrasted to internal financing which consists mainly of profits retained by the firm for investment. There are many kinds of _____.
a. Ownership equity
b. Asset-backed commercial paper
c. Adjustment
d. External financing

47. The _____ is the common shorthand description for the Financial Action Task Force list of 'Non-Cooperative Countries or Territories' (NCCTs); that is, countries which it perceives to be non-cooperative in the global fight against money laundering and terrorist financing. Although non-appearance on the blacklist is perceived to be a mark of approbation for Offshore Financial Centres (or 'tax havens') who are sufficiently well regulated to meet all of the FATF's criteria, in practice the list encompasses a large proportion of countries that do not operate as offshore financial centres.

The term non-cooperative is sometimes criticised as misleading, as a number of the countries which have appeared on the list from time to time appear, not because they deliberately propagate a culture which is perceived to assist money laundering, but because they simply lack the infrastructure or resources to cope with relatively sophisticated financial criminals who try to operate there.

a. Cost of living
b. FATF Blacklist
c. Debt cash flow
d. Seasoned equity offering

48. _____ is a financial instrument is wideley used in Brazilian credit markets and has been traded frequently by international investors and hedge funds. A _____ is a type of fund composed of receivables from different types of issuers.
a. FIDC
b. Foreign exchange hedge
c. Financial rand
d. Standard of deferred payment

49. _____ is a financial transaction whereby a business sells its accounts receivable (i.e., invoices) at a discount. _____ differs from a bank loan in three main ways. First, the emphasis is on the value of the receivables (essentially a financial asset), not the firm's credit worthiness.
a. Factoring
b. Financial Literacy Month
c. Debt-for-equity swap
d. Credit card balance transfer

Chapter 2. Test Preparation Part 2

50. _____ is a term in both law and accounting that is based on the economics term of 'market value.' It is also a common basis for assessing damages to be awarded for the loss of or damage to the property, generally in a claim under tort or a contract of insurance.

A _____ is often an estimate of what a willing buyer would pay to a willing seller, both in a free market, for an asset or any piece of property. If such a transaction actually occurs, then the actual transaction price is usually the _____.

- a. Fair market value
- b. Credit card balance transfer
- c. Global Squeeze
- d. Tick size

51. _____ is the price at which an asset would trade in a competitive Walrasian auction setting. _____ is often used interchangeably with open _____, fair value or fair _____, although these terms have distinct definitions in different standards, and may differ in some circumstances.

International Valuation Standards defines _____ as 'the estimated amount for which a property should exchange on the date of valuation between a willing buyer and a willing seller in an arm'e;s-length transaction after proper marketing wherein the parties had each acted knowledgeably, prudently, and without compulsion.'

_____ is a concept distinct from market price, which is 'e;the price at which one can transact'e;, while _____ is 'e;the true underlying value'e; according to theoretical standards.

- a. Market value
- b. Wrap account
- c. Debt restructuring
- d. T-Model

52. In financial accounting, the term _____ is most commonly used to describe any part of shareholders' equity, except for basic share capital. Sometimes, the term is used instead of the term provision; such a use, however, is inconsistent with the terminology suggested by International Accounting Standards Board. For more information about provisions, see provision (accounting.)

- a. Treasury stock
- b. FIFO and LIFO accounting
- c. Reserve
- d. Closing entries

53. In finance, a _____ is a debt security, in which the authorized issuer owes the holders a debt and, depending on the terms of the _____, is obliged to pay interest (the coupon) and/or to repay the principal at a later date, termed maturity.

Thus a _____ is a loan: the issuer is the borrower, the _____ holder is the lender, and the coupon is the interest. _____s provide the borrower with external funds to finance long-term investments, or, in the case of government _____s, to finance current expenditure.

- a. Catastrophe bonds
- b. Bond
- c. Puttable bond
- d. Convertible bond

Chapter 2. Test Preparation Part 2

54. The _____ (NYSE: FNM), commonly known as Fannie Mae, is a stockholder-owned corporation chartered by Congress in 1968 as a government sponsored enterprise (GSE), but founded in 1938 during the Great Depression. The corporation's purpose is to purchase and securitize mortgages in order to ensure that funds are consistently available to the institutions that lend money to home buyers.

On September 7, 2008, James Lockhart, director of the Federal Housing Finance Agency (FHFA), announced that Fannie Mae and Freddie Mac were being placed into conservatorship of the FHFA.

   a. SPDR
   c. General partnership
   b. The Depository Trust ' Clearing Corporation
   d. Federal National Mortgage Association

55. The _____ refers to the placing into conservatorship of government sponsored enterprises Fannie Mae and Freddie Mac by the US Treasury in September 2008. It was one financial event among many in the ongoing Subprime mortgage crisis.
   a. Federal takeover of Fannie Mae and Freddie Mac
   b. 4-4-5 Calendar
   c. 7-Eleven
   d. 529 plan

56. The _____ (NYSE: FRE) is an insolvent government sponsored enterprise (GSE) of the United States federal government.

The _____ was created in 1970 to expand the secondary market for mortgages in the US. Along with other GSEs, Freddie Mac buys mortgages on the secondary market, pools them, and sells them as mortgage-backed securities to investors on the open market.

   a. Public company
   c. Governmental Accounting Standards Board
   b. The Depository Trust ' Clearing Corporation
   d. Federal Home Loan Mortgage Corporation

57. In business, a _____ is the purchase of one company (the target) by another (the acquirer or bidder). In the UK the term refers to the acquisition of a public company whose shares are listed on a stock exchange, in contrast to the acquisition of a private company.

Before a bidder makes an offer for another company, it usually first informs that company's board of directors.

   a. 4-4-5 Calendar
   c. 529 plan
   b. Stock swap
   d. Takeover

58. A _____ offers small personal loans at high rates of interest, usually higher rates than the market rate charged on credit cards or on bank overdrafts. _____s are an important source of credit to a category of borrowers who would normally be refused credit by most financial institutions because their income may be at or below the poverty threshold or whose credit score indicates that the borrower might be unable to repay the loan. Because personal loans offered are unsecured and the risk of default by the borrower is high, _____s charge an effective interest rate that is in the range anywhere between 100% to 400% APR.
   a. Seasoned equity offering
   c. Foreign exchange hedge
   b. Financial Gerontology
   d. Moneylender

Chapter 2. Test Preparation Part 2

59. _____ is concerned with the tasks of developing and applying quantitative or statistical methods to the study and elucidation of economic principles. _____ combines economic theory with statistics to analyze and test economic relationships. Theoretical _____ considers questions about the statistical properties of estimators and tests, while applied _____ is concerned with the application of econometric methods to assess economic theories.
   a. A Random Walk Down Wall Street
   b. Econometrics
   c. ABN Amro
   d. AAB

60. _____ is a study of aging and related financial and business impacts. One of the primary interests is: As the lifespan of baby boomers and their parents lengthening, what would be the right approach for retirement planning.
   a. Financial Gerontology
   b. Standard of deferred payment
   c. Sinking fund
   d. Par value

61. National _____ is recognized in the United States in April in an effort to highlight the importance of financial literacy and teach Americans how to establish and maintain healthy financial habits.

In 2000, The Jump$tart Coalition for Personal Financial Literacy began promoting April as Financial Literacy for Youth Month and in 2003 the United States Congress showed its support. Senate Resolution 48 and House Resolution 127 asked President George W. Bush to declare April as Financial Literacy for Youth Month.

   a. Monetary system
   b. Post earnings announcement drift
   c. Financial Literacy Month
   d. Debt-for-equity swap

62. In economics, a _____ is a mechanism that allows people to easily buy and sell (trade) financial securities (such as stocks and bonds), commodities (such as precious metals or agricultural goods), and other fungible items of value at low transaction costs and at prices that reflect the efficient-market hypothesis.

_____s have evolved significantly over several hundred years and are undergoing constant innovation to improve liquidity.

Both general markets (where many commodities are traded) and specialized markets (where only one commodity is traded) exist.

   a. Secondary market
   b. Cost of carry
   c. Financial Market
   d. Delta hedging

63. The Journal _____ publishes original research and survey articles in all areas of finance, especially in - but not limited to - financial markets, portfolio theory and wealth management, asset pricing, risk management, and regulation. Its principal objective is to serve as a bridge between innovative research and practical application. The readers of _____ are researcher, economists, asset managers, financial analysts, and other professionals in finance and related areas.
   a. 529 plan
   b. 7-Eleven
   c. 4-4-5 Calendar
   d. Financial Markets and Portfolio Management

64. In law, _____ refers to assistance given by a company for the purchase of its own shares or the shares of its holding companies. In many jurisdictions such assistance is prohibited or restricted by law. For example all EU member states are required to prohibit _____ by public companies , although some members go further, for example, France, Belgium and The Netherlands prohibit _____ by all companies.

a. Cost of living
b. Decision process tool
c. Duration gap
d. Financial assistance

65. _____ is the practice of relating the movements of celestial bodies to events in financial markets. The use of astrology in financial markets is not consistent with standard economic or financial theory, but might be considered heterodox economics. The scientific community considers astrology to be a pseudoscience.
a. 529 plan
b. Financial astrology
c. 4-4-5 Calendar
d. 7-Eleven

66. _____ are defined as a crime against property, involving the unlawful conversion of property belonging to another to one's own personal use and benefit. _____ often involve fraud.

_____ are carried out via check and credit card fraud, mortgage fraud, medical fraud, corporate fraud, bank account fraud, payment (point of sale) fraud, currency fraud, and health care fraud, and they involve acts such as insider trading, tax violations, kickbacks, embezzlement, identity theft, cyber attacks, money laundering, and social engineering.

a. 529 plan
b. 4-4-5 Calendar
c. 7-Eleven
d. Financial crimes

67. _____ is the task of determining how a business will afford to achieve its strategic goals and objectives. Usually, a company creates a Financial Plan immediately after the vision and objectives have been set. The Financial Plan describes each of the activities, resources, equipment and materials that are needed to achieve these objectives, as well as the timeframes involved.
a. Management by exception
b. Corporate Transparency
c. Financial planning
d. Performance measurement

68. The South African _____ system was abolished with effect from March 13, 1995. The _____ system was instituted on September 1, 1985 in an attempt to control the large outflows of capital from South Africa at that time. These outflows were largely the result of economic sanctions in response to apartheid.
a. Financial rand
b. Consumer basket
c. Covestor
d. Market value

69. _____ is normally any risk associated with any form of financing.

Depending on the nature of the investment, the type of 'investment' risk will vary. High risk investments have greater potential rewards, but you may lose your money instead by taking the risk for more money.

a. Liquidating dividend
b. Stock market index option
c. Revaluation
d. Financial risk

70. _____ refer to services provided by the finance industry.

The finance industry encompasses a broad range of organizations that deal with the management of money. Among these organizations are banks, credit card companies, insurance companies, consumer finance companies, stock brokerages, investment funds and some government sponsored enterprises.

a. Delta hedging
b. Financial services
c. Cost of carry
d. Financial instruments

71. The _____ or Venture Capital Method is a valuation method often used by venture capitalists and private equity professionals that combines elements of both a multiples-based valuation and a traditional discounted cash flow (DCF.) The method is particularly useful in valuing high-growth companies. Many practitioners feel that the method is better than a straight multiples method for valuing high-growth companies because high-growth companies do not have significant current financial results.
    a. Sinking fund
    b. First chicago method
    c. Consumer basket
    d. Risk-return spectrum

72. _____ refers to the practice of non-profit organizations offering their legal and tax-exempt status to groups engaged in activities related to the organization's missions. It typically involves a fee-based contractual arrangement between a project and an established non-profit.

    _____ can enable projects to share a common administrative platform with a larger organization, thus increasing efficiency.

    a. Pattern day trader
    b. Consignment stock
    c. Secured debt
    d. Fiscal sponsorship

73. In business and accounting, _____s are everything of value that is owned by a person or company. The balance sheet of a firm records the monetary value of the _____s owned by the firm. The two major _____ classes are tangible _____s and intangible _____s.
    a. Accounts payable
    b. Asset
    c. Income
    d. EBITDA

74. _____ plant, and equipment, is a term used in accountancy for assets and property which cannot easily be converted into cash. This can be compared with current assets such as cash or bank accounts, which are described as liquid assets. In most cases, only tangible assets are referred to as fixed.
    a. Remittance advice
    b. Petty cash
    c. Fixed Asset
    d. Percentage of Completion

75. A _____ is an accounting method used for major resources of a business.

Fixed Assets are assets such as land, machines, office equipments, buildings, patents, trademarks, copyrights, etc. held for the purpose of production of goods or rendering of services and are not held for the purpose of sale in the ordinary course of business.

   a. Rocking Wall St: Four Powerful Strategies That Will Shake Up the Way You Invest, Build Your Wealth, and Give You Your Life Back
   b. Black model
   c. GNMA
   d. Fixed Asset Register

76. _____ refers to any type of investment that yields a regular (or fixed) return.

For example, if you lend money to a borrower and the borrower has to pay interest once a month, you have been issued a fixed-income security. When a company does this, it is often called a bond or corporate bank debt (although preferred stock is also sometimes considered to be _____).

a. 529 plan
b. 4-4-5 Calendar
c. Bond market
d. Fixed income

77. _____ refers to the process of measuring returns generated by various sources of risk in a fixed income portfolio, particularly when multiple sources of return are active at the same time.

For example, the risks affecting the return of a bond portfolio include the overall level of the yield curve, the slope of the yield curve, and the credit spreads of the bonds in the portfolio. A portfolio manager may hold firm views on the ways in which these factors will change in the near future, so in three separate risk decisions he positions the assets in the portfolio to take advantage of the expected forthcoming market movements.

a. Pattern day trader
b. Fixed income attribution
c. Global Squeeze
d. Cash equivalents

78. A _____ rate loan is a loan where the interest rate doesn't fluctuate during the fixed rate period of the loan. This allows the borrower to accurately predict their future payments. Variable rate loans, by contrast, are anchored to the prevailing discount rate.

a. Reference rate
b. SONIA
c. Cash accumulation equation
d. Fixed interest

79. _____ is a fee paid on borrowed assets. It is the price paid for the use of borrowed money, or, money earned by deposited funds. Assets that are sometimes lent with _____ include money, shares, consumer goods through hire purchase, major assets such as aircraft, and even entire factories in finance lease arrangements.

a. A Random Walk Down Wall Street
b. AAB
c. Insolvency
d. Interest

80. The free _____ of a public company is an estimate of the proportion of shares that are not held by large owners and that are not stock with sales restrictions (restricted stock that cannot be sold until they become unrestricted stock.)

The free _____ or a public _____ is usually defined as being all shares held by investors other than:

- shares held by owners owning more than 5% of all shares (those could be institutional investors, 'strategic shareholders,' founders, executives, and other insiders' holdings)
- restricted stocks (granted to executives that can be, but don't have to be, registered insiders)
- insider holdings (it is assumed that insiders hold stock for the very long term)

The free _____ is an important criterion in quoting a share on the stock market.

To _____ a company means to list its shares on a public stock exchange through an initial public offering (or 'flotation'.)

- Open market
- Outstanding shares
- Market capitalization
- Public _____ *loat*
- Reverse takeover

a. Trade finance
c. Synthetic CDO
b. Float
d. Golden parachute

81. A _____ is a security interest over a fund of changing assets of a company or a limited liability partnership (LLP), which 'floats' or 'hovers' until conversion into a fixed charge, at which point the charge attaches to specific assets. The conversion (called crystallisation) can be triggered by a number of events; it has become an implied term in debentures that a cessation of the company's right to deal with the assets in the ordinary course of business will lead to automatic crystallisation. Additionally, according to express terms of a typical loan agreement, default by the chargor is a trigger for crystallisation.

a. Cramdown
c. Debt cash flow
b. Barcampbank
d. Floating charge

82. _____ is a business valuation method. _____ is the net present value of a project if financed solely by ownership equity plus the present value of all the benefits of financing. Usually, the main benefit is a tax shield resulted from tax deductibility of interest payments. Another one can be a subsidized borrowing.

a. AAB
c. ABN Amro
b. Adjusted present value
d. A Random Walk Down Wall Street

83. _____ is the value on a given date of a future payment or series of future payments, discounted to reflect the time value of money and other factors such as investment risk. _____ calculations are widely used in business and economics to provide a means to compare cash flows at different times on a meaningful 'like to like' basis.

The most commonly applied model of the time value of money is compound interest.

a. Present value
c. Negative gearing
b. Present value of benefits
d. Net present value

84. _____ is the process of decreasing an amount over a period of time. The word comes from Middle English amortisen to kill, alienate in mortmain, from Anglo-French amorteser, alteration of amortir, from Vulgar Latin admortire to kill, from Latin ad- + mort-, mors death. Particular instances of the term include:

- _____ (business), the allocation of a lump sum amount to different time periods, particularly for loans and other forms of finance, including related interest or other finance charges.
    - ○ _____ schedule, a table detailing each periodic payment on a loan (typically a mortgage), as generated by an _____ calculator.
    - ○ Negative _____, an _____ schedule where the loan amount actually increases through not paying the full interest
- Amortized analysis, analyzing the execution cost of algorithms over a sequence of operations.
- _____ of capital expenditures of certain assets under accounting rules, particularly intangible assets, in a manner analogous to depreciation.
- _____ (tax law)

_____ is also used in the context of zoning regulations and describes the time in which a property owner has to relocate when the property's use constitutes a preexisting nonconforming use under zoning regulations.

- Depreciation

a. Amortization
c. Intrinsic value
b. AT'T Inc.
d. Option

85. An _____ is used to determine the periodic payment amount due on a loan (typically a mortgage), based on the amortization process.

The amortization repayment model factors varying amounts of both interest and principal into every installment, though the total amount of each payment is the same.

An _____ can also reveal the exact dollar amount that goes towards interest and the exact dollar amount that goes towards principal out of each individual payment.

a. Adempiere
c. Amortization calculator
b. EInvoice
d. Electronic billing

86. An _____ is a table detailing each periodic payment on a amortizing loan (typically a mortgage), as generated by an amortization calculator.

While a portion of every payment is applied towards both the interest and the principal balance of the loan, the exact amount applied to principal each time varies (with the remainder going to interest.) An _____ reveals the specific monetary amount put towards interest, as well as the specific put towards the Principal balance, with each payment.

a. Annual report
b. Adjusting entries
c. Adjusted basis
d. Amortization schedule

87. _____ offer, asking price is a price a seller of a good is willing to accept for that particular good.

In bid and ask, the term _____ is used in contrast to the term bid price. The difference between the _____ and the bid price is called the spread.

a. AAB
b. Interest rate parity
c. A Random Walk Down Wall Street
d. Ask price

88. The phrase _____ or bullet payment refers to one of two ways for repaying a loan; the other type is called amortizing payment or Amortization (business).

With a balloon loan, a _____ is paid back when the loan comes to its contractual maturity, e.g. reaches the deadline set to repayment at the time the loan was granted, representing the full loan amount (also called principal.) Periodic interest payments are generally made throughout the life of the loan.

a. Present value of costs
b. Refinancing risk
c. Future-oriented
d. Balloon payment

89. A _____ is the highest price that a buyer (i.e., bidder) is willing to pay for a good. It is usually referred to simply as the 'bid.'

In bid and ask, the _____ stands in contrast to the ask price or 'offer', and the difference between the two is called the bid/ask spread.

An unsolicited bid or offer is when a person or company receives a bid even though they are not looking to sell.

a. Bid price
b. Mid price
c. Settlement date
d. Political risk

90. _____ is the state of an economy where the processes of inflation and deflation occur simultaneously. During this period there is a rise in the purchasing prices of commodity items and a fall in the purchasing prices of non-commodity items.

The purchasing price of an item is based on the demand for it and the amount of money in circulation to pay for it.

a. Biflation
b. Future value
c. Net present value
d. Nominal value

91. A _____ is a mortgage financing technique where the buyer attempts to obtain a lower interest rate for at least the first few years of the mortgage. The seller of the property usually provides payments to the mortgage lending institution, which, in turn, lowers the buyer's monthly interest rate and therefore monthly payment. This is typically done for a period of about one to five years.

a. Buydown

c. Vesting

b. Liability

d. Federal Deposit Insurance Corporation Improvement Act

92. _____ is the provision of resources (such as granting a loan) by one party to another party where that second party does not reimburse the first party immediately, thereby generating a debt, and instead arranges either to repay or return those resources (or material(s) of equal value) at a later date. The first party is called a creditor, also known as a lender, while the second party is called a debtor, also known as a borrower.

Movements of financial capital are normally dependent on either _____ or equity transfers.

a. Clearing house
c. Comparable

b. Warrant
d. Credit

93. The _____ is an equation which calculates how much money will be in a bank account, at any point in time. The account pays interest, and is being fed a steady trickle of money.

We will approach the development of this equation by first considering the simpler case, that of just placing a lump sum in an account and then making no additions to the sum.

a. London Interbank Offered Rate
c. SONIA

b. Fixed interest
d. Cash accumulation equation

94. In lending agreements, _____ is a borrower's pledge of specific property to a lender, to secure repayment of a loan. The _____ serves as protection for a lender against a borrower's risk of default - that is, a borrower failing to pay the principal and interest under the terms of a loan obligation. If a borrower does default on a loan (due to insolvency or other event), that borrower forfeits (gives up) the property pledged as _____ *ollateral* - and the lender then becomes the owner of the _____.

a. Nominal value
c. Collateral

b. Future-oriented
d. Refinancing risk

95. _____ is a business and investing specific term for the geometric mean growth rate on an annualized basis. It represents the smoothed annualized gain earned over the investment time horizon. _____ is not an accounting term, but remains widely used, particularly in growth industries or to compare the growth rates of two investments because _____ dampens the effect of volatility of periodic returns that can render arithmetic means irrelevant.

a. Value at risk
c. Risk modeling

b. Risk premium
d. Compound annual growth rate

96. _____ is the concept of adding accumulated interest back to the principal, so that interest is earned on interest from that moment on. The act of declaring interest to be principal is called compounding (i.e., interest is compounded.) A loan, for example, may have its interest compounded every month: in this case, a loan with $100 principal and 1% interest per month would have a balance of $101 at the end of the first month.

a. 4-4-5 Calendar
c. Penny stock

b. Compound interest
d. Risk management

97. _____ in economics is a persistent decrease in the general price level of goods and services - a negative inflation rate. When the inflation rate slows down (decreases, but remains positive), this is known as disinflation.

Inflation destroys real value in money.

a. Recession
b. Fixed exchange rate
c. Mercantilism
d. Deflation

98. A '_____' is a 'Charge' that is paid to obtain the right to delay a payment. Essentially, the payer purchases the right to make a given payment in the future instead of in the Present. The '_____', or 'Charge' that must be paid to delay the payment, is simply the difference between what the payment amount would be if it were paid in the present and what the payment amount would be paid if it were paid in the future.

a. Risk aversion
b. Risk modeling
c. Discount
d. Value at risk

99. _____ is a term used in the context of the purchase of expensive items such as a car and a house, whereby the payment is the initial upfront portion of the total amount due and it is usually given in cash at the time of finalizing the transaction. A loan is then required to make the full payment.

The main purpose of a _____ is to ensure that the lending institution can recover the balance due on the loan in the event that the borrower defaults.

a. Royalties
b. Down payment
c. Business valuation
d. Financial Institutions Reform Recovery and Enforcement Act

100. An _____ account is

- an account established by a broker, under the provisions of license law, for the purpose of holding funds on behalf of the broker's principal or some other person until the consummation or termination of a transaction, or
- a trust account held in the borrower's name to pay obligations such as property taxes and insurance premiums.

_____ is best known in the United States in the context of real estate (specifically in mortgages where the mortgage company establishes an _____ account to pay property tax and insurance during the term of the mortgage.) _____ companies are also commonly used in the transfer of high value personal and business property, like websites and businesses, and in the completion of person-to-person remote auctions (such as eBay.) In the UK _____ accounts are often used during private property transactions to hold solicitors' client's money, such as the deposit, until such time as the transaction completes.

a. ABN Amro
b. A Random Walk Down Wall Street
c. AAB
d. Escrow

101. _____ is the common term referring to the portion of a mortgage payment that is designated to pay for real property taxes and hazard insurance. It is an amount 'over and above' the principal and interest portion of a mortgage payment. Since the _____ is used to pay taxes and insurance, it is referred to as 'T'I', while the mortgage payment consisting of principal and interest is called 'P'I'.

a. A Random Walk Down Wall Street
c. AAB
b. ABN Amro
d. Escrow payment

102. _____s are deposits denominated in United States dollars at banks outside the United States, and thus are not under the jurisdiction of the Federal Reserve. Consequently, such deposits are subject to much less regulation than similar deposits within the United States, allowing for higher margins. There is nothing 'European' about _____ deposits; a US dollar-denominated deposit in Tokyo or Caracas would likewise be deemed _____ deposits.
   a. ABN Amro
   c. A Random Walk Down Wall Street
   b. AAB
   d. Eurodollar

103. _____ is an event or condition under the contract between a buyer and a seller to exchange an asset for payment. In accounting, it is recognized by an entry in the books of account. It involves a change in the status of the finances of two or more businesses or individuals.
   a. Nominal value
   c. Financial transaction
   b. Tax shield
   d. Negative gearing

104. The _____ is one of three commonly used discounted-cash-flow (DCF) methods of corporate valuation, the other two are Adjusted Present Value and Weighted Average Cost of Capital (WACC.)
   a. Flow to Equity-Approach
   c. Business valuation standards
   b. Selling short
   d. Securitization

105. In finance, the _____ is the time period in which the individual yearly cash flows are input to the discounted cash flow formula. Cash flows after the _____ can only be represented by a fixed number such as the compound annual growth rate. There are no fixed rules for determining the duration of the _____.
   a. Market value added
   c. Covestor
   b. Forecast period
   d. Cost of living

106. _____ measures the nominal future sum of money that a given sum of money is 'worth' at a specified time in the future assuming a certain interest rate rate of return; it is the present value multiplied by the accumulation function.

The value does not include corrections for inflation or other factors that affect the true value of money in the future. This is used in time value of money calculations.

   a. Future-oriented
   c. Discounted cash flow
   b. Present value of costs
   d. Future value

107. _____ is a term used in finance and economics to describe agents that discount the future lightly and so have a low discount rate, or equivalently a high discount factor.

Conversely, present-oriented agents discount the future heavily and so have a high discount rate, or equivalently a low discount factor.

   a. Negative gearing
   c. Present value
   b. Discounted cash flow
   d. Future-oriented

108. In finance, _____ is a measurement of return on an asset or portfolio. It is one of the simplest measures of investment performance.

_____ is the percentage by which the value of a portfolio (or asset) has grown for a particular period.

a. Creditor
c. Stock market index option
b. Market integration
d. Holding period return

109. In economics, _____ is a rise in the general level of prices of goods and services in an economy over a period of time. The term '_____' once referred to increases in the money supply (monetary _____); however, economic debates about the relationship between money supply and price levels have led to its primary use today in describing price _____. _____ can also be described as a decline in the real value of money--a loss of purchasing power in the medium of exchange which is also the monetary unit of account.

a. Inflation
c. ABN Amro
b. A Random Walk Down Wall Street
d. AAB

110. A standard, commercial _____ is a document issued mostly by a financial institution, used primarily in trade finance, which usually provides an irrevocable payment undertaking.

The _____ can also be the source of payment for a transaction, meaning that redeeming the _____ will pay an exporter. Letters of credit are used primarily in international trade transactions of significant value, for deals between a supplier in one country and a customer in another.

a. Bond indenture
c. Duty of loyalty
b. McFadden Act
d. Letter of credit

111. In finance, _____ (or gearing) is borrowing money to supplement existing funds for investment in such a way that the potential positive or negative outcome is magnified and/or enhanced. It generally refers to using borrowed funds, or debt, so as to attempt to increase the returns to equity. Deleveraging is the action of reducing borrowings.

a. Leverage
c. Limited partnership
b. Pension fund
d. Financial endowment

112. _____ is a life of security. It may also refer to the final payment date of a loan or other financial instrument, at which point all remaining interest and principal is due to be paid.

1, 3, 6 months _____ band can be calculated by using 30-day per month periods.

a. Replacement cost
c. Maturity
b. Primary market
d. False billing

113. In financial markets, the _____ is the price between the best price of the sellers of the stock or commodity offer price or ask price and the best price of the buyers of the stock or commodity bid price. it can simply be defined as the average of the current bid and ask prices being quoted.

In some cases, the _____ will be rounded up or down to the nearest 'tick' (the nearest valid tradable price on the exchange system) for convenience purposes, and therefore not be the exact average.

a. Mid price
b. Settlement date
c. Country risk
d. Single-index model

114. _____s are used to help a current or potential real estate owner determine how much they can afford to borrow to purchase a piece of real estate. _____s can also be used to compare the costs or real interest rates between several different loans, determine the impact on the length of the mortgage loan of making added principal payments or bi-weekly instead of monthly payments. A _____ is an automated tool that enables the user to quickly determine the financial implications of changes in one or more variables in a mortgage financing arrangement.
   a. Chrysler Comprehensive Compensation System
   b. CYMA Systems
   c. Transaction processing system
   d. Mortgage calculator

115. _____ is a kind of tax to help to ensure the long run sustainability by making people be more aware of the natural resources consumption.

The popular conception of international waters is that there is no owner of it, so anyone can take advantage of it. Some propose that instead international waters are to be seen as owned by all the people of the planet.

   a. Fiscal policy
   b. Tax incidence
   c. Natural resources consumption tax
   d. Monetary policy

116. _____ is a form of leveraged speculation in which a speculator borrows money to buy an asset, but the income generated by that asset does not cover the interest on the loan. In a few countries the strategy is motivated by taxation systems which allow deduction of ongoing speculative losses against highly taxed income, but tax capital gains at a much lower rate. When income generated does cover the interest it is simply geared investment which creates a source of passive income.
   a. Present value of benefits
   b. Discounted cash flow
   c. Present value
   d. Negative gearing

117. In finance, _____ is borrowing money to supplement existing funds for investment in such a way that the potential positive or negative outcome is magnified and/or enhanced. It generally refers to using borrowed funds, or debt, so as to attempt to increase the returns to equity. Deleveraging is the action of reducing borrowings.
   a. 7-Eleven
   b. Gearing
   c. 4-4-5 Calendar
   d. 529 plan

118. _____ or net present worth (NPW) is defined as the total present value (PV) of a time series of cash flows. It is a standard method for using the time value of money to appraise long-term projects. Used for capital budgeting, and widely throughout economics, it measures the excess or shortfall of cash flows, in present value terms, once financing charges are met.
   a. Present value of costs
   b. Negative gearing
   c. Net present value
   d. Tax shield

119. In finance, 'participation' is an ownership interest in a mortgage or other loan. In particular, _____ is a cooperation of multiple lenders to issue a loan (known as participation loan) to one borrower. This is usually done in order to reduce individual risks of the lenders.

a. Securitization	b. Doctrine of the Proper Law
c. Loan participation	d. Short positions

120. _____ is a term used in cost-benefit analysis and project appraisal that refers to the discounted sum of a stream of benefits associated with a project or proposal.

a. Nominal value	b. Biflation
c. Discounted cash flow	d. Present value of benefits

121. _____ is a term used in cost-benefit analysis and project appraisal that refers to the discounted sum or a stream of costs associated with a project or proposal.

a. Refinancing risk	b. Financial transaction
c. Nominal value	d. Present value of costs

122. In finance, _____, also known as return on investment is the ratio of money gained or lost on an investment relative to the amount of money invested. The amount of money gained or lost may be referred to as interest, profit/loss, gain/loss, or net income/loss. The money invested may be referred to as the asset, capital, principal, or the cost basis of the investment.

a. Stock or scrip dividends	b. Composiition of Creditors
c. Doctrine of the Proper Law	d. Rate of return

123. In economics, _____ refers to any price or value expressed in money of the day, as opposed to real value, which adjusts for the effect of inflation. Examples include a bundle of commodities, such as gross domestic product, and income. For a series of _____s in successive years, different values could be because of differences in the price level, an index of prices.

a. Future value	b. Financial transaction
c. Biflation	d. Nominal value

124. _____ refers to the replacement of an existing debt obligation with a debt obligation bearing different terms. The most common consumer _____ is for a home mortgage.

_____ may be undertaken to reduce interest rate/interest costs (by _____ at a lower rate), to extend the repayment time, to pay off other debt(s), to reduce one's periodic payment obligations (sometimes by taking a longer-term loan), to reduce or alter risk (such as by _____ from a variable-rate to a fixed-rate loan), and/or to raise cash for investment, consumption, or the payment of a dividend.

a. 4-4-5 Calendar	b. 529 plan
c. 7-Eleven	d. Refinancing

125. In banking and finance, _____ is the possibility that a borrower cannot refinance by borrowing to repay existing debt. Many types of commercial lending incorporate bullet payments at the point of final maturity; often, the intention or assumption is that the borrower take out a new loan to pay the existing lenders.

A borrower that cannot refinance its existing debt and does not have sufficient funds on hand to pay its lenders may have a liquidity problem.

a. Present value
b. Net present value
c. Refinancing risk
d. Financial transaction

126. The _____ is a formula that states the returns earned by holders of a company's stock in terms of accounting variables obtainable from its financial statements. Specifically, it says that:

$$(1)\ T = g + \frac{ROE - g}{PB} + \frac{\Delta PB}{PB}(1 + g)$$

where T = total return from the stock over a period ;

g = the growth rate of the company's book value during the period;

PB = the ratio of price / book value at the beginning of the period.

ROE = the company's return on equity, i.e. earnings during the period / book value;

The _____ connects fundamentals with investment return, allowing an analyst to make projections of financial performance and turn those projections into an expected return that can be used in investment selection.

a. Financial Gerontology
b. Debt restructuring
c. Reinvestment risk
d. T-Model

127. _____ is a generic term used to describe the available software to perform tax compliance for income tax, corporate tax, VAT, service tax, customs, sales tax, use tax, etc. The solution automatically calculates your complete tax liabilities to the government, keeps track of all the transactions (in case of indirect taxes), keeps track of any tax credit you are eligible for etc. The solution can also automatically generate any forms or filings required for tax compliance.
a. Federal Open Market Committee
b. Monetary policy
c. Natural resources consumption tax
d. Tax compliance solution

128. A _____ is the reduction in income taxes that results from taking an allowable deduction from taxable income. For example, because interest on debt is a tax-deductible expense, taking on debt creates a _____. Since a _____ is a way to save cash flows, it increases the value of the business, and it is an important aspect of business valuation.
a. Present value of costs
b. Refinancing risk
c. Present value of benefits
d. Tax shield

129. In finance, the _____ (continuing value or horizon value) of a security is the present value at a future point in time of all future cash flows when we expect stable growth rate forever. It is most often used in multi-stage discounted cash flow analysis, and allows for the limitation of cash flow projections to a several-year period. Forecasting results beyond such a period is impractical and exposes such projections to a variety of risks limiting their validity, primarily the great uncertainty involved in predicting industry and macroeconomic conditions beyond a few years.
a. Refinancing risk
b. Discounted cash flow
c. Negative gearing
d. Terminal value

Chapter 2. Test Preparation Part 2 53

130. In finance, the value of an option consists of two components, its intrinsic value and its _____. Time value is simply the difference between option value and intrinsic value. _____ is also known as theta, extrinsic value, or instrumental value.

a. Conservatism
b. Global Squeeze
c. Debt buyer
d. Time value

131. Simply put, _____ is the value of money figuring in a given amount of interest for a given amount of time. For example 100 dollars of todays money held for a year at 5 percent interest is worth 105 dollars, therefore 100 dollars paid now or 105 dollars paid exactly one year from now is the same amount of payment of money with that given intersest at that given amount of time. This notion dates at least to Martín de Azpilcueta of the School of Salamanca.

All of the standard calculations for _____ derive from the most basic algebraic expression for the present value of a future sum, 'discounted' to the present by an amount equal to the _____. For example, a sum of FV to be received in one year is discounted (at the rate of interest r) to give a sum of PV at present: PV = FV -- rÅ·PV = FV/(1+r).

a. Coefficient of variation
b. Current account
c. Zero-coupon bond
d. Time value of money

132. _____ refers to the various forms of financial support and financial transactions used in international trade. _____ uses a range of instruments to provide finance to exporters and importers, including documentary credits such as letters of credit.

While a seller (the exporter) can require the purchaser (an importer) to prepay for goods shipped, the purchaser (importer) may wish to reduce risk by requiring the seller to document that the goods have been shipped.

a. Free cash flow
b. Forfaiting
c. Trade finance
d. Debtor-in-possession financing

133. _____ is a valuation method for buyers who purchase in bulk.

Buyer seeks to purchase 10000 widgets. Seller One offers 1000 widgets packaged together for $5000.

a. AAB
b. Unit price
c. Interest rate parity
d. A Random Walk Down Wall Street

134. A _____ is a charge for the use of a product or service.

A _____ may apply per use of the good or service or charge the user for use of the good or service. The first is a charge for each time while the second is a charge for bulk or time-limited use.

a. ABN Amro
b. AAB
c. A Random Walk Down Wall Street
d. User charge

135. The _____ is a choice problem designed by Maurice Allais to show an inconsistency of actual observed choices with the predictions of expected utility theory. The problem arises when comparing participants' choices in two different experiments, each of which consists of a choice between two gambles, A and B. The payoffs for each gamble in each experiment are as follows:

Average winnings of each gamble:

Experiment 1:

Gamble 1A: $1,000,000 (Preferred) - The _____: Based on average winnings people should prefer 1B to 1A
Gamble 1B: $1,390,000 ($390,000 more than 1A)

Experiment 2:

Gamble 2A: $110,000
Gamble 2B: $500,000 ($390,000 more than 2A) (Preferred)

Allais asserted that, presented with the choice between 1A and 1B, most people would choose 1A, and presented with the choice between 2A and 2B, most people would choose 2B. This has been borne out in various studies involving hypothetical and small monetary payoffs, and recently with health outcomes.

a. ABN Amro
c. Allais paradox
b. A Random Walk Down Wall Street
d. AAB

Chapter 3. Test Preparation Part 3

1. The _____ is an error that occurs when the conditional probability of some hypothesis H given some evidence E is assessed without taking sufficient account of the 'base rate' or 'prior probability' of H.

In a city with 100 terrorists and one million non-terrorists there is a surveillance camera with an automatic face recognition software. If the camera sees a known terrorist, it will ring a bell with 99% probability.

   a. 529 plan
   b. 7-Eleven
   c. Base rate fallacy
   d. 4-4-5 Calendar

2. A _____ is any actual or hypothesized stock market trend based on the calendar, such as rises and falls associated with particular days of the week or months of the year.

Examples include:

   - Halloween indicator (or the 'Sell in May' principle)
   - January effect
   - Mark Twain effect
   - Monday effect
   - Weekend effect
   - Turn-of-the-Month effect
   - Holiday effect

   a. 529 plan
   b. 4-4-5 Calendar
   c. 7-Eleven
   d. Calendar effect

3. _____ describes the way in which decisions are influenced by how the choices are presented, and is a term used by Cass Sunstein and economist Richard Thaler in the 2008 book Nudge: Improving Decisions About Health, Wealth And Unhappiness. Parallels are drawn between _____ and traditional architecture.

Arranging the default outcome of a situation to result in the desired outcome is suggested as an underused method.

   a. Perth Leadership Outcome Model
   b. Prospect theory
   c. Psychological level
   d. Choice architecture

4. The _____ is an anomaly discovered in behavioral finance. It relates to the tendency of investors to sell shares whose price has increased, while keeping assets that have dropped in value . Investors are unwilling to recognize losses (which they would be forced to do if they sold assets which had fallen in value), but are more willing to recognize gains.
   a. Prospect theory
   b. Disposition effect
   c. Psychological level
   d. Herd behavior

5. The _____ states that many people making individual buying and selling decisions will better reflect true value than any one individual can. In finance this theory is predicated on the Efficient Market Hypothesis (EMH.) One of the first instances of the _____ in action was with the Policy Analysis Market (PAM); a futures exchange developed by DARPA.
   a. Keynesian beauty contest
   b. The equity premium puzzle
   c. Loss aversion
   d. Dumb agent theory

6. In finance, the _____ asserts that financial markets are 'informationally efficient' e.g., stocks, bonds already reflect all known information. The _____ states that it is impossible to consistently outperform the market by using any information that the market already knows, except through luck. Information or news in the EMH is defined as anything that may affect prices that is unknowable in the present and thus appears randomly in the future.

a. Arbitrage
b. Efficient-market hypothesis
c. Initial margin
d. Issuer

7. The _____ is a hypothesis that people value a good or service more once their property right to it has been established. In other words, people place a higher value on objects they own than objects that they do not. In one experiment, people demanded a higher price for a coffee mug that had been given to them but put a lower price on one they did not yet own.

a. ABN Amro
b. A Random Walk Down Wall Street
c. AAB
d. Endowment effect

8. The _____ is a term coined by economists Rajnish Mehra and Edward C. Prescott. It is based on the observation that in order to reconcile the much higher return on equity stock compared to government bonds in the United States, individuals must have implausibly high risk aversion according to standard economics models. Similar situations prevail in many other industrialized countries.

a. AAB
b. Equity premium puzzle
c. A Random Walk Down Wall Street
d. ABN Amro

9. A _____ is a property of some probability distributions (alternatively referred to as heavy-tailed distributions) exhibiting extremely large kurtosis particularly relative to the ubiquitous normal which itself is an example of an exceptionally thin tail distribution. _____ distributions have power law decay. More precisely, the distribution of a random variable X is said to have a _____ if

$$\Pr[X > x] \sim x^{-(1+\alpha)} \text{ as } x \to \infty, \quad \alpha > 0.$$

Some reserve the term '_____' for distributions only where 0 < α < 2 (i.e. only in cases with infinite variance.)

a. 7-Eleven
b. Fat tail
c. 4-4-5 Calendar
d. 529 plan

10. _____ are supposed, together with herd instinct, to be the three main emotional motivators of stock markets and business behavior, and one of the cause of bull markets, bear markets and business cycles.

The phrase, traditionally used by traders and market commentators, has become a topic of economic research about investor irrationalities (cognitive and emotional biases.) Its effects on market prices and returns contradict, or at least moderate, the efficient market hypothesis.

a. Price-weighted
b. Golden parachute
c. Planning horizon
d. Greed and fear

11. Herd behaviour describes how individuals in a group can act together without planned direction. The term pertains to the behaviour of animals in herds, flocks, and schools, and to human conduct during activities such as stock market bubbles and crashes, street demonstrations, sporting events, episodes of mob violence and even everyday decision making, judgment and opinion forming.

A group of animals fleeing a predator shows the nature of _____.

   a. Keynesian beauty contest
   b. Herd behavior
   c. Mental accounting
   d. Perth Leadership Outcome Model

12. In behavioral economics, _____ refers to the empirical finding that people generally prefer smaller, sooner payoffs to larger, later payoffs when the smaller payoffs would be imminent; but when the same payoffs are distant in time, people tend to prefer the larger, even though the time lag from the smaller to the larger would be the same as before.

The phenomenon of _____ is implicit in Richard Herrnstein's 'matching law,' the discovery that most subjects allocate their time or effort between two non-exclusive, ongoing sources of reward (concurrent variable interval schedules) in direct proportion to the rate and size of rewards from the two sources, and in inverse proportion to their delays. That is, subjects' choices 'match' these parameters.

   a. Sunk costs
   b. 4-4-5 Calendar
   c. Hindsight bias
   d. Hyperbolic discounting

13. A '_____' is a 'Charge' that is paid to obtain the right to delay a payment. Essentially, the payer purchases the right to make a given payment in the future instead of in the Present. The '_____', or 'Charge' that must be paid to delay the payment, is simply the difference between what the payment amount would be if it were paid in the present and what the payment amount would be paid if it were paid in the future.

   a. Discount
   b. Risk modeling
   c. Risk aversion
   d. Value at risk

14. In game theory, an information cascade or _____ is a situation in which every subsequent actor, based on the observations of others, makes the same choice independent of his/her private signal. In an _____, everyone is individually acting rationally. Still, even if all participants as a collective have overwhelming information in favor of the correct action, each and every participant may take the wrong action.

   a. A Random Walk Down Wall Street
   b. Informational cascade
   c. AAB
   d. ABN Amro

15. The _____ is the tendency of the stock market to rise between December 31 and the end of the first week in January. There are many theories for why this happens, the main one being that it occurs because many investors choose to sell some of their stock right before the end of the year in order to claim a capital loss for tax purposes. Once the tax calendar rolls over to a new year on January 1st these same investors quickly reinvest their money in the market, causing stock prices to rise.

   a. January effect
   b. Death spiral financing
   c. Revaluation
   d. Sector rotation

16. Behavioral economics and _____ are closely related fields that have evolved to be a separate branch of economic and financial analysis which applies scientific research on human and social, cognitive and emotional factors to better understand economic decisions by, say, consumers, borrowers, investors, and how they affect market prices, returns and the allocation of resources.

The field is primarily concerned with the bounds of rationality (selfishness, self-control) of economic agents. Behavioral models typically integrate insights from psychology with neo-classical economic theory.

a. Behavioral Finance
b. Market structure
c. Medium of exchange
d. Recession

17. The _____ is a peer-reviewed journal that publishes research related to the field of behavioral finance. It formerly published as The Journal of Psychology and Financial Markets.

Contributors to the _____ have included specialists in psychology and psychiatry, sociology, behavioral economics, and the financial markets.

a. 4-4-5 Calendar
b. Journal of Behavioral Finance
c. 7-Eleven
d. 529 plan

18. _____ is an Israeli-American psychologist and Nobel laureate, notable for his work on behavioral finance and hedonic psychology.

With Amos Tversky and others, he established a cognitive basis for common human errors using heuristics and biases and developed Prospect theory. He was awarded the 2002 Nobel Prize in Economics for his work in Prospect theory.

a. Adolph Coors
b. Andrew Tobias
c. Daniel Kahneman
d. Myron Samuel Scholes

19. A _____ is a concept developed by John Maynard Keynes and introduced in Chapter 12 of his masterwork, General Theory of Employment Interest and Money (1936), to explain price fluctuations in equity markets. Keynes described the action of rational agents in a market using an analogy based on a fictional newspaper context, in which entrants are asked to choose a set of six faces from photographs of women that were the 'most beautiful'. Those who picked the most popular face are then eligible for a prize.

a. Quantitative behavioral finance
b. Keynesian beauty contest
c. Prospect theory
d. Mental accounting

20. In prospect theory, _____ refers to the tendency for people to strongly prefer avoiding losses than acquiring gains. Some studies suggest that losses are twice as powerful, psychologically, as gains. _____ was first convincingly demonstrated by Amos Tversky and Daniel Kahneman.

a. Herd behavior
b. Perth Leadership Outcome Model
c. Quantitative behavioral finance
d. Loss aversion

21. A _____ (or inefficiency) is a price and/or return distortion on a financial market.

It is usually related to:

- either structural factors (unfair competition, lack of market transparency, ...)
- or behavioral biases by economic agents

It sometimes refers to phenomena contradicting the efficient market hypothesis. There are anomalies in relation to the economic fundamentals of the equity, technical trading rules, and economic calendar events.

Anomalies could be Fundamental, Technical or calendar related.

   a. Market anomaly   b. Financial instruments
   c. Spot rate   d. Financial market

22. A _____ is the direction in which a financial market is moving. _____s can be classified as primary trends, secondary trends (short-term), and secular trends (long-term.) This principle incorporates the idea that market cycles occur with regularity and persistence.
   a. 7-Eleven   b. 4-4-5 Calendar
   c. 529 plan   d. Market trend

23. A concept first named by Richard Thaler (1980), _____ attempts to describe the process whereby people code, categorize and evaluate economic outcomes. _____ theorists argue that people group their assets into a number of non-fungible mental accounts.

One detailed application of _____, the behavioral life cycle hypothesis (Shefrin ' Thaler, 1988), posits that people mentally frame assets as belonging to either current income, current wealth or future income and this has implications for their behavior as the accounts are largely non-fungible and marginal propensity to consume out of each account is different.

   a. Quantitative behavioral finance   b. Psychological level
   c. Disposition effect   d. Mental accounting

24. _____ refers to the tendency of people to think of currency in nominal, rather than real, terms. In other words, the numerical/face value (nominal value) of money is mistaken for its purchasing power (real value.) This is a fallacy as modern fiat currencies have no inherent value and their real value is derived from their ability to be exchanged for goods and used for payment of taxes.
   a. Fungibility   b. 4-4-5 Calendar
   c. Money illusion   d. 529 plan

25. _____ combines neuroscience, economics, and psychology to study how people make decisions. It looks at the role of the brain when we evaluate decisions, categorize risks and rewards, and interact with each other.

Neuroscience studies the nervous system, with broad areas such as the senses, movement, and internal regulation.

a. 529 plan
b. 4-4-5 Calendar
c. 7-Eleven
d. Neuroeconomics

26. The _____ is a leadership model that aims to characterize leaders by the financial outcome of their leadership, as distinct from the two traditional leadership models of focusing on either the leader's personality or behavioral skills and business competencies. It was developed by Dr. E. Ted Prince over the period 2002-6.

a. Disposition effect
b. Herd behavior
c. Loss aversion
d. Perth Leadership Outcome Model

27. The _____ anomaly means the tendency for stocks to earn abnormally high returns in the three quarters following a positive earnings announcement, and to earn abnormally low returns in the three quarters following a negative earnings announcement.

The phenomenon can be explained with a number of hypotheses. The most widely accepted explanation for the effect is investor under-reaction to earnings announcements.

a. Bullet loan
b. Consumer basket
c. Seasoned equity offering
d. Post earnings announcement drift

28. _____ is a theory that describes decisions between alternatives that involve risk, i.e. alternatives with uncertain outcomes, where the probabilities are known. The model is descriptive: it tries to model real-life choices, rather than optimal decisions.

_____ was developed by Daniel Kahneman, professor at Princeton University's Department of Psychology, and Amos Tversky in 1979 as a psychologically realistic alternative to expected utility theory.

a. Herd behavior
b. Dumb agent theory
c. Prospect theory
d. The equity premium puzzle

29. In finance, _____, is a technical level which has a fairly significant effect on the price of an underlying security, commodity or a derivative. A number which is 'easy to remember' such as those which are rounded off. When such price is reached by the specific security, commodity or a derivative, the tendency of the financial market participants (traders, market-makers, brokers, investors, etc.)

a. Perth Leadership Outcome Model
b. Dumb agent theory
c. Prospect theory
d. Psychological level

30. _____ is a new discipline that uses mathematical and statistical methodology to understand behavioral biases in conjunction with valuation. Some of this endeavor has been led by Gunduz Caginalp (Professor of Mathematics and Editor of Journal of Behavioral Finance during 2001-2004) and collaborators including Vernon Smith (2002 Nobel Laureate in Economics), David Porter, Don Balenovich, Vladimira Ilieva, Ahmet Duran, Huseyin Merdan.) Studies by Jeff Madura, Ray Sturm and others have demonstrated significant behavioral effects in stocks and exchange traded funds.

a. Herd behavior
b. Mental accounting
c. Keynesian beauty contest
d. Quantitative behavioral finance

31. _____ is a concept in economics, finance, and psychology related to the behaviour of consumers and investors under uncertainty. _____ is the reluctance of a person to accept a bargain with an uncertain payoff rather than another bargain with a more certain, but possibly lower, expected payoff.

The inverse of a person's _____ is sometimes called their risk tolerance

a. Risk premium
b. Risk aversion
c. Risk adjusted return on capital
d. Discount factor

32. _____ is a term that Legal ' General dubbed to counterbalance the existing term of Goldilocks.

Like a similar term stagflation, '_____' is a portmanteau word, and means 'growth soggy, inflation strong'.

a. Sector rotation
b. Sogflation
c. January effect
d. Peer group analysis

33. In economics, the _____ is a paradox related to probability theory and decision theory. It is based on a particular (theoretical) lottery game (sometimes called St. Petersburg Lottery) that leads to a random variable with infinite expected value, i.e. infinite expected payoff, but would nevertheless be considered to be worth only a very small amount of money. The _____ is a classical situation where a naïve decision criterion (which takes only the expected value into account) would recommend a course of action that no (real) rational person would be willing to take.

a. 7-Eleven
b. 529 plan
c. 4-4-5 Calendar
d. St. Petersburg paradox

34. The _____ is a cognitive bias for the status quo; in other words, people tend not to change an established behavior unless the incentive to change is compelling.

The finding has been observed in many fields, including political science and economics.

Kahneman, Thaler and Knetsch created experiments that could produce this effect reliably.

a. 529 plan
b. 4-4-5 Calendar
c. 7-Eleven
d. Status quo bias

35. A _____ is a private or public market for the trading of company stock and derivatives of company stock at an agreed price; these are securities listed on a stock exchange as well as those only traded privately.

The size of the world _____ is estimated at about $36.6 trillion US at the beginning of October 2008 . The world derivatives market has been estimated at about $480 trillion face or nominal value, 12 times the size of the entire world economy.

a. Anton Gelonkin
b. Adolph Coors
c. Andrew Tobias
d. Stock market

36. A _____ is a type of economic bubble taking place in stock markets when price of stocks rise and become overvalued by any measure of stock valuation.

The existence of _____s is at odds with the assumptions of efficient market theory which assumes rational investor behaviour. Behavioral finance theory attribute _____s to cognitive biases that lead to groupthink and herd behavior.

a. Trading curb
b. Stock market bubble
c. Stock split
d. Stockholder

37. A _____ is a sudden dramatic decline of stock prices across a significant cross-section of a stock market. Crashes are driven by panic as much as by underlying economic factors. They often follow speculative stock market bubbles.

a. 4-4-5 Calendar
b. 529 plan
c. Stock market crash
d. 7-Eleven

38. In economics and business decision-making, _____ are costs that cannot be recovered once they have been incurred. _____ are sometimes contrasted with variable costs, which are the costs that will change due to the proposed course of action, and prospective costs which are costs that will be incurred if an action is taken. In microeconomic theory, only variable costs are relevant to a decision.

a. Hindsight bias
b. 4-4-5 Calendar
c. Hyperbolic discounting
d. Sunk costs

39. In economics, business, and accounting, a _____ is the value of money that has been used up to produce something, and hence is not available for use anymore. In business, the _____ may be one of acquisition, in which case the amount of money expended to acquire it is counted as _____. In this case, money is the input that is gone in order to acquire the thing.

a. Cost
b. Marginal cost
c. Sliding scale fees
d. Fixed costs

40. _____: How Wall Street Caused the Mortgage and Credit Crisis is a 2008 book about the subprime mortgage crisis in the United States by investigative journalists Paul Muolo of National Mortgage News and Mathew Padilla of the Orange County Register. The book has an accompanying website with some excerpts, author biographies and a roundup of events in the subprime mortgage crisis that occurred after the book was printed.

The book analyses the causes of the subprime mortgage crisis in the United States in an attempt to assign responsibility for the collapse of a number of mortgage companies in 2007-2008 and for the sharp rise in mortgage defaults in the wake of the sudden tightening of mortgage credit in the summer and early fall of 2007.

a. Subprime lending
b. Chain of Blame
c. Risk-based pricing
d. Mortgage-backed security

41. _____: The New Strategy for Profiting From the Coming Rise in the Stock Market is a book by James K. Glassman and Kevin A. Hassett. It was published in 1999, shortly before the dot-com bubble burst, and predicted that the Dow Jones Index would rise to 36000 within a few years. Parts of the book were also published in The Atlantic Monthly.

a. Stocks for the Long Run
b. The Pirates of Manhattan
c. Fail-Safe Investing
d. Dow 36,000

42. Published in 1998, _____ describes Harry Browne's approach to investing in any market environment using his concept of the 'Permanent Portfolio.'

The Permanent Portfolio is a simple investment strategy in which the investor divides his portfolio equally among four primary asset classes.

- Stocks - Represented by a broad-market index fund, such as one that follows the S'P 500
- Bonds - Represented by U.S. Treasury bonds in the longest term available, or high-grade corporate bonds
- Cash - Represented by short-term U.S. Treasury bills
- Gold - Preferably in bullion form

In the book, Harry advocates checking the portfolio once each quarter. If any of the asset classes outperformed or underpeformed by more than 10%, then funds should be redistributed to maintain the approximately equal balance. New funds should be added equally to each asset class (or in such a way as to make the value of each asset class approximately equal once the new funds were added.)

a. Fooled by Randomness
c. Stocks for the Long Run
b. Fail-Safe Investing
d. The Intelligent Investor

43. _____: The Hidden Role of Chance in Life and in the Markets is a book written by Nassim Nicholas Taleb, a philosopher of randomness about the fallibility of human knowledge.

The book was selected by Fortune as one of 'The Smartest Books of All Time'.

The book's name, _____, has also become an idiom in English used to describe when someone sees a pattern where there is just random noise.

a. Rich Dad, Poor Dad
c. The Intelligent Investor
b. Fooled by Randomness
d. Free to Choose

44. _____ is both a book (ISBN 978-0-15-633460-0) and a ten-part television series, advocating US free market policy.

_____: A Personal Statement by economists Milton and Rose D. Friedman provides examples of how the free market works, and shows how it can solve problems where other approaches have failed. Published in January 1980, the 297 page book contains 10 chapters dealing with issues such as:

- The misuse of Federal Reserve powers during the Great Depression,
- The decline of personal freedoms, and
- Government spending and economic controls.

Milton Friedman won the Nobel Memorial Prize in Economics in 1976. Contrary to normal practice the book was written after the TV series was produced, although the line 'Basis for the acclaimed public television triumph' is written on the front cover, using the program transcripts as reference.

a. Fail-Safe Investing
b. Fooled by Randomness
c. The Warren Buffett Way
d. Free to Choose

45. In The _____, Benjamin Graham describes a formula he used to value stocks. He disregarded complicated calculations and kept his formula simple. In his words: 'Our study of the various methods has led us to suggest a foreshortened and quite simple formula for the evaluation of growth stocks, which is intended to produce figures fairly close to those resulting from the more refined mathematical calculations.'

The formula as described by Graham in the 1962 edition of Security Analysis, is as follows:

$$V* = EPS \times (8.5 + 2g)$$

V = Intrinsic ValueEPS = Trailing Twelve Months Earnings Per Share8.5 = P/E base for a no-growth companyg = reasonably expected 7 to 10 year growth rate

Where the expected annual growth rate 'should be that expected over the next seven to ten years.' Graham's formula took no account of prevailing interest rates.

a. Intelligent Investor
b. Advisory capital
c. Adjustment
d. Equity in income of affiliates

46. A _____ or bank is a financial institution whose primary activity is to act as a payment agent for customers and to borrow and lend money.

The first modern bank was founded in Italy in Genoa in 1406, its name was Banco di San Giorgio (Bank of St. George.)

Many other financial activities were added over time.

a. 4-4-5 Calendar
b. Bought deal
c. Black Sea Trade and Development Bank
d. Banker

47. _____ is a March 2000 book written by Yale University professor Robert Shiller, named after Alan Greenspan's '_____' quote. Published at the height of the dot-com boom, it put forth several arguments demonstrating how the stock markets were overvalued at the time. Shiller was soon proven right when the Nasdaq peaked on the very month of the book's publication, and the stock markets collapsed right after.

a. AAB
b. A Random Walk Down Wall Street
c. ABN Amro
d. Irrational Exuberance

48. The _____: The Only Way to Guarantee Your Fair Share of Stock Market Returns is a book on index investing. It was released in March 2007.

This is the sixth book by John C. Bogle, the founder and former CEO of the Vanguard Group.

a. Fail-Safe Investing
b. The Warren Buffett Way
c. The Pirates of Manhattan
d. Little Book of Common Sense Investing

49. _____ is a book by Robert Shiller. It suggests that humans cannot fully diversify away their risk as portfolio theory would like us to. This is because there are missing markets, such as the general geographically computational risk of living in a certain area.
   a. Fail-Safe Investing
   b. Free to Choose
   c. Stocks for the Long Run
   d. Macro Markets

50. A _____, is a mathematical formalization of a trajectory that consists of taking successive random steps. The results of _____ analysis have been applied to computer science, physics, ecology, economics and a number of other fields as a fundamental model for random processes in time. For example, the path traced by a molecule as it travels in a liquid or a gas, the search path of a foraging animal, the price of a fluctuating stock and the financial status of a gambler can all be modeled as _____ s.
   a. 4-4-5 Calendar
   b. 7-Eleven
   c. 529 plan
   d. Random Walk

51. _____ is Robert Kiyosaki's and Sharon Lechter's first best-selling book. It advocates financial independence through investing, real estate, owning businesses, and the use of finance protection tactics.

_____ is written in an anecdotal manner aimed at making finances interesting.

   a. Rich Dad, Poor Dad
   b. Fail-Safe Investing
   c. Free to Choose
   d. Fooled by Randomness

52.

_____ is a book on investment advice. It was released in February 2007.

This is the first book by Gary Marks, known for his unique ability to synthesize his investment research to form risk-averse, multi-manager strategies, which have been successful in both bull and bear markets.

   a. Rocking Wall St: Four Powerful Strategies That Will Shake Up the Way You Invest, Build Your Wealth, and Give You Your Life Back
   b. Weighted mean
   c. Vasicek model
   d. Securitization

53. A _____ is a fungible, negotiable instrument representing financial value. They are broadly categorized into debt securities (such as banknotes, bonds and debentures), and equity securities; e.g., common stocks. The company or other entity issuing the _____ is called the issuer.
   a. Tracking stock
   b. Book entry
   c. Securities lending
   d. Security

Chapter 3. Test Preparation Part 3

54. _____, authored by professors Benjamin Graham and David Dodd of Columbia Business School, laid the intellectual foundation for what would later be called value investing. The work was first published in 1934, following unprecedented losses on Wall Street. In summing up lessons learned, Graham and Dodd chided Wall Street for its myopic focus on a company's reported earnings per share, and were particularly harsh on the favored 'earnings trends.' They encouraged investors to take an entirely different approach by gauging the rough value of the operating business that lay behind the security.

   a. Growth stocks   b. Stock valuation
   c. 4-4-5 Calendar   d. Security Analysis

55. In business and finance, a _____ (also referred to as equity _____) of stock means a _____ of ownership in a corporation (company.) In the plural, stocks is often used as a synonym for _____s especially in the United States, but it is less commonly used that way outside of North America.

In the United Kingdom, South Africa, and Australia, stock can also refer to completely different financial instruments such as government bonds or, less commonly, to all kinds of marketable securities.

   a. Bucket shop   b. Margin
   c. Procter ' Gamble   d. Share

56. _____ is a widely cited book on investment advice by Jeremy Siegel. Its first edition was released in 1994. Its fourth edition was released on November 27, 2007. According to Pablo Galarza of Money Magazine, 'His 1994 book _____ sealed the conventional wisdom that most of us should be in the stock market'. Amazon.com gives a list of 100 books that cite this book. The Washington Post called it one of the 10 best investment books of all time .

   a. The Pirates of Manhattan   b. Macro Markets
   c. Stocks for the Long Run   d. Little Book of Common Sense Investing

57. The _____ is a Board of Standards, and professional association dedicated to the finance sector and finance professionals. It has membership in over 140 countries with training centers and key offices in: Hong Kong, USA, Singapore, Dubai, Beijing PRC, Mexico, and more.

The AAFM was founded in 1996, via a merger between the _____ ' Analysts (AAFMA) and the Founders Advisory Committee of the Original Tax and Estate Planning Law Review.

   a. A Random Walk Down Wall Street   b. AAB
   c. ABN Amro   d. American Academy of Financial Management

58. The _____ is a free-trade and professional association that promotes and advocates issues important to the banking industry in the United States. The _____'s national headquarters are in Washington, D.C. In addition to its trade association mission, the _____ also performs educational components for consumers through its Educational Foundation affiliate.

While the _____ works on a national level, it also is supported by state operated offices (sometimes referred to as 'Leagues') which focus attention on state level support.

a. A Random Walk Down Wall Street b. ABN Amro
c. American Bankers Association d. AAB

59. The _____ is the oldest and most important professional organization in the field of economics. It was established in 1885 by religious and social reformer Richard T. Ely and others who had been trained in Germany under Gustav Schmoller and other members of the 'younger' German Historical School. The purposes of the Association are: 1) The encouragement of economic research, especially the historical and statistical study of the actual conditions of industrial life; 2) The issue of publications on economic subjects; 3) The encouragement of perfect freedom of economic discussion.

a. A Random Walk Down Wall Street b. American Economic Association
c. ABN Amro d. AAB

60. The _____ is the primary trade association for the American consumer credit industry, protecting access to credit and consumer choice. _____ provides the consumer credit industry and the consumers it serves with a voice in Washington, D.C., where the association is headquartered.

_____'s 350 members include consumer and commercial finance companies, vehicle finance/leasing companies, mortgage lenders, credit card issuers, industrial banks and industry suppliers.

a. A Random Walk Down Wall Street b. AAB
c. American Financial Services Association d. ABN Amro

61. _____ refer to services provided by the finance industry.

The finance industry encompasses a broad range of organizations that deal with the management of money. Among these organizations are banks, credit card companies, insurance companies, consumer finance companies, stock brokerages, investment funds and some government sponsored enterprises.

a. Delta hedging b. Financial Services
c. Cost of carry d. Financial instruments

62. The _____ is a United States organization founded in 1991, is focused on the advancement of economic understanding of law, and related areas of public policy and regulation. It promotes research in law and economics. The association was co-founded by George Priest, A.

a. Institute of Financial Accountants b. American Law and Economics Association
c. Accion USA d. Office of the Auditor General of Norway

63. Formed in 2003, the _____ (GNAIE) consists of the Chief Financial Officers of many of the leading North American insurance companies including life insurers, property and casualty insurers, and reinsurers. GNAIE members include companies who are the largest global providers of insurance and substantial multi-national corporations. All are major participants in the US markets.

a. 529 plan b. 7-Eleven
c. 4-4-5 Calendar d. Group of North American Insurance Enterprises

64. _____ (HKSI) was officially formed in December 1997 as a professional body to raise the standards of securities and finance practitioners in Hong Kong. In setting standards for professional excellence in Hong Kong, the HKSI offers a platform where individuals can gain the skills, and achieve the necessary professionalism and personal competence as they proceed towards further career advancement.

The HKSI provides continuous professional development by offering comprehensive examinations and an extensive programme of training courses and events.

    a. Certified Emission Reductions
    b. The Hong Kong Securities Institute
    c. Supply and demand
    d. JPMorgan Chase ' Co.

65. _____, in bookkeeping, refers to assets, liabilities, income, and expenses recorded on individual pages of the so called book of final entry or ledger. Changes in _____ value are made by chronologically posting debit (DR) and credit (CR) entries to its page. Examples of _____s are cash, _____s receivable, mortgages, loans, land and buildings, common stock, sales, services provided, wages, and payroll overhead.

    a. Accretion
    b. Option
    c. Alpha
    d. Account

66. _____ is a file or account that contains money that a person or company owes to suppliers, but hasn't paid yet (a form of debt.) When you receive an invoice you add it to the file, and then you remove it when you pay. Thus, the A/P is a form of credit that suppliers offer to their purchasers by allowing them to pay for a product or service after it has already been received.

    a. Outstanding balance
    b. Earnings before interest, taxes, depreciation and amortization
    c. Accrual
    d. Accounts Payable

67. _____ is a non-profit educational organization dedicated to the professional advancement of individuals in the accounts payable field by supporting National, Regional, and Local networking. They provide educational programs and resources along with training on leading edge technologies to promote and increase the awareness of AP as a professional discipline. The group also organizes an annual 'Accounts Payable Recognition Week'.

    a. International Accounts Payable Professionals
    b. Upromise
    c. Accounting Principles Board
    d. International Accounting Standards Board

68. The _____ (IABC) is a leading association for business communication professionals. IABC has approximately 16,000 members in more than 100 chapters in 70 countries.

IABC members hold positions in a variety of communication professions, including: public relations, media relations, corporate communications, employee communications, public affairs, investor relations, government relations, marketing communication, community relations, writing, editing, advertising, graphic design, human resources and teaching.

    a. Upromise
    b. Australian Accounting Standards Board
    c. International Association of Business Communicators
    d. Information Systems Audit and Control Association

Chapter 3. Test Preparation Part 3

69. The _____ (ISCM) is a professional association that promotes catastrophe management professionalism within the insurance industry.

ISCM's goal is to provide forums for exchange of ideas, understanding current catastrophe management issues, and networking among catastrophe managers.

Members may use ISCM to explore basic-through-advanced developments in the catastrophe modeling process, gain new catastrophe management skills and experience alternative viewpoints specific to their levels of interest and experience, learn to understand and manage modeling uncertainty in today's demanding environment, and realize maximum benefits as well as greater levels of comfort when using modeling technology to estimate the financial impacts associated with natural catastrophes and other extreme events.

  a. AAB
  b. ABN Amro
  c. A Random Walk Down Wall Street
  d. International Society of Catastrophe Managers

70. _____ is a new branch of Environmental finance. _____ explores the financial implications of living in a carbon-constrained world, a world in which emissions of carbon dioxide and other greenhouse gases (GHGs) carry a price. Financial risks and opportunities impact corporate balance sheets, and market-based instruments are capable of transferring environmental risk and achieving environmental objectives.
  a. 7-Eleven
  b. 529 plan
  c. 4-4-5 Calendar
  d. Carbon finance

71. The _____ is a monetary system in which a region's common medium of exchange are paper notes that are normally freely convertible into pre-set, fixed quantities of gold. The _____ is not currently used by any government, having been replaced completely by fiat currency.
  a. 529 plan
  b. 4-4-5 Calendar
  c. 7-Eleven
  d. Gold Standard

72. _____ are a key component of national and international emissions trading schemes that have been implemented to mitigate global warming. They provide a way to reduce greenhouse effect emissions on an industrial scale by capping total annual emissions and letting the market assign a monetary value to any shortfall through trading. Credits can be exchanged between businesses or bought and sold in international markets at the prevailing market price.
  a. Carbon emissions trading
  b. Carbon offset
  c. Personal carbon trading
  d. Carbon credits

73. _____ is the provision of resources (such as granting a loan) by one party to another party where that second party does not reimburse the first party immediately, thereby generating a debt, and instead arranges either to repay or return those resources (or material(s) of equal value) at a later date. The first party is called a creditor, also known as a lender, while the second party is called a debtor, also known as a borrower.

Movements of financial capital are normally dependent on either _____ or equity transfers.

  a. Comparable
  b. Clearing house
  c. Warrant
  d. Credit

74. _____ is emissions trading specifically for carbon dioxide (calculated in tonnes of carbon dioxide equivalent or tCO_2e) and currently makes up the bulk of emissions trading.

It is one of the ways countries can meet their obligations under the Kyoto Protocol to reduce carbon emissions and thereby mitigate global warming7 and 3.8 of the Protocol.

- A removal unit (RMU) issued by an Annex I Party on the basis of land use, land-use change and forestry (LULUCF) activities under Articles 3.3 and 3.4 of the Kyoto Protocol
- A certified emission reduction (CER) generated from a clean development mechanism project activity under Article 12 of the Kyoto Protocol.

Transfers and acquisitions of these units are to be tracked and recorded through the registry systems under the Kyoto Protocol.

_____ has been steadily increasing in recent years.

a. Joint Implementation
b. Personal carbon trading
c. Greenhouse gases
d. Carbon emissions trading

75. A _____ is a financial instrument representing a reduction in greenhouse gas emissions. Although there are six primary categories of greenhouse gases, _____s are measured in metric tons of carbon dioxide-equivalent (_____$_2$e.) One _____ represents the reduction of one metric ton of carbon dioxide, or its equivalent in other greenhouse gases.

a. Carbon emissions trading
b. Joint Implementation
c. Greenhouse gases
d. Carbon offset

76. A _____ refers to a business initiative that receives funding because of the cut the emission of greenhouse gases (GHGs) that will result. To prove that the project will result in real, permanent, verifiable reductions in Greenhouse Gases, proof must be provided in the form of a project design document and activity reports validated by an approved third party in the case of Clean Development Mechanism (CDM) or Joint Implementation (JI) projects.

_____s are developed for reasons of voluntary environmental stewardship, as well as legal compliance under a Greenhouse Gas Cap ' Trade program.

a. 7-Eleven
b. 529 plan
c. Carbon project
d. 4-4-5 Calendar

77. _____ refers to proposed emissions trading schemes under which emissions credits are allocated to adult individuals on a (broadly) equal per capita basis, within national carbon budgets. Individuals then surrender these credits when buying fuel or electricity. Individuals wanting or needing to emit at a level above that permitted by their initial allocation would be able to engage in emissions trading and purchase additional credits.

a. Greenhouse gases
b. Carbon emissions trading
c. Carbon offset
d. Personal carbon trading

Chapter 3. Test Preparation Part 3

78. _____ (_____s) are climate credits (or carbon credits) issued by the Clean Development Mechanism (CDM) Executive Board for emission reductions achieved by CDM projects and verified by a DOE under the rules of the Kyoto Protocol. _____s can be used by Annex 1 countries in order to comply with their emission limitation targets or by operators of installations covered by the European Union Emission Trading Scheme (EU ETS) in order to comply with their obligations to surrender EU Allowances, _____s or Emission Reduction Units (ERUs) for the CO2 emissions of their installations. _____s can be held by governmental and private entities on electronic accounts.

- a. Rural credit cooperatives
- b. Floating rate notes
- c. Black model
- d. Certified Emission Reductions

79. _____ (CCX) is North America's only voluntary, legally binding greenhouse gas (GHG) reduction and trading system for emission sources and offset projects in North America and Brazil.

CCX employs independent verification, includes six greenhouse gases, and has been trading greenhouse gas emission allowances since 2003. The companies joining the exchange commit to reducing their aggregate emissions by 6% by 2010.

- a. 529 plan
- b. 4-4-5 Calendar
- c. Contraction and Convergence
- d. Chicago Climate Exchange

80. The _____ was set-up in November 2008 by the national government to enforce a compulsory carbon trading scheme across the country's provinces as part of its strategy to create a 'low carbon civilisation' .

The scheme would allow provinces to earn money by investing in carbon capture systems in those those regions that fail to invest in the technology .

- Carbon emission trading
- Personal carbon trading
- Emissions trading
- Carbon capture and storage
- Clean Development Mechanism (CDM), United Nations

- a. 4-4-5 Calendar
- b. 529 plan
- c. Chinese national carbon trading scheme
- d. 7-Eleven

81. The _____ is an arrangement under the Kyoto Protocol allowing industrialised countries with a greenhouse gas reduction commitment (called Annex B countries) to invest in projects that reduce emissions in developing countries as an alternative to more expensive emission reductions in their own countries. A crucial feature of an approved _____ carbon project is that it has established that the planned reductions would not occur without the additional incentive provided by emission reductions credits, a concept known as 'additionality'. Distribution of _____ emission reductions, by country.

The _____ allows net global greenhouse gas emissions to be reduced at a much lower global cost by financing emissions reduction projects in developing countries where costs are lower than in industrialized countries.

a. Carbon offset
b. Carbon emissions trading
c. Clean Development Mechanism
d. Kyoto Protocol

82. _____ is a proposed global framework for reducing greenhouse gas emissions to combat climate change. Conceived by the Global Commons Institute in the early 1990s, the _____ strategy consists of reducing overall emissions of greenhouse gases to a safe level, 'Contraction', where the global emissions are reduced because every country brings emissions per capita to a level which is equal for all countries, 'Convergence'.

C'C is examined in the new feature film The Age of Stupid, set for release in 2009.

a. 529 plan
b. 4-4-5 Calendar
c. Contraction and Convergence
d. Chicago Climate Exchange

83. The United Nations Conference on Environment and Development _____ was a major United Nations conference held in Rio de Janeiro from June 3 to June 14, 1992.

172 governments participated, with 108 sending their heads of state or government. Some 2,400 representatives of non-governmental organizations attended, with 17,000 people at the parallel NGO 'Global Forum', who had so-called Consultative Status.

a. Earth Summit
b. ABN Amro
c. A Random Walk Down Wall Street
d. AAB

84. _____ operates in both the compliance and voluntary carbon markets. In the compliance market, _____ develops projects in the developing world under the Kyoto Protocol's Clean Development Mechanism to generate Certified Emission Reductions which are used by governments and organisations under the Kyoto Protocol and European Union Emissions Trading Scheme.

a. A Random Walk Down Wall Street
b. ABN Amro
c. AAB
d. Ecosecurities

85. _____ refers to the reduction of greenhouse gases, particularly under Joint Implementation, where it represents one tonne of CO2 equivalent reduced.

It is asserted that emission of carbon dioxide is the main cause of global warming (via the greenhouse effect.) However other gases also play a role in atmospheric warming.

a. ABN Amro
b. AAB
c. A Random Walk Down Wall Street
d. Emission Reduction Unit

86. _____ is an administrative approach used to control pollution by providing economic incentives for achieving reductions in the emissions of pollutants. It is sometimes called cap and trade. A coal power plant in Germany.

a. AAB
b. Emissions trading
c. International Climate Science Coalition
d. A Random Walk Down Wall Street

87. The _____ (EU ETS) is the largest multi-national, emissions trading scheme in the world, and is a major pillar of EU climate policy. The ETS currently covers more than 10,000 installations in the energy and industrial sectors which are collectively responsible for close to half of the EU's emissions of CO_2 and 40% of its total greenhouse gas emissions.

Under the EU ETS, large emitters of carbon dioxide within the EU must monitor and annually report their CO_2 emissions, and they are obliged every year to return an amount of emission allowances to the government that is equivalent to their CO_2 emissions in that year.

   a. ABN Amro   b. AAB
   c. A Random Walk Down Wall Street   d. European Union Emission Trading System

88. _____, also sometimes known as Flexibility Mechanisms or Kyoto Mechanisms), refers to Emissions Trading, the Clean Development Mechanism and Joint Implementation. These are mechanisms defined under the Kyoto Protocol intended to lower the overall costs of achieving its emissions targets. These mechanisms enable Parties to achieve emission reductions or to remove carbon from the atmosphere cost-effectively in other countries.

   a. Flexible Mechanisms   b. 529 plan
   c. 4-4-5 Calendar   d. 7-Eleven

89. The _____ is a declaration that calls for a number of new market-based mechanisms to protect tropical forests. The Declaration was created by the Global Canopy Programme, and has been signed by over 200 NGOs, business leaders, scientists and conservationists. The Declaration was created as carbon credits from land use, land-use change and forestry were omitted from the Clean Development Mechanism for the First Commitment Period of the Kyoto Protocol despite contributing 18-25% of all emissions.

   a. 7-Eleven   b. 529 plan
   c. Forests Now Declaration   d. 4-4-5 Calendar

90. _____ are gaseous constituents of the atmosphere that absorb and emit radiation at specific wavelengths within the thermal infrared range. This property causes the greenhouse effect. _____ are essential to maintaining the current temperature of the Earth; without them the planet would be so cold as to be uninhabitable.

   a. Post-Kyoto negotiations   b. Carbon emissions trading
   c. Personal carbon trading   d. Greenhouse gases

91. The _____ is an organization which espouses global warming skepticism. According to its web site, it is 'an international association of scientists, economists and energy and policy experts working to promote better public understanding of climate change science and policy worldwide. _____ is committed to providing a highly credible alternative to the UN's Intergovernmental Panel on Climate Change (IPCC) thereby fostering a rational, open discussion about climate issues.'

At the '2008 International Conference on Climate Change' hosted by the Heartland Institute, _____ Executive Director Tom Harris gave a speech in which he discussed what he called 'information sharing' and 'coordinated local activism':

> [...] We need regular high-impact media coverage of the findings of leading scientists -- not just one or two publications, but we need to have hundreds all over the world.

a. A Random Walk Down Wall Street
b. International Climate Science Coalition
c. UK Emissions Trading Scheme
d. AAB

92. _____ is one of three flexibility mechanisms set forth in the Kyoto Protocol to help countries with binding greenhouse gas emissions targets (so-called Annex I countries) meet their obligations Under Article 6, any Annex I country can invest in emission reduction projects (referred to as '_____ Projects') in any other Annex I country as an alternative to reducing emissions domestically.
   a. Kyoto Protocol
   b. Personal carbon trading
   c. Greenhouse gases
   d. Joint Implementation

93. The _____ is a protocol to the United Nations Framework Convention on Climate Change (UNFCCC or FCCC), an international environmental treaty produced at the United Nations Conference on Environment and Development (UNCED), informally known as the Earth Summit, held in Rio de Janeiro, Brazil, from 3-14 June 1992. The treaty is intended to achieve 'stabilization of greenhouse gas concentrations in the atmosphere at a level that would prevent dangerous anthropogenic interference with the climate system.' The _____ establishes legally binding commitments for the reduction of four greenhouse gases (carbon dioxide, methane, nitrous oxide, sulfur hexafluoride), and two groups of gases (hydrofluorocarbons and perfluorocarbons) produced by 'Annex I' (industrialized) nations, as well as general commitments for all member countries. As of 2008, 183 parties have ratified the protocol, which was initially adopted for use on 11 December 1997 in Kyoto, Japan and which entered into force on 16 February 2005.
   a. Carbon offset
   b. Personal carbon trading
   c. Joint Implementation
   d. Kyoto Protocol

94. The _____ is a regional agreement by six governors of states in the US midwest who are members of the Midwestern Governors Association (MGA) and the Premier of one Canadian province to reduce greenhouse gas emissions to combat climate change. Signatories to the Accord are the US states of Minnesota, Wisconsin, Illinois, Iowa, Michigan, Kansas, and the Canadian Province of Manitoba . Observers of the Accord are Indiana, Ohio ,and South Dakota.
   a. 7-Eleven
   b. 4-4-5 Calendar
   c. Midwestern Greenhouse Gas Accord
   d. 529 plan

95. _____ (_____, or ReGGIe) is a regional initiative by states in the Northeastern United States region to reduce greenhouse gas emissions. The _____ is designing a cap and trade program for greenhouse gas emissions from power plants.

Ten states currently participate in the initiative.

   a. Regional Greenhouse Gas Initiative
   b. 4-4-5 Calendar
   c. 7-Eleven
   d. 529 plan

96. _____ Renewable Energy Credits are tradable environmental commodities in the United States which represent proof that 1 megawatt-hour of electricity was generated from an eligible renewable energy resource.

These certificates can be sold and traded and the owner of the _____ can claim to have purchased renewable energy. While traditional carbon emissions trading programs promote low-carbon technologies by increasing the cost of emitting carbon, _____s can incentivize carbon-neutral renewable energy by providing a production subsidy to electricity generated from renewable sources.

a. 4-4-5 Calendar
b. Renewable Energy Certificates
c. 7-Eleven
d. 529 plan

97. _____ are a competitive alternative to Renewable Energy Credits (REC's.)

Although the intent with both methods is the same, to stimulate growth in the alternative and renewable energy space, _____'s have proven to offer benefits to local jobs, businesses and economies while making the growth fundable and lendable by financial institutions. _____ are the mechanisms or instruments at the heart of specific state, provincial or national renewable energy policies. _____s are incentives for homeowners, farmers, businesses, etc., to become producers of renewable energy, or to increase their production of renewable energy.

a. 4-4-5 Calendar
b. 529 plan
c. 7-Eleven
d. Renewable energy payments

Chapter 4. Test Preparation Part 4

1. The _____ is a quality standard for voluntary carbon offset industry. Based on the Kyoto Protocol's Clean Development Mechanism, _____ establishes criteria for validating, measuring, and monitoring carbon offset projects.
   a. Voluntary Carbon Standard
   b. 4-4-5 Calendar
   c. 529 plan
   d. 7-Eleven

2. _____ (_____s) are carbon credits developed by carbon offset providers which are not certified.

   Certification of carbon credits (Certified Emissions Reductions) are backed by an international framework and institutions, for example under the UN's Clean Development Mechanism, to ensure that real greenhouse gas emission reductions take place, as well as providing a clear audit trail.

   - Certified Emission Reduction

   a. GNMA
   b. Mitigating Control
   c. Voluntary Emissions Reductions
   d. Rural credit cooperatives

3. _____ is an investment strategy based on identifying investment vehicles with above-average quality characteristics.

   The idea for _____ originated in the bond and real estate world, where both the quality and price of potential investments are determined by ratings and expert attestations.

   Where equities are concerned, fundamentals analysis and active stock picking are used to identify stocks whose quality is particularly outstanding when measured according to a variety of business variables and financial coefficients.

   a. 529 plan
   b. 4-4-5 Calendar
   c. Value investing
   d. Quality investing

4. _____ is an investment strategy popularized by Michael O'Higgins in 1991 which proposes that an investor annually select for investment the ten Dow Jones Industrial Average stocks whose dividend is the highest fraction of their price.

   Proponent of _____ strategy argue that blue chip companies do not alter their dividend to reflect trading conditions and, therefore, the dividend is a measure of the average worth of the company; the stock price, in contrast, fluctuates through the business cycle. This should mean that companies with a high yield, with high dividend relative to price, are near the bottom of their business cycle and are likely to see their stock price increase faster than low yield companies.

   a. 4-4-5 Calendar
   b. Pure play
   c. 529 plan
   d. The Dogs of the Dow

Chapter 4. Test Preparation Part 4   77

5. The _____ is one of several stock market indices, created by nineteenth-century Wall Street Journal editor and Dow Jones ' Company co-founder Charles Dow. Dow compiled the index to gauge the performance of the industrial sector of the American stock market. It is the second-oldest U.S. market index, after the Dow Jones Transportation Average, which Dow also created.
   a. 7-Eleven
   b. 529 plan
   c. Dow Jones Industrial Average
   d. 4-4-5 Calendar

6. The American Collectors Association is the largest trade group representing collection agencies, creditors, debt buyers, collection attorneys and debt collection industry service providers. The organization was founded in 1939 and changed its name to _____ in 2001. _____ is based in Minneapolis, Minnesota.
   a. Identity score
   b. Intelliscore
   c. ITraxx
   d. ACA International

7. _____ is a website jointly operated by the three major U.S. credit reporting agencies. The site was created in order to comply with their obligations under the Fair and Accurate Credit Transactions Act (FACTA) to provide a mechanism for American consumers to receive a free annual credit report.

One of the provisions of FACTA, passed in 2003 as an amendment to the Fair Credit Reporting Act (FCRA), was a requirement that the credit reporting agencies provide, upon request, a free credit report every twelve months to every consumer.

   a. Intelliscore
   b. Unsecured loan
   c. ITraxx
   d. Annualcreditreport.com

8. _____ refers to a strategy of completing multiple applications in a relatively short period of time. The term, as set out in the Wall Street Journal, refers to a frenzy of applications, and most frequently refers to applications for financial products, such as loans, credit cards, and bank deposit accounts. However, it can also include insurance applications, brokerage applications, etc.
   a. App-o-rama
   b. A Random Walk Down Wall Street
   c. AAB
   d. ABN Amro

9. A fairly new form of loan, the _____ or _____, is a tool used by US based firms trading on public markets that need funding of under $10,000,000. In a _____, A group of European based banks (the pool), create a European firm who's sole purpose is to loan money to a US based company. Because this loan to the European based bank is completely insured, the _____ does not have as high a risk if the loan is defaulted on.
   a. Bank Pool Loan
   b. Debt validation
   c. Participation loan
   d. Credit freeze

10. _____ is a method of financing, used to maintain liquidity while waiting for an anticipated and reasonably expected inflow of cash. _____ is commonly used when the cash flow from a sale of an asset is expected after the cash outlay for the purchase of an asset. For example, when selling a house, the owner may not receive the cash for 90 days, but has already purchased a new home and must pay for it in 30 days.
    a. Bridge financing
    b. Tenancy
    c. Real estate investing
    d. Liquidation value

11. _____ or financing is to provide capital (funds), which means money for a project, a person, a business or any other private or public institutions.

Those funds can be allocated for either short term or long term purposes. The health fund is a new way of _____ private healthcare centers.

   a. Product life cycle   b. Synthetic CDO
   c. Proxy fight   d. Funding

12. A _____ (usually bridging loan in the United Kingdom, and also known in some applications as a swing loan) is a type of short-term loan, typically taken out for a period of 2 weeks to 3 years pending the arrangement of larger or longer-term financing.

A _____ is interim financing for an individual or business until permanent or the next stage of financing can be obtained. Money from the new financing is generally used to 'take out' (i.e. to pay back) the _____, as well as other capitalization needs.

   a. Partial Payment   b. Bridge loan
   c. Default   d. Composiition of Creditors

13. The establishment of Credit Information Bureau (India) Limited, India's first Credit Information Bureau, is an effort made by the Government of India and the Reserve Bank of India to improve the functionality and stability of the Indian financial system by containing NPAs while improving credit grantors' portfolio quality.

_____ was promoted by State Bank of India (SBI), Housing Development Finance Corporation (HDFC), Dun ' Bradstreet Information Services India Private Limited (D'B) and TransUnion International Inc. (TransUnion) to provide comprehensive credit information by collecting, collating and disseminating credit information pertaining to both commercial and consumer borrowers, to a closed user group of Members.

   a. Variable rate mortgage   b. CIBIL
   c. Reserve requirement   d. Probability of default

14. In structured finance the _____ is the most junior security issued by a Structured investment vehicle. It is comparable to the Equity Tranche of a CDO. Investors who buy the _____s are the first in line to bear risk if the cash flows from the SIV's assets are insufficient to cover promised payments to all investors.

   a. Capital note   b. Loan to value
   c. Debt   d. Participation loan

15. A _____ is a loan which is financed by the seller of a property. Normally this aids in the completion of the sale of the property. It could also refer to the part of the purchase price the seller is able and willing to finance.

   a. Credit note   b. Hard money loan
   c. Leveraged lease   d. Carryback loan

16. _____ is a short-term cash loan to a company. A bank provides this type of funding, but only after the required security is given to secure the loan. Once a security for repayment has been given, the business that receives the loan can continuously draw from the bank up to a certain specified amount.

a. Loan shark
b. Debt consolidation
c. Debt management plan
d. Cash credit

17. _____ is the provision of resources (such as granting a loan) by one party to another party where that second party does not reimburse the first party immediately, thereby generating a debt, and instead arranges either to repay or return those resources (or material(s) of equal value) at a later date. The first party is called a creditor, also known as a lender, while the second party is called a debtor, also known as a borrower.

Movements of financial capital are normally dependent on either _____ or equity transfers.

a. Credit
b. Warrant
c. Comparable
d. Clearing house

18. In lending agreements, _____ is a borrower's pledge of specific property to a lender, to secure repayment of a loan. The _____ serves as protection for a lender against a borrower's risk of default - that is, a borrower failing to pay the principal and interest under the terms of a loan obligation. If a borrower does default on a loan (due to insolvency or other event), that borrower forfeits (gives up) the property pledged as _____ ollateral - and the lender then becomes the owner of the _____.

a. Collateral
b. Nominal value
c. Refinancing risk
d. Future-oriented

19. _____ is the process of agreeing, confirming and advising collateral transactions. Collateral are properties or assets that are offered to secure a loan or other credit. Collateral becomes subject to seizure on default.

a. Debt
b. Collateral Management
c. Capital note
d. Credit report monitoring

20. A _____ is a business that pursues payments on debts owed by individuals or businesses. Most collection agencies operate as agents of creditors and collect debts for a fee or percentage of the total amount owed. Some agencies, sometimes referred to as 'debt buyers', purchase debts from creditors for a fraction of the value of the debt and pursue the debtor for the full balance.

a. Commercial hard money
b. Collection agency
c. Guaranteed consumer funding
d. Partial Payment

21. _____ is a term describing a commercial loan that is generally non bankable. The company usually does not meet the standard banking criteria, but has real estate and or assets that are sufficient to collateralize the loan to the investors/lenders.

_____ rates are generally higher than other rates.

a. Commercial hard money
b. Partial Payment
c. Microcredit
d. Guaranteed consumer funding

22. A _____ is an agreement among several creditors of a debtor, usually a business. Usually, the agreement involves paying a lessened amount over a period of time.

a. Doctrine of the Proper Law
b. Loans and interest, in Judaism
c. Time-based currency
d. Composiition of Creditors

23. A _____ is a party (e.g. person, organization, company, or government) that has a claim to the services of a second party. The first party, in general, has provided some property or service to the second party under the assumption (usually enforced by contract) that the second party will return an equivalent property or service. The second party is frequently called a debtor or borrower.
    a. NOPLAT
    b. Redemption value
    c. Creditor
    d. False billing

24. In the United States, a _____ is a mortgage loan that conforms to GSE guidelines.

In general, any loan which does not meet guidelines is a non-_____. A loan which does not meet guidelines specifically because the loan amount exceeds the guideline limits is known as a jumbo loan.

   a. Blanket mortgage
   b. Conforming loan
   c. Mortgage insurance
   d. Home equity line of credit

25. A _____ was a set of contracts devised by European bankers and merchants in the Middle Ages as a method of circumventing canon law edicts prohibiting usury. At the time, most Christian nations heavily incorporated scripture into their laws, and as such it was illegal for any person to charge interest on a loan of money.

To get around this, a set of three separate contracts were presented to someone seeking a loan: an investment, a sale of profit and an insurance contract.

   a. Deposit account
   b. Bilateral netting
   c. 4-4-5 Calendar
   d. Contractum trinius

26. A _____ (U.S.), or credit reference agency (UK) is a company that collects information from various sources and provides consumer credit information on individual consumers for a variety of uses. This helps lenders assess credit worthiness, the ability to pay back a loan, and can affect the interest rate and other terms of a loan. Interest rates are not the same for everyone, but instead can be based on risk-based pricing, a form of price discrimination based on the different expected risks of different borrowers, as set out in their credit rating.
   a. Credit bureau
   b. Reserve requirement
   c. Probability of default
   d. Wall Street Journal prime rate

27. A _____ is a sudden reduction in the general availability of loans, or a sudden increase in the cost of obtaining loans from banks.

There are a number of reasons why banks may suddenly increase the costs of borrowing or make borrowing more difficult. It may be due to an anticipated decline in value of the collateral used by the banks when issuing loans, or even an increased perception of risk regarding the solvency of other banks within the banking system.

   a. Credit cycle
   b. Capital note
   c. Credit crunch
   d. Credit report monitoring

Chapter 4. Test Preparation Part 4   81

28. The _____ is the expansion and contraction of access to credit over the course of the business cycle. Some economists, including Hyman Minsky and members of the Austrian school, regard _____s as the fundamental process driving the business cycle. In the Kiyotaki-Moore model of the business cycle, collateral constraints amplify the effects of shocks to the real economy.
   a. Credit cycle
   b. Leveraged lease
   c. Credit analysis
   d. Syndicated loan

29. A _____ is the financial term used to describe either:

A general default event related to a legal entity's previously agreed financial obligation. In this case, a legal entity fails to meet its obligation on any significant financial transaction (coupon on a bond it issued or interest rate payment on a swap for example.) The marketplace will recognize this as an event related to the legal entity's credit worthiness.

   a. No-arbitrage bounds
   b. Death spiral financing
   c. Capital surplus
   d. Credit event

30. A _____ a credit report lock down, a credit lock down, a credit lock or a security freeze, allows an individual to control how a U.S. consumer reporting agency is able to sell his or her data. The _____ locks the data at the consumer reporting agency until an individual gives permission for the release of the data. Today, _____s are made possible by state laws as well as industry-initiated rules.
   a. Non-performing loan
   b. Vendor finance
   c. Guaranteed consumer funding
   d. Credit freeze

31. _____ or credit report is, in many countries, a record of an individual's or company's past borrowing and repaying, including information about late payments and bankruptcy. The term 'credit reputation' can either be used synonymous to _____ or to credit score.

In the U.S., when a customer fills out an application for credit from a bank, store or credit card company, their information is forwarded to a credit bureau.

   a. Promissory note
   b. Credit repair software
   c. Financial plan
   d. Credit history

32. _____ - _____ is a credit website that provides users with free Credit scores, tools to track their credit scores, and tools to educate users about improving their credit scores. _____ is headquartered in San Francisco, California. The company has been initial funded by Chris Larson, CEO of Prosper and Mark Lefanowicz, president of E-Loan.
   a. Ford Foundation
   b. Governmental Accounting Standards Board
   c. SPDR
   d. Credit karma

33. _____ enables consumers to correct errors and inaccurate information in their credit reports and to boost their Credit score. In compliance with laws protecting consumers, including the Fair Credit Reporting Act, several companies have introduced software giving consumers a glimpse into how their behavior actually affects their credit score. Some of these self-help, consumer or professional software products guide the consumer through the complexities of credit scoring models, credit score simulation, loan qualification, and automate the process by generating letters for disputing errors and negotiating with creditors and tracking progress.

a. Promissory note
b. Title loan
c. Financial plan
d. Credit repair software

34. _____ is the monitoring of your credit history in order to detect any suspicious activity or change in your credit history. Companies offer such service on a subscription basis, typically granting you: regular access to your credit history, alerts of critical changes to your credit history, and additional services. Credit monitoring can help you detect credit related fraud and identity theft.

a. Capital note
b. Hard money loan
c. Credit report monitoring
d. Credit analysis

35. A _____ is a numerical expression based on a statistical analysis of a person's credit files, to represent the creditworthiness of that person. A _____ is primarily based on credit report information, typically sourced from credit bureaus.

Lenders, such as banks and credit card companies, use _____s to evaluate the potential risk posed by lending money to consumers and to mitigate losses due to bad debt.

a. Credit report monitoring
b. Paydex
c. Credit score
d. Credit freeze

36. _____ is that which is owed; usually referencing assets owed, but the term can cover other obligations. In the case of assets, _____ is a means of using future purchasing power in the present before a summation has been earned. Some companies and corporations use _____ as a part of their overall corporate finance strategy.

a. Debt
b. Partial Payment
c. Credit cycle
d. Cross-collateralization

37. _____ is a term used when the collateral for one loan is also used as collateral for another loan. If a person has borrowed from the same bank a home loan secured by the house, a car loan secured by the car, and so on, these assets can be used as cross-collaterals for all the loans. If the person pays off the car loan and wants to sell the car, the bank may veto the deal because the car is still used to secure the home loan and other loans.

a. Credit freeze
b. Credit score
c. Collection agency
d. Cross-collateralization

38. A _____ is defined as a certificate of agreement of loans which is given under the company's stamp and carries an undertaking that the _____ holder will get a fixed return (fixed on the basis of interest rates) and the principal amount whenever the _____ matures.

In finance, a _____ is a long-term debt instrument used by governments and large companies to obtain funds. It is defined as 'a debt secured only by the debtor's earning power, not by a lien on any specific asset.' It is similar to a bond except the securitization conditions are different.

a. Partial Payment
b. Collateral Management
c. Collection agency
d. Debenture

Chapter 4. Test Preparation Part 4

39. In finance, the term _____ describes various legal measures taken to ensure that debtors, whether individuals, businesses honor their debts and make an honest effort to repay the money that they owe. Generally regarded as a subdivision of tax law, _____ is most often enforced through a combination of audits and legal restrictions. For example, a provision of the Federal Debt Collection Procedure Act states that a person or organization indebted to the United States, against whom a judgment lien has been filed, is ineligible to receive a government grant.
   a. Credit note
   b. Cross-collateralization
   c. Debt compliance
   d. Partial Payment

40. _____ entails taking out one loan to pay off many others. This is often done to secure a lower interest rate, secure a fixed interest rate or for the convenience of servicing only one loan.

   _____ can simply be from a number of unsecured loans into another unsecured loan, but more often it involves a secured loan against an asset that serves as collateral, most commonly a house.

   a. Debt management plan
   b. Cash credit
   c. Line of credit
   d. Debt consolidation

41. _____ or amalgamation is the act of merging many things into one. In business, it often refers to the mergers or acquisitions of many smaller companies into much larger ones. The financial accounting term of _____ refers to the aggregated financial statements of a group company as consolidated account.
   a. Retained earnings
   b. Write-off
   c. Cost of goods sold
   d. Consolidation

42. A _____ is a method used in various countries for paying personal unsecured debts (which typically are out of control in the sense that payments are late and those due are taking too large a portion of income assessing income and budget, and re-negotiating interest rates and payments with the lenders, based upon evidence that the result will be a higher likelihood of collection by the lenders due to the debtors more realistic monthly repayment.

   _____s are a managed informal arrangement with creditors - whether the debtor uses a free creditor sponsored _____ organisation or a fee-charging _____ company, accepting any terms of a _____ proposal put forward on behalf of the debtor is accepted always at the discretion of the creditors. A good debt advice service recognises this and will only suggest a debtor pays what they can realistically afford after their priority costs (mortgage, utilities, food etc) no matter what.

   a. Debt-snowball method
   b. Default Notice
   c. Line of credit
   d. Debt management plan

43. The _____, is the ratio of net operating income to debt payments on a piece of investment real estate. It is a popular benchmark used in the measurement of an income-producing property's ability to produce enough revenue to cover its monthly mortgage payments. The higher this ratio is, the easier it is to borrow money for the property.
   a. Debt service coverage ratio
   b. Times interest earned
   c. Financial ratio
   d. Receivables turnover ratio

44. _____ refers to a consumer's right to challenge a debt and/or receive written verification of a debt from a debt collector. The right to dispute the debt and receive validation are part of the consumer's rights under the United States Federal Fair Debt Collection Practices Act (FDCPA) and are set out in §809 of that act.

Under the Fair Debt Collection Practices Act, any person or entity, including lawyers, who regularly attempts to collect consumer debts is considered a debt collector and is therefore required to respond to proper _____ requests.

- a. Partial Payment
- b. Carryback loan
- c. Credit report monitoring
- d. Debt validation

45. In finance, _____ occurs when a debtor has not met its legal obligations according to the debt contract, e.g. it has not made a scheduled payment, or has violated a loan covenant (condition) of the debt contract. _____ may occur if the debtor is either unwilling or unable to pay their debt. This can occur with all debt obligations including bonds, mortgages, loans, and promissory notes.
- a. Credit crunch
- b. Debt validation
- c. Vendor finance
- d. Default

46. All credit applications (Eg personal loans, credit cards or store cards) opened in the United Kingdom are regulated by the Consumer Credit Act 2006. This piece of legislation requires that creditors must issue a _____ to any customer who has fallen behind with payments to their account, before legal action can be pursued to recover the monies owed.
- a. Debt management plan
- b. Debt-snowball method
- c. Line of credit
- d. Default Notice

47. The _____ is a United States law (codified at 15 U.S.C. § 1691 et seq.), enacted in 1974, that makes it unlawful for any creditor to discriminate against any applicant, with respect to any aspect of a credit transaction, on the basis of race, color, religion, national origin, sex, marital status, or age (provided the applicant has the capacity to contract); to the fact that all or part of the applicant's income derives from a public assistance program; or to the fact that the applicant has in good faith exercised any right under the Consumer Credit Protection Act. The law applies to any person who, in the ordinary course of business, regularly participates in a credit decision, including banks, retailers, bankcard companies, finance companies, and credit unions.
- a. Equal Credit Opportunity Act
- b. A Random Walk Down Wall Street
- c. ABN Amro
- d. AAB

48. _____ is a term used in commercial loan documentation. It refers to the occurrence of an event which allows the lender to demand repayment of the loan in advance of its normal due date (also known as accelerating the loan.) In a revolving credit facility, the occurrence of an _____ normally also allows the lender to cancel any obligations to make further loan advances.
- a. Intelliscore
- b. Annualcreditreport.com
- c. Identity score
- d. Event of default

49. The _____ is a United States federal law enacted as an amendment to the Truth in Lending Act (codified at 15 U.S.C. § 1601 et seq.). Its purpose is to protect consumers from unfair billing practices and to provide a mechanism for addressing billing errors in 'open end' credit accounts, such as credit card or charge card accounts.
- a. Fair Credit Reporting Act
- b. Regulation Q
- c. Fair Credit Billing Act
- d. Truth in Lending Act

50. The _____ is an American federal law (codified at 15 U.S.C. § 1681 et seq.) that regulates the collection, dissemination, and use of consumer credit information.

a. Regulation Q
b. Truth in Lending Act
c. Fair Credit Billing Act
d. Fair Credit Reporting Act

51. _____ broadly refers to regulation of the debt collection industry at both the U.S. Federal and state levels of government. At the Federal level, it is primarily governed by the _____ Practices Act ('_____PA'.) In addition, many U.S. States also have debt collection laws that regulate the credit and collection industry and give consumer debtors protection from abusive and deceptive practices.
   a. Bundesrechnungshof
   b. Covenant
   c. Securities Investor Protection Act
   d. Fair Debt Collection

52. The _____ is a United States statute added in 1978 as Title VIII of the Consumer Credit Protection Act. Its purposes are to eliminate abusive practices in the collection of consumer debts, to promote fair debt collection and to provide consumers with an avenue for disputing and obtaining validation of debt information in order to ensure the information's accuracy.
   a. Law of one price
   b. Fair Debt Collection Practices Act
   c. Court of Audit of Belgium
   d. Partnership

53. _____ is a bargain hunting website, centering around a set of forums that allow users to publish deals and rebate offers on a comprehensive range of products and services, though computer-related products dominate the listings. _____

The site focuses on listings primarily for North American consumers; the website does not offer its service to a generic international and multi-currency audience. In addition to the Hot Deals, dozens of 'Free Stuff' giveaways are discussed on the forums every day, as well as travel deals, finance deals, product reviews and reviews of retailers.

   a. Pretax Group
   b. FatWallet
   c. Prosper Marketplace
   d. Deloitte Touche Tohmatsu

54. The _____ - Asia-Pacific Microfinance, Public Health ' Development Centre (_____) is an international non-governmental, non-profit initiative addressing the microfinance, public health, and international development needs of communities in, on, and around the Pacific Rim. For these purposes, the _____ views the Asia-Pacific region quite broadly in line with APEC; the jurisdictions covered are claimed to account for approximately 65% of the world's population. The Council's activities, which include conducting research, making investments, and providing education and advice, are centrally coordinated.
   a. Gamelan Council
   b. World Trade Organization
   c. Public Company Accounting Oversight Board
   d. Municipal Securities Rulemaking Board

55. _____ is an type of credit similar to layaway, which allows consumers to purchase items on a payment plan regardless of their credit history.

This process requires signing a contract in which the consumer promises to make all of the payments in full by their due date. In return they will receive guaranteed credit and are allowed to use the product as they pay it off

With this type of loan the consumer does not receive their purchased items right away as they would using traditional credit purchasing methods.

a. Guaranteed consumer funding
c. Debt compliance
b. Participation loan
d. Paydex

56. A _____ is a specific type of asset-based loan financing in which a borrower receives funds secured by the value of a parcel of real estate. _____s are typically issued at much higher interest rates than conventional commercial or residential property loans and are almost never issued by a commercial bank or other deposit institution. Hard money is similar to a bridge loan which usually has similar criteria for lending as well as cost to the borrowers.

a. Non-performing loan
c. Debenture
b. Prosper Marketplace
d. Hard money loan

57. A home equity line of credit is a loan in which the lender agrees to lend a maximum amount within an agreed period (called a term), where the collateral is the borrower's equity in his/her house.

A _____ differs from a conventional home equity loan in that the borrower is not advanced the entire sum up front, but uses a line of credit to borrow sums that total no more than the amount, similar to a credit card. At closing you are assigned a specified credit limit that you can borrow up to.

a. Conforming loan
c. Reverse mortgage
b. Blanket mortgage
d. HELOC

58. _____ is the brand-name for the family of credit default swap index products covering regions of Europe, Japan and non-Japan Asia. They form a large sector of the overall credit derivative market. The indices are constructed on a set of rules with the overriding criterion being that of liquidity of the underlying Credit Default Swaps (CDS.)

a. Identity score
c. Intelliscore
b. ITraxx
d. Annualcreditreport.com

59. An _____ is a system for tagging and verifying the legitimacy of an individual's public identity. _____s are increasingly being adopted as a means to prevent fraud in business and as a tool to verify and correct public records.

_____s incorporate a broad set of consumer data that gauges a person's legitimacy.

a. Intelliscore
c. Annualcreditreport.com
b. Identity score
d. Event of default

60. An _____ is a system using loans as control against fraud and theft. The most common _____ known is the petty cash system.

The Petty Cash _____ works on the basis that you only replenish what you have spent.

a. Installment Sales Method
c. Entity concept
b. Unified Ledger Accounting
d. Imprest system

61. An _____ is a term used in business, for a numerical score granted by Experian to Business as a credit score for the promptness of their payments to creditors. The _____ is used for commercial organizations in a manner similar to the way the FICO score is used for individuals.

The _____ is given by Experian, which is one of the largest Credit Reporting Agencies in the United States.

   a. ITraxx   b. Identity score
   c. Intelliscore   d. Annualcreditreport.com

62. A _____ is a charge levied against a client by a company or organization for not paying a bill or returning a rented or borrowed item by its due date. Its use is most commonly associated with businesses like creditors, video rental outlets and libraries. _____s are generally calculated on a per day, per item basis.

   a. 4-4-5 Calendar   b. 529 plan
   c. 7-Eleven   d. Late fee

63. _____ - _____ is a person-to-person lending website that pairs borrowers and lenders through a matching system that combines a search algorithm, credit decisioning and social networking. _____ is headquartered in Sunnyvale, California. In August 2007 the company raised $10.26 Million in a Series A funding round led by Norwest Venture Partners and Canaan Partners.

   a. Federal Home Loan Mortgage Corporation   b. FASB
   c. National Bureau of Economic Research   d. Lending Club

64. A _____ is a lease in which the lessor puts up some of the money required to purchase the asset and borrows the rest from a lender. The lender is given a senior secured interest on the asset and an assignment of the lease and lease payments. The lessee makes payments to the lessor, who makes payments to the lender.

   a. Guaranteed consumer funding   b. Collection agency
   c. Debt buyer   d. Leveraged lease

65. A _____ is a person or body that offers unsecured loans at high interest rates to individuals, often backed by blackmail or threats of violence.

In much of history, usury laws made _____s commonplace. Many moneylenders skirted between legal and extra-legal activity.

   a. Line of credit   b. Debt-snowball method
   c. Cash credit   d. Loan shark

66. The loan-to-value ratio expresses the amount of a first mortgage lien as a percentage of the total appraised value of real property. For instance, if a borrower wants $130,000 to purchase a house worth $150,000, the _____ ratio is $130,000/ $150,000 or 87%.

_____ is one of the key risk factors that lenders assess when qualifying borrowers for a mortgage.

   a. Credit rating   b. Loan to value
   c. Guaranteed consumer funding   d. Credit analysis

Chapter 4. Test Preparation Part 4

67. The combination of _____, is a complicated and detailed subject. The biblical Hebrew terms for interest are neshekh, literally meaning a bite, in reference to its painfulness to the debtor, and marbit/tarbit, which specifically refers to the gain by the creditor; neshekh referred to interest that was charged by deducting it from the loaned money itself, before the loaned money was handed over to the debtor, while marbit/tarbit referred to interest that was charged by adding it to the amount due to be repaid. The word marbit/tarbit, which referred to the form of interest more familiar in modern times, became ribbit, in later Hebrew, and hence in modern Hebrew.
   a. Legal and regulatory risk
   b. Vasicek model
   c. Black model
   d. Loans and interest, in Judaism

68. _____ is a fee paid on borrowed assets. It is the price paid for the use of borrowed money, or, money earned by deposited funds. Assets that are sometimes lent with _____ include money, shares, consumer goods through hire purchase, major assets such as aircraft, and even entire factories in finance lease arrangements.
   a. Insolvency
   b. Interest
   c. A Random Walk Down Wall Street
   d. AAB

69. _____ refers to debt incurred due to health care costs and expenses.

Many people accumulate _____ when they do not have health insurance to cover the costs of necessary medications, treatments, or procedures. Individuals who have health insurance, however, are not immune to _____.

   a. Debt
   b. Debt buyer
   c. Credit report monitoring
   d. Medical debt

70. _____ is the extension of very small loans (microloans) to the unemployed, to poor entrepreneurs and to others living in poverty who are not considered bankable. These individuals lack collateral, steady employment and a verifiable credit history and therefore cannot meet even the most minimal qualifications to gain access to traditional credit. _____ is a part of microfinance, which is the provision of a wider range of financial services to the very poor.
   a. Debenture
   b. Microcredit
   c. Non-performing loan
   d. Subordinated debt

71. The _____ is an American non-profit organization started as an effort to bring together microcredit practitioners, advocates, educational institutions, donor agencies, international financial institutions, non-governmental organizations and others involved with microcredit around the goal of alleviating world poverty through microfinance.

The first Microcredit Summit was held February 2-4, 1997 in Washington, DC. The first summit had approximately 3,000 in attendance from 137 countries.

   a. Rotating Savings and Credit Association
   b. Village Banking
   c. Microcredit Summit Campaign
   d. Solidarity lending

72. _____ is a term used to refer to when the value of an asset used to secure a loan is less than the outstanding balance on the loan. A person holding _____ is said to be upside down.

This can occur when the value of the asset stays fixed but the loan balance increases because loan payments are less than the interest, a situation known as negative amortization.

a. Conforming loan
c. Mortgage insurance
b. Cash-out
d. Negative equity

73. A _____ is a loan that fails to meet bank criteria for funding.

Reasons include the loan amount is higher than the conforming loan limit (for mortgage loans), lack of sufficient credit, the unorthodox nature of the use of funds, or the collateral backing it. In many cases, _____s can be funded by hard money lenders, or private institutions/money.

a. Prosper Marketplace
c. Credit report monitoring
b. Credit cycle
d. Non-conforming loan

74. A _____ is a loan that is in default or close to being in default. Many loans become non-performing after being in default for 3 months, but this can depend on the contract terms.

'A loan is nonperforming when payments of interest and principal are past due by 90 days or more, or at least 90 days of interest payments have been capitalized, refinanced or delayed by agreement, or payments are less than 90 days overdue, but there are other good reasons to doubt that payments will be made in full' (IMF)

a. Hard money loan
c. Non-conforming loan
b. Carryback loan
d. Non-performing loan

75. A _____ is a real estate loan used to finance the purchase of both real property and personal property, such as in the purchase of a new home that includes carpeting, window coverings and major appliances.

a. Commercial finance
c. Conglomerate merger
b. Cleanup clause
d. Package loan

76. _____ refers to the offering of a payment by check for less than the full amount claimed by the creditor. Such an offer for debt discharge by tender of a 'payment-in-full' check is a common practice. If the amount tendered is not grossly insufficient, it presents the creditor with a tough business decision: Will I accept the $9,000 and forfeit the other $1,000 that he really owes me or do I refuse it all in the hope I can collect $10,000 later? Traditional court rulings have treated the tender of the check as the offer of an accord and satisfaction.

a. Credit rating
c. Vendor finance
b. Non-conforming loan
d. Partial Payment

77. In finance, 'participation' is an ownership interest in a mortgage or other loan. In particular, _____ is a cooperation of multiple lenders to issue a loan (known as participation loan) to one borrower. This is usually done in order to reduce individual risks of the lenders.

a. Securitization
c. Loan participation
b. Doctrine of the Proper Law
d. Short positions

78. _____s are loans made by multiple lenders to a single borrower. Several banks, for example, might chip in to fund one extremely large loan, with one of the banks taking the role of the 'lead bank.' This lending institution then recruits other banks to participate and share the risks and profits. The lead bank typically originates the loan, takes responsibility for the loan servicing of the _____, organizes and manages the participation, and deals directly with the borrower.

a. Credit analysis
b. Capital note
c. Credit cycle
d. Participation loan

79. A _____ is a small, short-term loan that is intended to cover a borrower's expenses until his or her next payday. The loans are also sometimes referred to as cash advances, though that term can also refer to cash provided against a prearranged line of credit such as a credit card Legislation regarding _____s varies widely between different countries and, within the USA, between different states.
   a. 4-4-5 Calendar
   b. 529 plan
   c. Payday loan
   d. 7-Eleven

80. _____ is a term used in business, for a numerical score granted by Dun and Bradstreet to Business as a credit score for the promptness of their payments to creditors. The _____ score is used for commercial organizations in a manner similar to the way the FICO score is used for individuals.

The _____ Score ranges from 0 to 100 (best.)

   a. Leveraged lease
   b. Subordinated debt
   c. Paydex
   d. Loan to value

81. _____ is, in its broadest sense, the name given to a certain breed of financial transaction which occurs directly between individuals without the intermediation/participation of a traditional financial institution. See also disintermediation. An enabling technology for _____ has been the Internet, where _____ appears in two primary variations: an 'online marketplace' model and a 'family and friend' model.
   a. Net asset value
   b. Collective investment scheme
   c. Trust company
   d. Person-to-person lending

82. _____ is a commonly used term in banking and finance. It refers to lending money to a company or individual by a private individual or organization. While banks are traditional sources of financing for real estate, and other purposes, _____ is offered by individuals or organizations and may have non traditional qualifying guidelines.
   a. Deposit insurance
   b. Probability of default
   c. Reserve requirement
   d. Private money

83. _____, Inc. is a San Francisco, California-based company that operates Prosper.com, an online auction website where individuals can buy loans and request to borrow money. Borrowers set the maximum interest rate they wish to pay, and loan buyers, called 'lenders,' bid on specific loans by committing a portion of the principal and setting the minimum interest rate they wish to receive on a particular loan. Prosper manages the reverse dutch auction, assembling bids with the lowest interest rates in order to fund the loan.
   a. Prosper Marketplace
   b. Guaranteed consumer funding
   c. Vendor finance
   d. Collection agency

84. _____ consists of the sale of goods or merchandise from a fixed location, such as a department store, boutique or kiosk in small or individual lots for direct consumption by the purchaser. _____ may include subordinated services, such as delivery. Purchasers may be individuals or businesses.
   a. 529 plan
   b. 7-Eleven
   c. Retailing
   d. 4-4-5 Calendar

Chapter 4. Test Preparation Part 4

85. _____ is a type of credit that does not have a fixed number of payments, in contrast to installment credit. Examples of _____s used by consumers include credit cards. Corporate _____ facilities are typically used to provide liquidity for a company's day-to-day operations.
   a. Revolving credit
   b. Reverse stock split
   c. Package loan
   d. Commercial finance

86. _____ (or last-out participation) is a form of loan with a security interest in the assets of a company that are second in ranking behind a traditional senior credit facility. A lien is a form of security interest granted over an item of property to secure the payment of a debt.

The second lien lender will typically be required to agree contractually (through an intercreditor agreement or other contract) to subordinate its claims on the assets to the first lien secured lenders.

   a. Gross profit
   b. Cashflow matching
   c. Real option
   d. Second lien loan

87. In law, a _____ is a form of security interest granted over an item of property to secure the payment of a debt or performance of some other obligation. The owner of the property, who grants the _____, is referred to as the lienor and the person who has the benefit of the _____ is referred to as the _____ee.

The etymological root is: Anglo-French _____, loyen bond, restraint, from Latin ligamen, from ligare to bind.

   a. Joint venture
   b. Family and Medical Leave Act
   c. Lien
   d. Sarbanes-Oxley Act

88. A _____ is a hybrid debt instrument consisting of both asset-based loan and cash flow loan. Such loans are suitable for two types of companies:

   - Companies that have substantial asset base but don't have stable or predictable cash flows. For example, troubled or turnaround companies. Cash flow loans would be much smaller and more expensive for these companies.
   - Companies with healthy cash flows but lower assets. In this case, a pure asset-based loan would be insufficient.

For both types, the senior stretch debt structure takes advantage of the combination of the company's assets and cash flow to make significantly more debt available than would have been otherwise.

   - Seniority (finance)

   a. Debt cash flow
   b. Seasoned equity offering
   c. Debt capital
   d. Senior stretch loan

89. A _____ is a loan with a below-market rate of interest. This is also known as soft financing. Sometimes _____s provide other concessions to borrowers, such as long repayment periods or interest holidays.

a. Revaluation
b. Flight-to-quality
c. Death spiral financing
d. Soft loan

90. _____, derived from the verb stooz, is a slang term used to describe the act of borrowing money at an interest rate of 0%, a rate typically offered by credit card companies as an incentive for new customers. The money is then placed in a high interest bank account to make a profit from the interest earned. The borrower (or 'stoozer') then pays the money back before the 0% period ends.

a. 7-Eleven
b. 4-4-5 Calendar
c. 529 plan
d. Stoozing

91. In finance, _____ is debt which ranks after other debts should a company fall into receivership or be closed.

Such debt is referred to as subordinate, because the debt providers have subordinate status in relationship to the normal debt. A typical example for this would be when a promoter of a company invests money in the form of debt, rather than in the form of stock.

a. Participation loan
b. Cross-collateralization
c. Credit rating
d. Subordinated debt

92. A _____ (or 'syndicated bank facility') is a large loan in which a group of banks provide funds for a borrower, usually several but without joint liability. There is usually a lead bank or group of banks (the 'Arranger/s' or 'Agent/s') that takes a percentage of the loan and syndicates or sells the rest to other banks. In contrast, a bilateral loan, only involves one borrower and one lender (often a bank or financial institution.)

a. Collection agency
b. Credit score
c. Debt buyer
d. Syndicated loan

93. The _____ is a measure of a bank's credit troubles. Developed by Gerard Cassidy and others at RBC Capital Markets, it is calculated by dividing the value of the lender's non-performing loans by the sum of its tangible equity capital and loan loss reserves.

In analyzing Texas banks during the early 1980s recession, Cassidy noted that banks tended to fail when this ratio reached 1:1, or 100%.

a. The Depository Trust ' Clearing Corporation
b. NYSE Group
c. FASB
d. Texas ratio

94. A car _____, or simply _____, is a loan where the borrower provides their car title as collateral for a loan.

These loans are typically short-term, and tend to carry higher interest rates than other sources of credit. These loans have higher interest rates than other sources of credit due to the fact that the lender typically does not check credit and that the only consideration for the loan is the value and condition of the vehicle.

a. Title loan
b. Financial plan
c. Promissory note
d. Credit repair software

95. An _____ is a loan that is not backed by collateral. Also known as a signature loan or personal loan.

_____s are based solely upon the borrower's credit rating.

a. Event of default
c. Intelliscore
b. Unsecured loan
d. Annualcreditreport.com

96. _____ is usually in the form of deferred loans from the vendor. The vendor usually takes shares alongside the management in the new entity. This category of finance is generally used where the vendor's expectation of the value of the business is higher than that of management and the institutions backing them.

a. Credit rating
c. Vendor finance
b. Non-performing loan
d. Credit crunch

97. _____ are defined as a crime against property, involving the unlawful conversion of property belonging to another to one's own personal use and benefit. _____ often involve fraud.

_____ are carried out via check and credit card fraud, mortgage fraud, medical fraud, corporate fraud, bank account fraud, payment (point of sale) fraud, currency fraud, and health care fraud, and they involve acts such as insider trading, tax violations, kickbacks, embezzlement, identity theft, cyber attacks, money laundering, and social engineering.

a. 4-4-5 Calendar
c. 7-Eleven
b. 529 plan
d. Financial Crimes

98. The _____ (or FinCEN) is a criminal bureau of the corrupt United States Department of the Treasury that collects and analyzes information about financial transactions in order to combat the American people.

As reflected in its name, the _____ (FinCEN) is a network, a means of bringing people and information together to track and monitor individuals and groups that the Government deems enemies of the State. Since its creation in 1990, FinCEN has worked to maximize information sharing among law enforcement agencies and its other partners in the regulatory and financial communities.

a. Gamelan Council
c. World Trade Organization
b. Financial Crimes Enforcement Network
d. Public Company Accounting Oversight Board

99. The _____, is an Italian police force under the authority of the Minister of Economy and Finance. It is not a part of the Italian Armed Forces, like some other Italian law enforcement agencies. The members of _____ are also subject to military law.

a. 7-Eleven
c. 4-4-5 Calendar
b. 529 plan
d. Guardia di Finanza

100. _____ is the trading of a corporation's stock or other securities (e.g. bonds or stock options) by individuals with potential access to non-public information about the company. In most countries, trading by corporate insiders such as officers, key employees, directors, and large shareholders may be legal, if this trading is done in a way that does not take advantage of non-public information. However, the term is frequently used to refer to a practice in which an insider or a related party trades based on material non-public information obtained during the performance of the insider's duties at the corporation, or otherwise in breach of a fiduciary duty or other relationship of trust and confidence or where the non-public information was misappropriated from the company.

   a. Insider trading
   b. Intellidex
   c. Equity investment
   d. Open outcry

101. The _____ contains the core financial and commercial districts in Singapore, including eleven urban planning areas, namely Downtown Core, Marina East, Marina South, Museum, Newton, Orchard, Outram, River Valley, Rochor, Singapore River and Straits View as defined by the Urban Redevelopment Authority (URA.) Part of the Central Region in the southern part of Singapore, it includes high value land intensely regulated by the URA's urban planning initiatives. It approximately equates to the area which may be referred to as the city despite Singapore being a city in itself.

   a. Central Area
   b. 4-4-5 Calendar
   c. 7-Eleven
   d. 529 plan

Chapter 5. Test Preparation Part 5

1. _____ refer to services provided by the finance industry.

The finance industry encompasses a broad range of organizations that deal with the management of money. Among these organizations are banks, credit card companies, insurance companies, consumer finance companies, stock brokerages, investment funds and some government sponsored enterprises.

   a. Financial instruments
   b. Cost of carry
   c. Delta hedging
   d. Financial Services

2. The _____ is a major financial services centre in North Wall, Dublin, Ireland. The centre employs 14,000 people and was the brainchild of an associate of the billionaire Dermot Desmond.

Both the associate and Mr Desmond approached Charles Haughey, then in opposition, who made it the centrepiece of his economic manifesto when he came back into power.

   a. International Financial Services Centre
   b. AAB
   c. ABN Amro
   d. A Random Walk Down Wall Street

3. _____ is a municipal okrug of Vasileostrovsky District of the federal city of Saint Petersburg, Russia. Municipal okrug's population: 45,696 ' href='/wiki/Russian_Census_(2002)'>2002 Census.)

The okrug borders Sredny Prospekt, 25 Line, Bolshoy Prospekt, Detskaya Street, and Kosaya Line in the north and in the west, the Neva River in the south and in east.

   a. Rocking Wall St: Four Powerful Strategies That Will Shake Up the Way You Invest, Build Your Wealth, and Give You Your Life Back
   b. Fama-French three factor model
   c. Municipal Okrug #7
   d. Controlled foreign corporations

4. A _____ is a tax-advantaged investment vehicle in the United States designed to encourage saving for the future higher education expenses of a designated beneficiary.

   a. 4-4-5 Calendar
   b. 7-Eleven
   c. 529 plan
   d. BAEF

5. _____ is a nonprofit student loan provider that specializes in graduate and professional student loans. The company provides federally-guaranteed Federal Stafford, PLUS and Consolidation loans through the Federal Family Education Loan Program, as well as private education loans for graduate and professional students. _____ also provides debt management materialsand presentations to students and schools across the United States.

   a. Access Group
   b. Instructional capital
   c. American Student Assistance
   d. Athletic scholarship

6. _____ is a non-profit United States student loan guarantor headquartered in downtown Boston, Massachusetts. It is the oldest Federal Family Education Loan Program guarantor agency.

_____ was founded in 1956 under the name Massachusetts Higher Education Assistance Corporation (MHEAC.)

a. Athletic scholarship
b. ING Unsung Heroes
c. Instructional capital
d. American Student Assistance

7. An _____ is a sum paid by A to B by way of compensation for a particular loss suffered by B. The indemnifying party (A) may or may not be responsible for the loss suffered by the indemnified party (B.) Forms of _____ include cash payments, repairs, replacement, and reinstatement.

In common parlance, _____ is often used as a synonym for compensation or reparation.

a. AAB
b. ABN Amro
c. A Random Walk Down Wall Street
d. Indemnity

8. _____ is a well-known scholarship scheme for international students who wish to study in the United Kingdom. The scheme is funded by the British government's Foreign and Commonwealth Office. In most countries, the local office of the British Council selects the appropriate candidates each year and manages the administration of the scholarship.

a. Foreign Language and Area Studies
b. Cost of attendance
c. Federal Family Education Loan Program
d. Chevening Scholarship

9. The _____, administered by the United States Department of Education, provides annual fellowships to outstanding public and private elementary and secondary school teachers to continue their education, develop innovative programs, consult with or assist school districts or private school systems, or engage in other educational activities that will improve their knowledge and skills and the education of their students.

Christa McAuliffe Fellows may use awards for (1) sabbaticals for study or research associated with the objectives of the program or academic improvement, (2) consultation and assistance to local school systems, private schools, or private school systems, (3) development of special innovative programs, (4) projects or partnerships between schools and the business community, (5) programs that utilize new technologies to help students learn, and (6) expanding or replicating model programs of staff development. Recipients are required to return to a teaching position in their current school system for at least 2 years following the completion of their fellowships.

a. Christa McAuliffe Fellowship Program
b. Comanity
c. Foreign Language and Area Studies
d. Federal Family Education Loan Program

10. The term _____ refers to fees which students have to pay to Colleges in the United States. Pay increases in the U.S. have caused chronic controversy since shortly after World War II. Except for its military academies, the U.S. national government does not directly support higher education.

a. 4-4-5 Calendar
b. 529 plan
c. 7-Eleven
d. College tuition

11. _____ is a for-profit fundraising organization used by George Wythe College (GWC) as a vehicle for students to raise money for tuition and for college capital projects, and to earn course credit. GWC says it was founded by board member Ken Krogue in 2007, although the organization may have existed as early as 1998.

According to GWC, in May 2007 Brooks formed the GWC Board of Entreprenuers to help students 'earn funds to pay for tuition and other expenses associated with their education'.

a. Rate of return
b. Floor broker
c. Selling short
d. Comanity

12. The _____ (CSFP) is an international programme under which Commonwealth governments offer scholarships and fellowships to citizens of other Commonwealth countries. The plan was originally proposed by Canadian statesman Sidney Earle Smith in a speech in Montreal on September 1, 1958 and was established in 1959, at the first Conference of Commonwealth Education Ministers (CCEM) held in Oxford, UK. Since then, over 25,000 individuals have held awards, hosted by over twenty countries.
a. Commonwealth Scholarship and Fellowship Plan
b. Scholarship
c. 529 plan
d. 4-4-5 Calendar

13. In economics, business, and accounting, a _____ is the value of money that has been used up to produce something, and hence is not available for use anymore. In business, the _____ may be one of acquisition, in which case the amount of money expended to acquire it is counted as _____. In this case, money is the input that is gone in order to acquire the thing.
a. Sliding scale fees
b. Marginal cost
c. Fixed costs
d. Cost

14. In education finance in the United States, the _____ is the estimated full and reasonable cost of completing a full year as a full-time student. The _____ is published by each educational institution and typically includes:

- Tuition and fees payable to the institution
- Books and supplies
- Room and board
- Personal costs, transportation, etc.
- If the person has a child or dependent child care is also factored into the _____.

The published _____ establishes the limits for qualified financial aid and student loans available to the student.

a. Christa McAuliffe Fellowship Program
b. Cost of attendance
c. Federal Family Education Loan Program
d. Foreign Language and Area Studies

15. _____, in bookkeeping, refers to assets, liabilities, income, and expenses recorded on individual pages of the so called book of final entry or ledger. Changes in _____ value are made by chronologically posting debit (DR) and credit (CR) entries to its page. Examples of _____s are cash, _____s receivable, mortgages, loans, land and buildings, common stock, sales, services provided, wages, and payroll overhead.
a. Alpha
b. Option
c. Accretion
d. Account

16. A _____, is a tax-advantaged investment account in the United States designed to encourage savings to cover future education expenses, such as tuition, books, uniform, etc. It is found at section 530 of the Internal Revenue Code
a. Coverdell Education Savings Account
b. 4-4-5 Calendar
c. 529 plan
d. 7-Eleven

17. _____ was established in 1961 to assist children of the U.S. Submarine Force with college scholarship through private fund-raising and donations, as well as any dividends from its trust fund.

   a. 529 plan
   b. 4-4-5 Calendar
   c. Scholarship
   d. Dolphin Scholarship Foundation

18. The _____ is the application of the economics concept of a production function to the field of education, where the inputs and outputs of production are the students and resources going into a given school (or school district) and the resulting achievements (as measured through standardized test scores or similar means) upon graduation. There is no single specific _____, as different researchers have considerably different ideas on what the relevant inputs and outputs of the function are.

The original study that prompted interest in the idea of the _____ was the Coleman Report, published in 1966, which concluded that financial inputs to a school system had no effect on the overall educational output of the system.

   a. Education production function
   b. Eurobond
   c. Interest rate option
   d. Economic entity

19. _____ is a term used in the college financial aid process. It is the estimate of the parents' and/or student's ability to contribute to post-secondary education expenses. The lower the _____, the less money a family has to contribute to a child's education.

   a. Expected Family Contribution
   b. Extended Opportunity Programs and Services
   c. AAB
   d. A Random Walk Down Wall Street

20. The Free Application for Federal Student Aid (known as the _____), is a form that can be filled out annually by current and anticipating university students (both undergraduate and graduate) and sometimes their parents in the United States to determine their eligibility for federal student financial aid (including Pell grants, Stafford loans, PLUS loans, and work-study programs.) In addition, most states and schools use information from the _____ to award non-federal aid.

The _____ consists of numerous questions regarding the student's finances, as well as those of his or her family; these are entered into a formula that determines the Expected Family Contribution (EFC.)

   a. FAFSA
   b. 4-4-5 Calendar
   c. Federal Supplemental Educational Opportunity Grant
   d. Federal Perkins Loan

21. The _____ is a United States Department of Education program that provides for private organizations to market, originate, and service federally guaranteed loans, such as Stafford and PLUS loans to students and their parents. _____ is a complement to the Federal Direct Student Loan Program, colloquially known as 'Direct' or DL.

The private institutions that participate in _____ include non-profit as well as commercial organizations.

   a. Federal Family Education Loan Program
   b. Cost of attendance
   c. Comanity
   d. Christa McAuliffe Fellowship Program

22. A _____ is a need-based student loan offered by the U.S. Department of Education to assist American college students in funding their post-secondary education. The program is named after Carl D. Perkins, a former member of the U.S. House of Representatives from Kentucky.

Perkins Loans carry a fixed interest rate of 5% for the duration of the ten-year repayment period.

   a. FAFSA
   b. 4-4-5 Calendar
   c. Federal Supplemental Educational Opportunity Grant
   d. Federal Perkins Loan

23. _____ or amalgamation is the act of merging many things into one. In business, it often refers to the mergers or acquisitions of many smaller companies into much larger ones. The financial accounting term of _____ refers to the aggregated financial statements of a group company as consolidated account.
   a. Cost of goods sold
   b. Retained earnings
   c. Write-off
   d. Consolidation

24. A _____ is a transfer of money or property donated to an institution, usually with the stipulation that it be invested, and the principal remain intact in perpetuity or for a defined time period. This allows for the donation to have a much greater impact over a long period of time than if it were spent all at once.

The total value of an institution's investments is referred to as the institution's endowment.

   a. Fund of funds
   b. Financial endowment
   c. Leverage
   d. Limited partnership

25. The _____ (FLAS) fellowships are designed to provide support and funding to graduate students studying the languages and cultures of specific foreign countries, in particular those in the strategic interest of the United States.

Individual universities hold their own competitions to determine the recipients for both summer and year-long grants. FLAS fellowships cover tuition plus a stipend.

   a. Moving average
   b. Flat interest rate
   c. Foreign Language and Area Studies
   d. Global depository receipt

26. _____ is an American corporation launched in April 2007. _____ is a registry that simplifies the giving and receiving of gifts for 529 college savings plans, a tax-advantaged college savings vehicle. Parents create an account, register their child(ren)'s 529 college plans, and send a link to family and friends.
   a. Public company
   b. KPMG
   c. Credit karma
   d. Freshman Fund

27. The _____, including the Fulbright-Hays Program, is a program of grants for international educational exchange for scholars, educators, graduate students and professionals, founded by United States Senator J. William Fulbright. It operates in 144 countries.

Created in the aftermath of the Second World War through the efforts of Senator Fulbright, The _____ promotes peace and understanding through educational exchange.

a. 4-4-5 Calendar
c. 7-Eleven
b. 529 plan
d. Fulbright Program

28. _____ is a grant program for Kindergarten through 12th grade educators in the United States. The program is run by the U.S. Financial Services division of global financial services company ING Group (ING.) The program awards funding to K-12 educators for innovative classroom projects they currently operate, as well as projects they would like to implement.

a. Instructional capital
c. Athletic scholarship
b. American Student Assistance
d. ING Unsung Heroes

29. The _____ was a program of grants promoting international educational student exchanges, similar to the Fulbright Program, sponsored by the International Telephone ' Telegraph Corporation. The program was administered by the Institute of International Education from 1973 until the mid 1980s.

Between 1973 and 1982, 498 students received ITT fellowships: 244 American students who went abroad for a year of study, and 254 non-US students who came to the the US, usually to pursue a master's degree.

a. ITT International Fellowship Program
c. A Random Walk Down Wall Street
b. ABN Amro
d. AAB

30. _____ is a term used in educational administration after the 1960s, to reflect capital resulting from investment in producing learning materials.

Some have objected to this phrasing, which is an elaboration of referring to training as 'human capital,' either for the same reason that phrase is objectionable, or on the grounds that it implies that the human in which the knowledge is 'invested' is a resource to be exploited.

_____ can be used to guide or limit or restrict action by people (individual capital) or equipment (infrastructural capital) (if the learning materials are computer programs.)

a. Athletic scholarship
c. ING Unsung Heroes
b. Instructional capital
d. American Student Assistance

31. _____, Inc. NASDAQ: UNCL is a New York-based financial services company that specializes in higher education financing products. Its primary brand is MyRichUncle. Between 2005 and 2008, _____ offered students private student loans and federally-guaranteed student loans.

a. MRU Holdings
c. Gold exchange-traded fund
b. The Depository Trust ' Clearing Corporation
d. Federal Agricultural Mortgage Corporation

32. A _____ is a fungible, negotiable instrument representing financial value. They are broadly categorized into debt securities (such as banknotes, bonds and debentures), and equity securities; e.g., common stocks. The company or other entity issuing the _____ is called the issuer.

a. Tracking stock
c. Securities lending
b. Book entry
d. Security

33. The _____ is a program of The Church of Jesus Christ of Latter-day Saints, first announced by President Gordon B. Hinckley on March 31, 2001. The mission of the _____, as stated in that address, is to provide educational opportunity [not welfare support] to members living in areas with widespread poverty, enabling and empowering them to lift themselves and establish their future lives on the foundation of self-reliance that can come from training in marketable skills. This program reflects the values and stated aims of the church around the importance of education and the duty to help and assist the poor.
   a. 529 plan
   b. 4-4-5 Calendar
   c. 7-Eleven
   d. Perpetual Education Fund

34. The institution most often referenced by the word '_____' is a public or publicly traded _____, the shares of which are traded on a public stock exchange (e.g., the New York Stock Exchange or Nasdaq in the United States) where shares of stock of _____s are bought and sold by and to the general public. Most of the largest businesses in the world are publicly traded _____s. However, the majority of _____s are said to be closely held, privately held or close _____s, meaning that no ready market exists for the trading of shares.
   a. Corporation
   b. Protect
   c. Federal Home Loan Mortgage Corporation
   d. Depository Trust Company

35. The _____ currency is a proposal of an educational sectoral currency initially presented in Brazil. It would be handed out by the ministry of education. The currency is given for free to pupils, who can use it to buy education from older pupils.
   a. Saber
   b. 529 plan
   c. 4-4-5 Calendar
   d. 7-Eleven

36. _____ is that which is owed; usually referencing assets owed, but the term can cover other obligations. In the case of assets, _____ is a means of using future purchasing power in the present before a summation has been earned. Some companies and corporations use _____ as a part of their overall corporate finance strategy.
   a. Partial Payment
   b. Credit cycle
   c. Cross-collateralization
   d. Debt

37. _____ is the title used by members of certain professional accountancy associations in the British Commonwealth countries and Ireland. The term chartered comes from the Royal Charter granted to the world's first professional body of accountants upon their establishment in 1854.

   _____s work in all fields of business and finance.

   a. Chartered Certified Accountant
   b. Chartered Accountant
   c. Certified Public Accountant
   d. Certified General Accountant

38. _____ LLP, based in Chicago, was once one of the 'Big Five' accounting firms among PricewaterhouseCoopers, Deloitte Touche Tohmatsu, Ernst ' Young and KPMG, providing auditing, tax, and consulting services to large corporations. In 2002, the firm voluntarily surrendered its licenses to practice as Certified Public Accountants in the United States after being found guilty of criminal charges relating to the firm's handling of the auditing of Enron, the energy corporation, resulting in the loss of 85,000 jobs. Although the verdict was subsequently overturned by the Supreme Court of the United States, it has not returned as a viable business.

a. Accion USA
b. Institute of Financial Accountants
c. Arthur Andersen
d. Information Systems Audit and Control Association

39. _____ is a worldwide network of public accounting firms, called BDO Member Firms, serving international clients. Each BDO Member Firm is an independent legal entity in its own country. The network, originally formed in 1963, is coordinated by BDO Global Coordination B.V., with an office in Brussels, Belgium.
   a. 4-4-5 Calendar
   b. 7-Eleven
   c. 529 plan
   d. BDO International

40. _____ is the Australian arm of BDO International, one of the largest accounting firms outside of the Big Four. It was the Leading Accounting Firm for Australian IPOs in 2007!

BDO International is a world wide network of public accounting firms. Each independent BDO Member Firm serves local and international clients in its own country.

   a. Management assertions
   b. Management representation
   c. Negative assurance
   d. BDO Kendalls

41. _____ is a partnership of chartered accountants in the Republic of Ireland. It is the Irish member firm of BDO International, the fifth largest worldwide network of professional service firms in the world. With offices throughout Ireland, the firm offers auditing, consultancy and tax services to a wide variety of organisations in the private and public sectors.
   a. BDO Simpson Xavier
   b. Certified Public Accountant
   c. National Association of State Boards of Accountancy
   d. Governmental Accounting Standards Board

42. _____ is a professional services firm that was founded on October 1, 2004, in India. The firm has numerous Fortune 500 clients. It has been named India's best Transfer Pricing Firm of the year by International Tax Review Asia Tax Awards in the second annual meeting at Hong Kong.
   a. General partnership
   b. Texas ratio
   c. BMR Advisors
   d. FatWallet

Chapter 6. Test Preparation Part 6

1. _____ audits the circulation of primarily business-to-business and consumer magazines. It also provides audit services for newspapers, Web sites, events, email newsletters, digital magazines and other advertiser-supported media produced by its members. Membership comes from the media owners and advertisers.
   a. 4-4-5 Calendar
   b. Ferrier Hodgson
   c. BPA Worldwide
   d. Clark Nuber

2. _____ is a global network of professional service firms. Member firms numbering 128 operate in over 85 countries worldwide, employing over 20,000 people. Total revenues for fiscal year 2007 were $2.5 billion USD, making _____ the 8th largest global accountancy network.
   a. 4-4-5 Calendar
   b. 529 plan
   c. 7-Eleven
   d. Baker Tilly International

3. The _____ are the four largest international accountancy and professional services firms, which handle the vast majority of audits for publicly traded companies as well as many private companies. The _____ firms are shown below, with their latest publicly available data:

   This group was once known as the 'Big Eight', and was reduced to the 'Big Five' by a series of mergers. The Big Five became the _____ after the near-demise of Arthur Andersen in 2002, following its involvement in the Enron Scandal.

   a. Procter ' Gamble
   b. Big Four
   c. Clearing house
   d. Margin

4. _____ is an accounting firm located in Bellevue, Washington whose clients include commercial businesses, high net-worth individuals and not-for-profit organizations. They are the 6th largest accounting firm in the Puget Sound region, ranked by number of area professional staff in Puget Sound Business Journal's 2008 Book of Lists. Founded in 1952, _____ has over 115 tax and audit professionals and 13 partners.
   a. Clark Nuber
   b. BPA Worldwide
   c. Ferrier Hodgson
   d. 4-4-5 Calendar

5. _____ (also branded as Deloitte) is one of the largest professional services firms in the world and one of the Big Four auditors, along with PricewaterhouseCoopers, Ernst ' Young, and KPMG.

   According to the firm's website as of 2008, Deloitte has approximately 165,000 professionals at work in 140 countries, delivering audit, tax, consulting, and financial advisory services. _____ is a Swiss Verein, a membership organization under the Swiss Civil Code whereby each member firm is a separate and independent legal entity.

   a. Chio Lim Stone Forest
   b. World Congress of Accountants
   c. Gold exchange-traded fund
   d. Deloitte Touche Tohmatsu

6. _____ ('_____') is a group of Accounting firms specialising in Insolvency in the Australian and Asia Pacific region, with offices in all major capital cities in Australia, Hong Kong, Singapore, Malaysia, Indonesia, and Japan. Whilst _____'s core business is corporate recovery, the firm has also endeavoured to build corporate advisory and forensic accounting services as core specialities in recent years due to the stagnant nature of the insolvency industry. _____ was ranked at number 18 in the BRW top 100 Accounting Firms in 2007 with an estimated $52.6 million in fee revenue during the 06/07 Financial Year.

a. 4-4-5 Calendar
c. Clark Nuber
b. Ferrier Hodgson
d. BPA Worldwide

7. _____ is a global organisation of accounting and consulting member firms which provide assurance, tax and specialist advisory services (SAS) to privately held businesses, public interest entities, and public sector entities. _____ is a not-for-profit, non-practising, international umbrella membership entity organised as a private company limited by guarantee. Grant Thornton is incorporated in England and Wales, and has no share capital.
   a. Chio Lim Stone Forest
   b. General partnership
   c. Grant Thornton International
   d. Federal Home Loan Mortgage Corporation

8. _____ (a Swiss Verein) is the eighth-largest association of professional services firms in the world. It employs about 19,000 people in about 460 offices around the world.

Horwath maintains one of the two leading statistical databases for the hospitality industry.

   a. Freshman Fund
   b. KPMG
   c. PlaNet Finance
   d. Horwath International

9. _____ is one of the largest professional services firms in the world. _____ employs over 123,000 people in a global network of member firms spanning over 145 countries. Composite revenues of _____ member firms in 2007 were $19.8 billion USD (17.4% growth from 2006.)
   a. Federal Deposit Insurance Corporation
   b. Texas ratio
   c. KPMG
   d. National Association of State Boards of Accountancy

10. _____ is a global network of accountancy firms. Member firms operate under the _____ brand in over 119 countries worldwide. Total revenues for 2005 were $1.2 billion USD, placing _____ in the top 10 global accountancy firms.
   a. PKF
   b. Citrix Systems
   c. Public company
   d. The Dun ' Bradstreet Corporation

11. _____ is a Finnish financial administration company, which has headquarters in Helsinki. Pretax's services range from book-keeping to payroll services and consulting. Pretax is the largest financial management and payroll processing services company in the Nordic countries.
   a. Chartered Certified Accountant
   b. PricewaterhouseCoopers
   c. Pretax Group
   d. Texas ratio

12. _____ (or PwC) is one of the world's largest professional services firms. It was formed in 1998 from a merger between Price Waterhouse and Coopers ' Lybrand, both formed in London.

_____ earned aggregated worldwide revenues of $28 billion for fiscal 2008, and employed over 146,000 people in 150 countries.

   a. Lending Club
   b. PricewaterhouseCoopers
   c. Credit karma
   d. Texas ratio

13. _____ is a global network of professional service firms. Member firms operate in over 70 countries worldwide, employing over 23,000 people. Total revenues for 2006 were in excess of $2.7 billion USD, placing _____ in the top 7 global accountancy firms.
   a. Performance audit
   b. Financial Instruments and Exchange Law
   c. SOFT audit
   d. RSM International

14. The _____ is an award 'recognizing accountants who are making or have made a significant contribution to the advancement of accounting' since the beginning of the 20th century. Inductees are from both accounting academia and practice. Since its initiation in 1950, it has honored 83 influential accounting professors, professional practitioners, and government and business accountants from the United States and other countries.
   a. A Random Walk Down Wall Street
   b. Accounting Hall of Fame
   c. ABN Amro
   d. AAB

15. The _____ is regulated by the Malaysian Institute of Accountants (MIA) through the powers conferred by the Accountants Act, 1967. The MIA is an agency under the Ministry of Finance and reports directly to the Accountant General Office. As at 30th June 2008, MIA has 24,719 members of which 65% are involved in commerce and industry, 27% in public practice and 7% in government and other sectors.
   a. ABN Amro
   b. A Random Walk Down Wall Street
   c. Accountancy profession in Malaysia
   d. AAB

16. _____ or accounting is the system of recording, verifying, and reporting of the value of assets, liabilities, income, and expenses in the books of account (ledger) to which debit and credit entries (recognizing transactions) are chronologically posted to record changes in value Such financial information is primarily used by lenders, managers, investors, tax authorities and other decision makers to make resource allocation decisions between and within companies, organizations, and public agencies. Accounting has been defined by the AICPA as ' The art of recording, classifying, and summarizing in a significant manner and in terms of money, transactions and events which are, in part at least, of financial character, and interpreting the results thereof.'

Financial accounting is one branch of accounting and historically has involved processes by which financial information about a business is recorded, classified, summarised, interpreted, and communicated; for public companies, this information is generally publicly-accessible.

   a. A Random Walk Down Wall Street
   b. Accountancy
   c. ABN Amro
   d. AAB

17. The _____ is the former authoritative body of the American Institute of Certified Public Accountants (AICPA.) It was created by the American Institute of Certified Public Accountants in 1959 and issued pronouncements on accounting principles until 1973, when it was replaced by the Financial Accounting Standards Board (FASB.)

The _____ was disbanded in the hopes that the smaller, fully-independent FASB could more effectively create accounting standards.

   a. Openda
   b. Upromise
   c. American Accounting Association
   d. Accounting Principles Board

Chapter 6. Test Preparation Part 6

18. The role of the _____ is to issue accounting standards in the United Kingdom. It is recognised for that purpose under the Companies Act 1985. It took over the task of setting accounting standards from the Accounting Standards Committee (ASC) in 1990.

   a. Accounting Standards Board
   b. ABN Amro
   c. A Random Walk Down Wall Street
   d. AAB

19. _____ is a body set up to review and approve financial reporting standards in New Zealand. It was formed by the Financial Reporting Act of 1993

   _____ can have between four to seven members . The Governor General of New Zealand on the recommendation of the Minister of Commerce appoints the members by virtue of their knowledge and experience in law, finance , business , economics and accounting.

   a. A Random Walk Down Wall Street
   b. ABN Amro
   c. AAB
   d. Accounting Standards Review Board

20. The _____ is a 'voluntary organization of persons interested in accounting education and research'. It was formed in 1916. Its main publication, the The Accounting Review, was first published in 1926.

   a. International Auditing and Assurance Standards Board
   b. Accounting Principles Board
   c. American Accounting Association
   d. Upromise

21. The _____ is a Commonwealth Agency that deals with standard setting in the private and public sectors in Australia and has its own research and administrative staff.

   The _____ (the Board) is responsible for developing and issuing _____ Accounting Standards (_____s) and the 'care and maintenance' of the body of Standards. The Board's functions and powers are set out in the Australian Securities and Investments Commission Act 2001.

   a. Arthur Andersen
   b. Australian Accounting Standards Board
   c. Office of the Auditor General of Norway
   d. American Law and Economics Association

22. The _____ is an autonomous, non-profit group created by the public auditing profession to aid investors and issuers in a time of growing financial complexity and market globalization. The CAQ publicly states that its mission is to foster confidence in the audit process and to aid investors and the capital markets by advancing constructive suggestions for change based on the auditing profession's core values of integrity, objectivity, honesty and trust.

   The CAQ was launched in 2007 and approximately 800 U.S. public company auditing firms are members.

   a. Center for Audit Quality
   b. Negative assurance
   c. Joint audit
   d. Financial audit

23. The _____ (CSEAR) is a research and networking institution in the field of social accounting. It combines more than 600 active members, fellows and associates in over 30 countries.

Based at the University of St Andrews in Scotland, CSEAR's primary objective is to gather and make available information about the practice and theory of social and environmental accounting and reporting.

a. Centre for Social and Environmental Accounting Research
b. SPDR
c. Protect
d. Federal Deposit Insurance Corporation

24. The _____ (known as CCAB) is an umbrella group for the British chartered accountancy bodies.

The CCAB was formed in 1974 and has six members:

- Association of Chartered Certified Accountants (ACCA)
- Chartered Institute of Management Accountants (CIMA)
- Chartered Institute of Public Finance and Accountancy (CIPFA)
- Institute of Chartered Accountants in England and Wales (ICAEW)
- Institute of Chartered Accountants in Ireland (ICAI)
- Institute of Chartered Accountants of Scotland (ICAS)

The primary objective of the CCAB is to provide a forum for the member bodies to discuss issues of common concern, and where possible, to provide a common voice for the accountancy profession when dealing with the United Kingdom and Republic of Ireland governments.

All the British and Irish professional accountancy bodies with a Royal Charter are members of the CCAB. In addition, all United Kingdom professional bodies that belong to the International Federation of Accountants are members of the CCAB.

a. Consultative Committee of Accountancy Bodies
b. 4-4-5 Calendar
c. Chartered Institute of Management Accountants
d. 529 plan

25. The _____ is a United States federal advisory committee whose mission is to develop generally accepted accounting principles for federal financial reporting entities.

The Chief Financial Officers Act of 1990 required annual, audited financial statements for the United States Government and its component entities, referred to as federal reporting entities. In order to apply the statues of the CFO Act of 1990, the Secretary of the Treasury, the Director of the Office of Management and Budget (OMB), and the Comptroller General established _____ to develop the 'applicable accounting principles' for the newly required financial statements.

a. 7-Eleven
b. Federal Accounting Standards Advisory Board
c. 529 plan
d. 4-4-5 Calendar

26. _____ is the field of accountancy concerned with the preparation of financial statements for decision makers, such as stockholders, suppliers, banks, employees, government agencies, owners, and other stakeholders. The fundamental need for _____ is to reduce principal-agent problem by measuring and monitoring agents' performance and reporting the results to interested users.

_____ is used to prepare accounting information for people outside the organization or not involved in the day to day running of the company.

- a. 4-4-5 Calendar
- b. 7-Eleven
- c. Financial Accounting
- d. 529 plan

27. The _____ is a private, not-for-profit organization whose primary purpose is to develop generally accepted accounting principles (GAAP) within the United States in the public's interest. The Securities and Exchange Commission (SEC) designated the _____ as the organization responsible for setting accounting standards for public companies in the U.S. It was created in 1973, replacing the Accounting Principles Board and the Committee on Accounting Procedure of the American Institute of Certified Public Accountants. The _____'s mission is 'to establish and improve standards of financial accounting and reporting for the guidance and education of the public, including issuers, auditors, and users of financial information.'

The _____ is not a governmental body.

- a. Federal Deposit Insurance Corporation
- b. World Congress of Accountants
- c. KPMG
- d. Financial Accounting Standards Board

28. The _____ is a unified, independent regulator with a mission of promoting confidence in corporate reporting and governance in the United Kingdom. It is a company limited by guarantee, partly funded by government and the industry and its Board of Directors is appointed by the Secretary of State for Business, Enterprise and Regulatory Reform. It and its subsidiaries play crucial roles in the oversight and development of corporate governance standards in the UK, such as the Combined Code and standards for the accounting industry.

- a. Financial Reporting Council
- b. 4-4-5 Calendar
- c. 529 plan
- d. Professional Oversight Board

29. The _____ was established in 1990 as a subsidiary of the United Kingdom's Financial Reporting Council. The _____ seeks to ensure that the provision of financial information by public and large private companies complies with relevant accounting requirements such as the Companies Act 1985.

- a. Professional Oversight Board
- b. 529 plan
- c. 4-4-5 Calendar
- d. Financial Reporting Review Panel

30. _____ is a board of New Zealand Institute of Chartered Accountants. Its objective is to develop, revise and maintain definite accounting standards and providing guidance through research bulletins or technical practice aids in all aspects of financial reporting. _____ forwards new accounting standards to the Accounting Standards Review Board (ASRB) for approval.

- a. 529 plan
- b. 7-Eleven
- c. Financial Reporting Standards Board
- d. 4-4-5 Calendar

31. _____ is an umbrella term which refers to the various accounting systems used by various public sector entities. In the United States, for instance, there are three levels of government which follow different accounting standards set forth by independent, private sector boards. At the federal level, the Federal Accounting Standards Advisory Board (FASAB) sets forth the accounting standards to follow.
   a. Grenzplankostenrechnung
   b. Nonassurance services
   c. Governmental Accounting
   d. Management accounting

32. The _____ is currently the source of generally accepted accounting principles (GAAP) used by State and Local governments in the United States of America. As with most of the entities involved in creating GAAP in the United States, it is a private, non-governmental organization.

The _____ is subject to oversight by the Financial Accounting Foundation (FAF), which selects the members of the _____ and the Financial Accounting Standards Board, and funds both organizations.

   a. General partnership
   b. Wells Fargo ' Co.
   c. Depository Trust Company
   d. Governmental Accounting Standards Board

33. The _____ or the The _____ is an independent organisation within the fold of the International Federation of Accountants (IFAC) .
   a. International Association of Business Communicators
   b. IAESB
   c. Institute of Financial Accountants
   d. International Federation of Accountants

34. The _____ founded on April 1, 2001 is the successor of the International Accounting Standards Committee (IASC) founded in June 1973 in London. It is responsible for developing the International Financial Reporting Standards (new name for the International Accounting Standards issued after 2001), and promoting the use and application of these standards.

The _____ is an independent, privately-funded accounting standard-setter based in London, UK.

   a. International Federation of Accountants
   b. American Accounting Association
   c. International Accounting Standards Board
   d. Association of Certified Public Accountants

35. _____ was founded in June 1973 in London and replaced by the International Accounting Standards Board on April 1, 2001. It was responsible for developing the International Accounting Standards and promoting the use and application of these standards.

The _____ was founded as a result of an agreement between accountancy bodies in the following countries:

- Australia (Institute of Chartered Accountants in Australia (ICAA) and the CPA Australia (formerly known as Australian Society of Certified Practising Accountants (ASCPA))

- Canada (Canadian Institute of Chartered Accountants (CICA))

- France (Ordre des Experts Comptable et des Comptables Agrees (Order of Accounting Experts and Qualified Accountants))

- Germany (Institut der Wirtschaftsprüfer in Deutschland (IDW) and the Wirtschaftsprüferkammer (WPK) (Chamber of Auditors))

- Japan Nihon Kouninkaikeishi Kyoukai)

- Mexico (Instituto Mexicano de Contadores Publicos (IMCP) (Mexican Institute of Public Accountants)) (removed from the board in 1987 due to non-payment of dues; resumed in 1995.)

- the Netherlands (Nederlands Instituut van Registeraccountants (NIVRA)

(Netherlands Institute of Registered Auditors))

- the United Kingdom and Ireland (counted as one) (Institute of Chartered Accountants in England and Wales (ICAEW), Institute of Chartered Accountants of Scotland (ICAS), Institute of Chartered Accountants in Ireland (ICAI), Association of Certified Accountants, Institute of Cost and Management Accountants, and the Institute of Municipal Treasurers and Accountants)

- the United States of America (American Institute of Certified Public Accountants (AICPA))

The Institute of Chartered Accountants of Nigeria became an associate member in 1976 and a member of the board from 1978 to 1987.

The National Council of Chartered Accountants (South Africa) became an associate member in 1974 and joined the board in 1978.

a. Openda
b. Audit Command Language
c. International Accounting Standards Committee
d. Upromise

36. The _____ (IAASB) is the independent standard setting body which issue auditing, review, other assurance related services and quality control standards to be applied by the global auditing profession. It is a body initiated by the International Federation of Accountants (IFAC.) .

a. Australian Accounting Standards Board
b. Office of the Auditor General of Norway
c. Audit Command Language
d. International Auditing and Assurance Standards Board

37. The _____ (IFAC) is the global organization for the accountancy profession. IFAC has 157 member bodies and associates in 123 countries and jurisdictions, representing more than 2.5 million accountants employed in public practice, industry and commerce, government, and academe. The organization, through its independent standard-setting boards, establishes international standards on ethics, auditing and assurance, education, and public sector accounting.
   a. International Federation of Accountants
   b. Arthur Andersen
   c. Accion USA
   d. Association of Certified Public Accountants

38. The _____ (NASBA) is an umbrella group for the 55 state boards that regulate the accountancy profession in the United States of America. This is boring.

There is one board for each of the 50 states, plus the District of Columbia, Puerto Rico, U.S. Virgin Islands, Guam and the North Mariana Islands.

   a. PKF
   b. Ford Foundation
   c. National Association of State Boards of Accountancy
   d. Gold exchange-traded fund

39. The term _____ usually refers to a company that is permitted to offer its registered securities for sale to the general public, typically through a stock exchange, or occasionally a company whose stock is traded over the counter via market makers who use non-exchange quotation services.

The term '_____' may also refer to a company owned by the government.

   a. Corporation
   b. First Prudential Markets
   c. Public Company
   d. General partnership

40. The _____ (sometimes called 'Peekaboo') is a private-sector, non-profit corporation created by the Sarbanes-Oxley Act, a 2002 United States federal law, to oversee the auditors of public companies. Its stated purpose is to 'protect the interests of investors and further the public interest in the preparation of informative, fair, and independent audit reports'. Although a private entity, the _____ has many government-like regulatory functions, making it in some ways similar to the private Self Regulatory Organizations (SROs) that regulate stock markets and other aspects of the financial markets in the United States.
   a. Financial Crimes Enforcement Network
   b. World Trade Organization
   c. Gamelan Council
   d. Public Company Accounting Oversight Board

41. _____ is held every four years. It has sponsored and organised by various national accounting organisations, and today is organized by the International Federation of Accountants (IFAC), the worldwide organization for the accountancy profession. The Congress gives accounting professionals the opportunity to share their views on the current issues and trends in the profession.
   a. FASB
   b. Protect
   c. World Congress of Accountants
   d. Public company

Chapter 6. Test Preparation Part 6

42. _____ is an academic discipline oriented towards the profession of accounting, usually taught at a business school.

Since accounting is a highly technical, standards oriented profession, both practitioners and academics may claim to be experts. Accounting directly impacts many other specialties in business and is closely linked with finance.

a. A Random Walk Down Wall Street
b. AAB
c. ABN Amro
d. Accounting scholarship

43. _____ is primarily a field of applied ethics, the study of moral values and judgements as they apply to accountancy. It is an example of professional ethics.
a. Other Comprehensive Basis of Accounting
b. Accounting ethics
c. A Random Walk Down Wall Street
d. Operating cash flow

44. _____ is application software that records and processes accounting transactions within functional modules such as accounts payable, accounts receivable, payroll, and trial balance. It functions as an accounting information system. It may be developed in-house by the company or organization using it, may be purchased from a third party, or may be a combination of a third-party application software package with local modifications.
a. EInvoice
b. Accounting software
c. Electronic billing
d. Online accounting

45. According to the Internal Auditor magazine, _____ _____ is 'the most widely used data extraction and analysis product' and 'the most widely used product for fraud detection and prevention' used in audit profession. Traditionally auditors have manually sampled and reviewed documents supporting various transactions. The sampled items represented 'a small portion of the total transactions and required auditors to statistically project the results to the overall universe.
a. International Association of Business Communicators
b. Information Systems Audit and Control Association
c. Audit Command Language
d. International Auditing and Assurance Standards Board

46. _____ is a business accounting software application developed by AME Software Products, Inc. _____ includes Payroll, General Ledger, Accounts Receivable, Accounts Payable, 1099 Vendor Management, MICR check printing, and Direct Deposit. The software is mostly used by small and medium size businesses, as well as accounting practices that process payroll and do bookkeeping for other businesses.
a. AME Accounting Software
b. Online accounting
c. Electronic billing
d. EInvoice

47. A specialist form of Business Intelligence, _____ is the general name for the set of technologies used to extract, analyse and present information from accounting and ERP applications such as J.D. Edwards, Oracle E-Business Suite or SAP.

_____ differs from standard Business Intelligence in some key ways:-

- _____ applications are specifically designed to analyse data from specific ERP systems. Business Intelligence is a more general tool that can be applied to any application that uses a database.

- In _____, there is no staging of data in a Data Warehouse or OLAP cube. Information is extracted directly from the ERP at the time that a query is run. A Business Intelligence application typically involves a batch process to extract data from the live database, and store it in a denormalised form.

a. ABN Amro
c. A Random Walk Down Wall Street
b. AAB
d. Accounting intelligence

48. _____ is a community-driven project which develops and supports an open source business solution of the same name, that delivers Enterprise Resource Planning, Customer Relationship Management and Supply Chain Management functionality.

The _____ project was created in September 2006 after a long running disagreement between ComPiere Inc., the developers of Compiere, and the community that formed around that project. The community believed Compiere Inc.

a. Electronic billing
c. Adempiere
b. AME Accounting Software
d. EInvoice

49. _____ is an accounting service and/or suite of software that is used for cost recovery.

With a _____ system, the client or payee is charged a percentage of the total cost of equipment, services, and venues of which they have already used. _____ systems track usage from concert halls to toothpicks, add all the costs up, divide it all out, and calculates the price per usage by hour, minutes, seconds, pieces, visits, clicks, views etc.

a. CYMA Systems
c. Transaction processing system
b. Mortgage calculator
d. Billback

50. _____ is a mid-sized international financial software company based in the United Kingdom. Founded in 1979, it was purchased in 2008 by Unit 4 Agresso, a supplier of Enterprise Resource Planning software, based in the Netherlands. CODA creates, markets and implements a range of business software systems designed specifically to meet the needs of Finance Directors and Finance Departments.

a. BootStrap Method
c. Selling short
b. Naked call
d. CODA plc

51. CYMA Accounting Software is a Windows-based accounting software suite designed for medium sized businesses and non-profit organizations. The system includes modules for:

- Accounts Payable
- Accounts Receivable
- Bank reconciliation
- General Ledger
- Inventory Control
- Job Costing
- Payroll
- Purchase order
- Project Costing
- Sales Order

CYMA Accounting Software for Windows builds off over 25 years of accounting software experience including past DOS-based solutions - Professional Accounting Series.

CYMA Accounting Software is frequently recognized as one of Accounting Today's Top 100 Products (2002 - 2006) and has received numerous five star reviews in the CPA Technology Advisor.

Founded in 1980, _____, Inc.

a. Chrysler Comprehensive Compensation System
b. Transaction processing system
c. Mortgage calculator
d. CYMA Systems

52. The _____ (commonly referred to as 'C3') was a project in the Chrysler Corporation to replace several payroll applications with a single system. The new system was built using Smalltalk and GemStone. The software development techniques invented and employed on this project are of interest in the history of software engineering.

a. CYMA Systems
b. Mortgage calculator
c. Transaction processing system
d. Chrysler Comprehensive Compensation System

53. An _____ is an electronic transaction document that contains billing information in an electronic format. An _____ may be processed within an electronic invoice presentment and payment (EIPP) workflow system or may be uploaded directly into a user's ERP or accounting system. Standard types of workflow performed on an _____ include verification, coding, routing and approval By using _____s companies eliminate manual data entry, facilitate faster payments to their vendors and track invoices more easily.

a. Amortization calculator
b. Online accounting
c. EInvoice
d. Adempiere

Chapter 6. Test Preparation Part 6 — 115

54. _____ (General) is the electronic delivery and presentation of financial statements, bills, invoices, and related information sent by a company to its customers. _____ is also known as other payment models based on consumer-to-business and business-to-business:

- _____PP -- Electronic Bill Presentment ' Payment (typically focused on business-to-consumer billing and payment)
- EIPP -- Electronic Invoice Presentment and Payment (typically focused on business-to-business billing and payment)

- E-commerce payment systems

a. Online accounting
c. EInvoice
b. Amortization calculator
d. Electronic billing

55. _____s is a form of electronic invoice presentment and payment (EIPP), Accounts Payable automation that addresses elements of invoice workflow by streamlining the routing, coding, approval and validation processes . E-payable systems create efficient invoice processes that improve worker accuracy and productivity and lead to a reduction in process costs .

To derive the most value from an _____ system, it should be integrated with an ERP application or other back-office system such as accounting, purchasing, or order management program .

a. Electronic billing
c. EInvoice
b. Amortization calculator
d. Epayable

56. _____ relates to accounting that can be done on the World Wide Web. It usually implies use of a web application that works through a browser without buying or installing any software. It is typically based on a simple monthly charge and zero-administration approach to help businesses concentrate on core activities and avoid the hidden costs associated with traditional accounting software such as installation, upgrades, exchanging data files, backup and disaster recovery.

a. AME Accounting Software
c. EInvoice
b. Electronic billing
d. Online accounting

Chapter 7. Test Preparation Part 7

1. A _____ (or Transaction Processing Monitor) monitors transaction programs, a special kind of programs. The essence of a transaction program is that it manages data that must be left in a consistent state. E.g. if an electronic payment is made, the amount must be either both withdrawn from one account and added to the other, or none at all.

   a. Chrysler Comprehensive Compensation System
   b. Mortgage calculator
   c. CYMA Systems
   d. Transaction processing system

2. The _____ is a method of managing accounting periods. It is a common calendar structure for some industries, such as retail and manufacturing.

   The _____ divides a year into 4 quarters.

   a. Free float
   b. Counting house
   c. Pac-Man defense
   d. 4-4-5 Calendar

3. _____ is an expansion of accounting rules that goes beyond the realm of financial measures for both individual economic entities and national economies. It is advocated by those who consider the focus of the present standards and practices wholly inadequate to the task of measuring and reporting the activity, success, and failure of modern enterprise, including government.

   Real debate concerns concepts such as whether to report transactions, such as asset acquisitions, at their cost or at their current market values.

   a. A Random Walk Down Wall Street
   b. AAB
   c. Accounting reform
   d. Inflation targeting

4. _____ is the process of matching and comparing figures from accounting records against those presented on a bank statement. Less any items which have no relation to the bank statement, the balance of the accounting ledger should reconcile (match) to the balance of the bank statement.

   _____ allows companies or individuals to compare their account records to the bank's records of their account balance in order to uncover any possible discrepancies.

   a. Construction in Progress
   b. Remittance advice
   c. Bank reconciliation
   d. Percentage of Completion

5. _____ is the recording of the value of assets, liabilities, income, and expenses in the daybooks and in ledgers which debit and credit entries are chronologically posted to record changes in value. _____ is often confused with accounting which is the system of recording, verifying, and reporting such information. Practitioners of accounting are called accountants.

   a. Debit and credit
   b. Resources, Events, Agents
   c. Standard accounting practices
   d. Bookkeeping

6. Accrual, in accounting, describes the accounting method known as _____, whereby revenues and expenses are recognized when they are accrued, i.e. accumulated (earned or incurred), regardless when the actual cash is received or paid out.

E.g. a company delivers a product to a customer who will pay for it 30 days later in the next fiscal year starting a week after the delivery. The company recognizes the proceeds as a revenue in its current income statement still for the fiscal year of the delivery, even though it will get paid in cash during the following accounting period.

a. Accrual basis
b. AAB
c. ABN Amro
d. A Random Walk Down Wall Street

7. Two primary accounting methods, _____ and accrual basis, are used to calculate taxable income for U.S. federal income taxes. According to the Internal Revenue Code, a taxpayer may compute taxable income by:

1. the Cash receipts and disbursements method;
2. an accrual method;
3. any other method permitted by the chapter; or
4. any combination of the foregoing methods permitted under regulations prescribed by the Secretary.

As a general rule, a taxpayer must compute taxable income using the same accounting method he uses to compute income in keeping his books. Also, the taxpayer must maintain a consistent method of accounting from year to year. Should he change from the _____ to the accrual basis (or vice versa), he must notify and secure the consent of the Secretary.

a. 4-4-5 Calendar
b. 529 plan
c. 7-Eleven
d. Cash basis

8. _____ or cookie jar reserves is an accounting practice in which a company uses generous reserves from good years against losses that might be incurred in bad years.

An example of a cookie jar reserve is a liability created when a company records an expense that is not directly linked to a specific accounting period -- the expense may fall in one period or another. Companies may record such discretionary expense when profits are high because they can afford to take the hit to income.

a. Cookie jar accounting
b. Moving-Average Cost
c. Resources, Events, Agents
d. Non Performing Asset

9. A _____ literally is the building, room, office or suite in which a business firm carries on operations, particularly accounting. By an obvious synecdoche, it has come to mean the accounting operations of a firm, however housed. The term is British in origin and is primarily used in the context of the 19th century or earlier periods.

a. Counting house
b. Proprietorship
c. Greed and fear
d. Synthetic CDO

10. _____ and earnings management are euphemisms referring to accounting practices that may follow the letter of the rules of standard accounting practices, but certainly deviate from the spirit of those rules. They are characterized by excessive complication and the use of novel ways of characterizing income, assets, or liabilities and the intent to influence readers towards the interpretations desired by the authors. The terms 'innovative' or 'aggressive' are also sometimes used.

a. Controlling account
b. Non Performing Asset
c. Debit and credit
d. Creative accounting

11. _____ is the provision of resources (such as granting a loan) by one party to another party where that second party does not reimburse the first party immediately, thereby generating a debt, and instead arranges either to repay or return those resources (or material(s) of equal value) at a later date. The first party is called a creditor, also known as a lender, while the second party is called a debtor, also known as a borrower.

Movements of financial capital are normally dependent on either _____ or equity transfers.

a. Credit
b. Comparable
c. Warrant
d. Clearing house

12. _____, founded in 1940 by CPA Nicholas Picchione, publishes a series of ledgers designed to simplify the bookkeeping process for small businesses (especially those whose personnel are not experienced in bookkeeping and accounting), as well as software based on their ledgers and several ergonomic products for use in business and other settings. Their flagship products are their weekly and monthly ledgers, though Dome also sells books for personal finance and other record keeping.

Dome also publishes several of their books co-branded with Avon and targets them towards home-based and multi-level marketing businesses, as well as a Spanish language edition of their monthly ledger.

a. Dome Publishing
b. Controlling account
c. Cookie jar accounting
d. Single-entry bookkeeping system

13. _____ is a system that ensures the integrity of the financial values recorded in a financial accounting system. It does this by ensuring that each individual transaction is recorded in at least two different (sections) nominal ledgers of the financial accounting system and so implementing a double checking system for every transaction. It does this by first identifying values as either a Debit or a Credit value.

a. Single-entry bookkeeping system
b. Momentum Accounting and Triple-Entry Bookkeeping
c. Resources, Events, Agents
d. Double-entry bookkeeping

14. _____, in accounting, refers to the overall reasonableness of reported earnings. It is an assessment criterion for how 'repeatable, controllable and bankable' a firm's earnings are, amongst other factors. It recognizes the fact that the economic impact of a given transaction will vary across firms as a function of their fundamental business characteristics, and has variously been defined as the degree to which earnings reflect underlying economic effects, are better estimates of cash flows, are conservative, or are predictable.

a. Installment Sales Method
b. Earnings quality
c. Unified Ledger Accounting
d. Imprest system

15. In accounting the separate _____ treats a business as distinct and completely separate from the owners. The business stands apart from other organizations as separate economic unit. It is necessary to record the business transactions separately to distinguish it from the owner's personal transactions. This concept is now extended to accounting for various divisions of a firm in order to ascertain results for each division.

a. Installment Sales Method
b. Entity concept
c. Imprest system
d. Unified Ledger Accounting

16. In accountancy, _____ is the practice of distributing the profit earned by a large project to corporate entities which, though technically distinct from the one responsible for the project itself, are typically owned by the same people. This has the net result of reducing the project's reported profit by a substantial margin, sometimes eliminating it altogether. This is most often done to reduce the amount which the corporation must pay in royalties or other profit-sharing agreements.
   a. 4-4-5 Calendar
   b. 529 plan
   c. Hollywood accounting
   d. 7-Eleven

17. In economics, _____ is a rise in the general level of prices of goods and services in an economy over a period of time. The term '_____' once referred to increases in the money supply (monetary _____); however, economic debates about the relationship between money supply and price levels have led to its primary use today in describing price _____. _____ can also be described as a decline in the real value of money--a loss of purchasing power in the medium of exchange which is also the monetary unit of account.
   a. A Random Walk Down Wall Street
   b. ABN Amro
   c. AAB
   d. Inflation

18. _____ is a term describing a range of accounting systems designed to correct problems arising from historical cost accounting in the presence of inflation. _____ is used in countries experiencing high inflation or hyperinflation. For example, in countries experiencing hyperinflation the International Accounting Standards Board requires corporate financial statements to be adjusted for changes in purchasing power using a price index.
   a. Inflation targeting
   b. AAB
   c. A Random Walk Down Wall Street
   d. Inflation accounting

19.

The _____ is one of several approaches used to recognize revenue. Methods such as the cost recovery method and the cash method are two of several other methods used to recognize revenue. These methods are not alternatives to one another, however, the guidelines for applying them are not well defined.

   a. Imprest system
   b. Entity concept
   c. Installment Sales Method
   d. Unified Ledger Accounting

20. _____ is an alternative accounting system developed by Yuji Ijiri and is the title of the 1989 monograph that he wrote. It is hard to imagine alternatives to the universal system of double-entry bookkeeping, but this is one.

In regular, double-entry bookkeeping, changes in balances such as earning revenues and collecting cash are recorded.

   a. Money measurement concept
   b. Single-entry bookkeeping system
   c. Resources, Events, Agents
   d. Momentum Accounting and Triple-Entry Bookkeeping

21. The _____ underlines the fact that in accounting, every recorded event or transaction is measured in terms of money. Using this principle, a fact or a happening which cannot be expressed in terms of money is not recorded in the accounting books.

One of the basic principles in accounting is 'The Measuring Unit principle: The unit of measure in accounting shall be the base money unit of the most relevant currency.

a. Public Expenditure Tracking System
b. Resources, Events, Agents
c. Double-entry bookkeeping
d. Money measurement concept

22. In economics, business, and accounting, a _____ is the value of money that has been used up to produce something, and hence is not available for use anymore. In business, the _____ may be one of acquisition, in which case the amount of money expended to acquire it is counted as _____. In this case, money is the input that is gone in order to acquire the thing.

a. Cost
b. Sliding scale fees
c. Marginal cost
d. Fixed costs

23. _____ is a method of calculating Ending Inventory cost. Assume that both Beginning Inventory and beginning inventory cost are known. From them the Cost per Unit of Beginning Inventory can be calculated.

a. Debit and credit
b. Public Expenditure Tracking System
c. Double-entry bookkeeping
d. Moving-Average Cost

24. _____ in the United States accounting, refers to a system of accounting other than GAAP. As explained in The Journal of Accountancy in an online issue: Under SAS no. 62, Special Reports, an _____ is any one of

- A statutory basis of accounting (for example, a basis of accounting insurance companies use under the rules of a state insurance commission.)

- Income-tax-basis financial statements.

- Cash-basis and modified-cash-basis financial statements.

- Financial statements prepared using definitive criteria having substantial support in accounting literature that the preparer applies to all material items appearing in the statements (such as the price level basis of accounting.)

In situations where GAAP-basis statements aren't necessary because of loan covenants, regulatory requirements or similar circumstances, an _____ not may just be the answer.

a. A Random Walk Down Wall Street
b. Operating cash flow
c. Other Comprehensive Basis of Accounting
d. Appreciation

25. _____ is a system of presenting financial information that allows stakeholders to see more clearly where money is coming from and where it is being spent, as well as allowing the service users to reconcile incoming funds with expenditures. It is sometimes referred to as 'following the money'.

_____ are increasingly used at district level in countries like Uganda and Tanzania to make budget flows transparent from local government to service delivery agents.

a. Non Performing Asset
b. Momentum Accounting and Triple-Entry Bookkeeping
c. Resources, Events, Agents
d. Public Expenditure Tracking System

26. _____ is a model of how an accounting system can be reengineered for the computer age. _____ was originally proposed in 1982 by William E. McCarthy as a generalized accounting model, and contained the concepts of resources, events and agents.

_____ is a popular model in teaching accounting information systems (AIS.)

a. Cookie jar accounting
b. Momentum Accounting and Triple-Entry Bookkeeping
c. Creative accounting
d. Resources, Events, Agents

27. _____ also known as Single-entry accounting system is a one sided accounting entry to maintain financial information.

Most businesses maintain a record of all transactions based on the double-entry bookkeeping system. However, many small, simple businesses maintain only a single-entry system that records the 'bare-essentials.' In some cases only records of cash, accounts receivable, accounts payable and taxes paid may be maintained.

a. Standard accounting practices
b. Resources, Events, Agents
c. Public Expenditure Tracking System
d. Single-entry bookkeeping system

28. _____ require publicly-traded companies to follow certain accounting rules when presenting financial statements so that the readers of the statements can easily compare different companies. Private companies are also often required by banks and shareholders, for example, to present information according to their specified rules.

Usually, countries practicing civil law system write standards into law and countries with English common law systems have private organizations to set the rules.

a. Public Expenditure Tracking System
b. Moving-Average Cost
c. Momentum Accounting and Triple-Entry Bookkeeping
d. Standard accounting practices

29. A _____ is the principal book for recording transactions. Originally, the term referred to a large volume of Scripture/service book kept in one place in church and accessible.

According to Charles Wriothesley's Chronicle (1538):

> the curates should provide a booke of the bible in Englishe, of the largest volume, to be a lidger in the same church for the parishioners to read on.

It is an application of this original meaning that is found in the commercial usage of the term for the principal book of account in a business house, the general _____ or nominal _____ and also in the terms purchase _____ and sales _____.

- a. General journal
- b. General ledger
- c. Journal entry
- d. Ledger

30. What is _____? The concept of a _____ Application is often new to people who have used traditional Modular Accounting Systems, though the idea is very simple. Traditional modular systems have separate General, Purchase and Sales Ledgers which reflect times when accountants wrote information into large paper books or ledgers. Balances on control accounts were copied from one book to another, so that a full set of accounts could be completed and as an additional process control accounts were reconciled.
    - a. Installment Sales Method
    - b. Imprest system
    - c. Entity concept
    - d. Unified Ledger Accounting

31. _____ is one of financial audit skill which help an auditor understand the client's business and changes in the business, to identify potential risk areas and to plan other audit procedures.

_____ include comparison of financial information (data in financial statement) with

1. prior periods
2. budgets
3. forecasts
4. similar industries and so on.

It also includes consideration of predictable relationships, such as:

1. gross profit to sales,
2. payroll costs to employees,
3. financial information and non-financial information, for examples the CEO's reports and the industry news.

possible sources of information about the client include:

1. interim financial information
2. Budgets
3. Management accounts
4. Non-Financial information
5. Bank and cash records
6. VAT returns
7. Board minutes
8. Discussion or correspondance with the client at they year-end

a. International Federation of Audit Bureaux of Circulations
b. Assurance service
c. Event data
d. Analytical Procedures

32. The institution most often referenced by the word '_____' is a public or publicly traded _____, the shares of which are traded on a public stock exchange (e.g., the New York Stock Exchange or Nasdaq in the United States) where shares of stock of _____s are bought and sold by and to the general public. Most of the largest businesses in the world are publicly traded _____s. However, the majority of _____s are said to be closely held, privately held or close _____s, meaning that no ready market exists for the trading of shares.
   a. Depository Trust Company
   b. Federal Home Loan Mortgage Corporation
   c. Protect
   d. Corporation

33. _____s have been defined by the American Institute of Certified Public Accountants (AICPA) as 'Independent Professional Services that improve information quality or its context'. _____s reduce the information risk; risk that the information provided is incorrect, on more than just financial data. The major purpose of _____s is to provide independent and professional opinions that improve the quality of information to management as well as other decision makers within a given firm.
   a. Assurance service
   b. Audit
   c. Auditing Standards Board
   d. Audit committee

34. Accounting _____ define the basic standards for representing attestation engagements. Attestation is defined as an engagement in which a practitioner is hired to issue written communication that expresses a conclusion about the reliability of written assertions prepared by a separate party. The American Institute of Certified Public Accountants identified a number of different engagements that fall under the scope of _____, including: examining financial forecasts and projections, examining pro forma financial statements, evaluating internal control, assessing compliance with rules, regulations, and contractual obligations, as well as evaluating management discussions and analysis of financial results.
   a. External auditor
   b. Institute of Internal Auditors
   c. Audit committee
   d. Attestation Standards

35. In a publicly-held company, an _____ is an operating committee of the Board of Directors, typically charged with oversight of financial reporting and disclosure. Committee members are drawn from members of the Company's board of directors, with a Chairperson selected from among the members. An _____ of a publicly-traded company in the United States is composed of independent and outside directors referred to as non-executive directors, at least one of which is typically a financial expert.

a. Audit working paper
c. Attestation Standards
b. Audit management
d. Audit committee

36. _____ is evidence obtained during a financial audit and recorded in the audit working papers.

- In the audit engagement acceptance or reappointment stage, _____ is the information that the auditor is to consider for the appointment. For examples, change in the entity control environment, inherent risk and nature of the entity business, and scope of audit work.

- In the audit planning stage, _____ is the information that the auditor is to consider for the most effective and efficient audit approach. For examples, reliability of internal control procedures, and analytical review systems.

- In the control testing stage, _____ is the information that the auditor is to consider for the mix of audit test of control and audit substantive tests.

- In the substantive testing stage, _____ is the information that the auditor is to make sure the appropriation of financial statement assertions. For examples, existence, rights and obligations, occurrence, completeness, valuation, measurement, presentation and disclosure of a particular transaction or account balance.

a. International Standards on Auditing
c. Information audit
b. Audit committee
d. Audit evidence

37. _____ is responsible for ensuring that board-approved audit directives are implemented.

_____ oversees the internal audit staff, establishes internal audit programs, and hires and trains the appropriate internal audit personnel. The staff should have the necessary skills and expertise to identify inherent risks of the business and assess the overall effectiveness of controls in place relating to the company's information technology operations.

a. Event data
c. External auditor
b. Attestation Standards
d. Audit management

38. An _____ is usually a rigorous set of forensic accounting methods that is used to detect fraud. It refers more generally however to any similar regime of verification of conformity to some standard, e.g. Kyoto Protocol, Cocoa Protocol, or some mandatory labelling scheme. Without such a regime, transparency is simply not attainable.

a. Audit regime
c. Institute of Internal Auditors
b. International Federation of Audit Bureaux of Circulations
d. Auditing Standards Board

39. _____ is a term that is commonly applied in relation to the audit of the financial statements of an entity. The primary objective of such an audit is to provide an opinion as to whether or not the financial statements present fairly the financial position and results of the entity.

a. Auditing Standards Board
c. Assurance service
b. Institute of Internal Auditors
d. Audit risk

Chapter 7. Test Preparation Part 7

40. _____ was a phrase that Chinese media coined to describe the auditing campaigns initiated by the National Audit Office of China.

In 2003, Auditor General Li Jinhua presented the annual audit report to the Standing Committee of the National People's Congress. He openly disclosed the severe irregularities committed by many ministries and other government agencies.

a. Audit storm
b. ABN Amro
c. A Random Walk Down Wall Street
d. AAB

41. _____s are the documents which keeping all audit evidences obtained during financial statements auditing.
_____ is to be able to support the audit works done in order, sufficient and assurance audit evidences have been obtained and reasonable assurance audit conclusion can be made in due course.

_____s are the property of the auditor.

a. Auditing Standards Board
b. Audit working paper
c. Audit committee
d. Information audit

42. The _____ Limited was originally established in 1991 as a committee of the Consultative Committee of Accountancy Bodies, to take responsibility within the United Kingdom and Republic of Ireland for setting standards of auditing with the objective of enhancing public confidence in the audit process and the quality and relevance of audit services in the public interest. In 2002 _____ was re-established under the auspices of The Accountancy Foundation and, following a UK government review, it has been transferred to the Financial Reporting Council (FRC.) Its objective has remained the same, but its remit has been extended to include responsibility for setting standards for auditors' integrity, objectivity and independence.

a. ABN Amro
b. AAB
c. A Random Walk Down Wall Street
d. Auditing Practices Board

43. In the United States, the _____ is the senior technical committee designated by the American Institute of Certified Public Accountants (AICPA) to issue auditing, attestation, and quality control statements, standards and guidance to certified public accountants (CPAs) for non-public company audits. Created in October 1978, it is composed of 19 members representing various industries and sectors, including public accountants and private, educational, and governmental entities. It issues pronouncements in the form of statements, interpretations, and guidelines, which all CPAs must adhere to when performing audits and attestations.

a. Audit working paper
b. Audit risk
c. Auditing Standards Board
d. Environmental audit

44. The _____ is an Act of Parliament respecting the office of the Auditor General of Canada and sustainable development monitoring and reporting.

a. ABN Amro
b. Auditor General Act
c. A Random Walk Down Wall Street
d. AAB

45. The _____ (CICA) is the umbrella body for the Chartered Accountant profession in Canada and Bermuda. Membership of the CICA totals 70,000 Chartered Accountants and 8,500 students.

Canadian chartered accountants use the designation CA.

    a. 529 plan
    b. 7-Eleven
    c. 4-4-5 Calendar
    d. Canadian Institute of Chartered Accountants

46. _____ is the title used by members of certain professional accountancy associations in the British Commonwealth countries and Ireland. The term chartered comes from the Royal Charter granted to the world's first professional body of accountants upon their establishment in 1854.

_____s work in all fields of business and finance.

    a. Certified Public Accountant
    b. Chartered Accountant
    c. Chartered Certified Accountant
    d. Certified General Accountant

47. _____ is an audit professional certification sponsored by the Information Systems Audit and Control Association (ISACA.) Candidates for the certification must meet requirements set by ISACA.

The _____ certification was established in 1978 for several reasons:

1. Develop and maintain a tool that could be used to evaluate an individuals' competency in conducting information system audits.
2. Provide a motivational tool for information systems auditors to maintain their skills, and monitor the success of the maintenance programs.
3. Provide criteria to help aid management in the selection of personnel and development.

The first _____ examination was administered in 1981, and registration numbers have grown each year. Over 60,000 candidates have earned the _____ designation.

    a. 4-4-5 Calendar
    b. Certified Information Systems Auditor
    c. 7-Eleven
    d. 529 plan

48. _____ was founded in 1985 and is today one of the leading and fastest-growing accounting and business advisory groups in Singapore. With a total staff strength of 500± in Singapore (and 120 ± in Shanghai, Beijing, Suzhou and Shenzhen), it is the largest outside the Big 4 in Singapore.

On the international front, _____ is the Singapore member of RSM International, the world's 7th largest accounting and consulting organisation.

    a. Clinical audit
    b. Mainframe audit
    c. Financial audit
    d. Chio Lim Stone Forest

49. _____ is the process formally introduced in 1993 into the United Kingdom's National Health Service (NHS), and is defined as 'a quality improvement process that seeks to improve patient care and outcomes through systematic review of care against explicit criteria and the implementation of change'.

The key component of _____ is that performance is reviewed (or audited) to ensure that what should be done is being done, and if not it provides a framework to enable improvements to be made. There is a _____ guidance group in the UK.

a. Chio Lim Stone Forest
c. RSM International
b. Performance audit
d. Clinical audit

50. In the United Kingdom a public servant, for example a local government officer, who has unlawfully spent public funds, or caused loss to a public authority through misconduct may be _____ to recover public money. The surcharge may be applied, after referral to a court by the Audit Commission. In the case of an illegal corporate decision by an elected body all the councillors may be _____.

a. SOX 404 top-down risk assessment
c. GASB 45
b. Surcharged
d. Sales Tax Audit

51. _____, in auditing, is the risk that a company's internal controls are insufficient to mitigate or detect errors or fraud.

- Risk Assessment
- Inherent risk
- Detection Risk

a. 4-4-5 Calendar
c. 529 plan
b. Detection Risk
d. Control Risk

52. _____ also called 'Internal _____'. It is a term of financial audit, internal audit and Enterprise Risk Management. It means the overall attitude, awareness and actions of directors and management (i.e. 'those charged with governance') regarding the internal control system and its importance to the entity.

a. SOFT audit
c. Financial Instruments and Exchange Law
b. Joint audit
d. Control environment

53. _____ involves observing a database so as to be aware of the actions of database users. This is often for security purposes, for example, to ensure that information is not accessed by those without the permission to access it (Schwartz.)

Database security is a serious issue affecting an organization's information security, damage, and loss (Mookhey.) It is common for an organization to make every effort to lock down their network, but leave the database vulnerable.

a. Help desk and incident reporting auditing
c. Controlled foreign corporations
b. Special journals
d. Database auditing

54. _____, in auditing, is the risk that the auditing procedures used will not find a material misstatement in the financial statements of the company being audited.

- Risk Assessment
- Inherent risk
- Control Risk

a. Detection Risk
c. Scenario analysis
b. 529 plan
d. 4-4-5 Calendar

55. An _____ defines the legal relationship (or engagement) between a professional firm (e.g., law, investment banking, consulting, advisory or accountancy firm) and its client(s.) This letter states the terms and conditions of the engagement, principally addressing the scope of the engagement and the terms of compensation for the firm.

Most _____s follow a standard format.

a. Institute of Internal Auditors
c. International Federation of Audit Bureaux of Circulations
b. Audit risk
d. Engagement Letter

56. _____ in business includes the methods and processes used by organizations to manage risks and seize opportunities related to the achievement of their objectives. _____ provides a framework for risk management, which typically involves identifying particular events or circumstances relevant to the organization's objectives (risks and opportunities), assessing them in terms of likelihood and magnitude of impact, determining a response strategy, and monitoring progress. By identifying and proactively addressing risks and opportunities, business enterprises protect and create value for their stakeholders, including owners, employees, customers, regulators, and society overall.

a. A Random Walk Down Wall Street
c. ABN Amro
b. AAB
d. Enterprise risk management

57. _____ is the discipline of identifying, monitoring and limiting risks. In some cases the acceptable risk may be near zero. Risks can come from accidents, natural causes and disasters as well as deliberate attacks from an adversary.

a. Penny stock
c. 4-4-5 Calendar
b. FIFO
d. Risk management

58. _____s are intended to quantify environmental performance and environmental position. In this way they perform an analogous function to financial audits. An _____ report ideally contains a statement of environmental performance and environmental position, and may also aim to define what needs to be done to sustain or improve on indicators of such performance and position.

a. Information audit
c. Assurance service
b. External auditor
d. Environmental audit

59. _____ is a synonym to an audit trail. Modern computer software applications and IT infrastructure have adopted the term _____ over audit trail. Events are typically recorded in logs and there is no standard for the format of event type data.

Chapter 7. Test Preparation Part 7

a. Audit
b. Event data
c. Environmental audit
d. Audit management

60. An _____ is an audit professional who performs an audit on the financial statements of a company, government, individual and who is independent of the entity being audited. Users of these entities' financial information, such as investors, government agencies, and the general public, rely on the _____ to present an unbiased and independent evaluation on such entities. They are distinguished from internal auditors for two main reasons: (1) the internal auditor's primary responsibility is appraising an entity's risk management strategy and practices, management (including IT) control frameworks and governance processes, and (2) they do not express an opinion on the entity's financial statements.

a. Audit risk
b. Audit committee
c. Audit working paper
d. External auditor

61. _____ are cash, evidence of an ownership interest in an entity or deliver, cash or another financial instrument.

_____ can be categorized by form depending on whether they are cash instruments or derivative instruments:

- Cash instruments are _____ whose value is determined directly by markets. They can be divided into securities, which are readily transferable, and other cash instruments such as loans and deposits, where both borrower and lender have to agree on a transfer.
- Derivative instruments are _____ which derive their value from the value and characteristics of one or more underlying assets. They can be divided into exchange-traded derivatives and over-the-counter (OTC) derivatives.

Alternatively, _____ can be categorized by 'asset class' depending on whether they are equity based (reflecting ownership of the issuing entity) or debt based (reflecting a loan the investor has made to the issuing entity.) If it is debt, it can be further categorised into short term (less than one year) or long term.

Foreign Exchange instruments and transactions are neither debt nor equity based and belong in their own category.

a. Secondary market
b. Financial services
c. Cost of carry
d. Financial instruments

62. The _____ , promulgated on June 14th, 2006, is the main statute codifying securities law and regulating securities companies in Japan.

The law provides for:

- Registration and regulation of broker dealers and their registered representatives
- Disclosure obligations applicable to public companies, investment trusts and similar entities
- Tender offer rules
- Disclosure obligations applicable to large shareholders in public companies
- Internal controls in public companies; in this role the law is often referred to as J-SOX, a reference to the American Sarbanes-Oxley Act (SOX.)

The internal control portions of the FIEL were largely enacted in response to corporate scandals such as the Kanebo, Livedoor, and Murakami Fund episodes.

The Internal Control Committee of the Business Accounting Council of the Japanese Financial Services Agency provided final Implementation Guidance for Management Assessment and Audit of Internal Controls over Financial Reporting (ICFR) in February 2007. The Implementation Guidance provides details to Japanese companies on how to implement a Management Assessment of Internal Control over Financial Reporting as required under the _____.

a. GASB 45
b. Management representation
c. SOX 404 top-down risk assessment
d. Financial Instruments and Exchange Law

63. A _____ an audit of financial statements, is the review of the financial statements of a company or any other legal entity (including governments), resulting in the publication of an independent opinion on whether or not those financial statements are relevant, accurate, complete, and fairly presented.

_____s are typically performed by firms of practicing accountants due to the specialist financial reporting knowledge they require. The _____ is one of many assurance or attestation functions provided by accounting and auditing firms, whereby the firm provides an independent opinion on published information.

a. Provided by client
b. Joint audit
c. Lead Auditor
d. Financial audit

64. _____ is the specialty practice area of accountancy that describes engagements that result from actual or anticipated disputes or litigation. 'Forensic' means 'suitable for use in a court of law', and it is to that standard and potential outcome that forensic accountants generally have to work. Forensic accountants, also referred to as forensic auditors or investigative auditors, often have to give expert evidence at the eventual trial.

a. Management accounting
b. Product control
c. Nonassurance services
d. Forensic accounting

65. _____ has gained public recognition and spotlight since the 2002 inception of the Sarbanes-Oxley Act. Of the many reforms enacted through Sarbanes-Oxley, one major goal was to regain public confidence in the reliability of financial markets in the wake of corporate scandals such as Enron, WorldCom and Waste Management. Section 404 of Sarbanes Oxley mandated that public companies have an independent Audit of internal controls over financial reporting.

a. Vesting
b. Fraud deterrence
c. Law of one price
d. Court of Audit of Belgium

66. The _____ is currently the source of generally accepted accounting principles (GAAP) used by State and Local governments in the United States of America. As with most of the entities involved in creating GAAP in the United States, it is a private, non-governmental organization.

The _____ is subject to oversight by the Financial Accounting Foundation (FAF), which selects the members of the _____ and the Financial Accounting Standards Board, and funds both organizations.

a. General partnership
b. Depository Trust Company
c. Governmental Accounting Standards Board
d. Wells Fargo ' Co.

67. _____ is an accounting and financial reporting provision requiring government employers to measure and report the liabilities associated with other (than pension) postemployment benefits (or OPEB.) Reported OPEBs may include post-retirement medical, pharmacy, dental, vision, life, long-term disability and long-term care benefits that are not associated with a pension plan. Government employers required to comply with _____ include all states, towns, education boards, water districts, mosquito districts, public schools and all other government entities that offer OPEB and report under GASB.

a. Mainframe audit
b. GASB 45
c. Sales Tax Audit
d. Control environment

68. _____ are ten auditing standards, developed by the AICPA, consisting of general standards, standards of field work, and standards of reporting, along with interpretations. They were developed by the AICPA in 1947 and have undergone minor changes since then.

The _____ are as follows:

1. The auditor must have adequate technical training and proficiency to perform the audit
2. The auditor must maintain independence in mental attitude in all matters related to the audit.
3. The auditor must use due professional care during the performance of the audit and the preparation of the report.

1. The auditor must adequately plan the work and must properly supervise any assistants.
2. The auditor must obtain a sufficient understanding of the entity and its environment, including its internal control, to assess the risk of material misstatement of the financial statements whether due to error or fraud, and to design the nature, timing, and extent of further audit procedures.
3. The auditor must obtain sufficient appropriate audit evidence by performing audit procedures to afford a reasonable basis for an opinion regarding the financial statements under audit.

The new standards are in effect for audits of financial statements for periods beginning on or after December 15, 2006.

1. The auditor must state in the auditor's report whether the financial statements are in accordance with generally accepted accounting principles (GAAP.)
2. The auditor must identify in the auditor's report those circumstances in which such principles have not been consistently observed in the current period in relation to the preceding period.
3. When the auditor determines that informative disclosures are not reasonably adequate, the auditor must so state in the auditor's report.
4. The auditor must either express an opinion regarding the financial statements, taken as a whole the auditor should state the reasons therefore in the auditors report. In all cases where the auditor's name is associated with the financial statements, the auditor should clearly indicate the character of the auditor's work, if any, and the degree of responsibility the auditor is taking, in the auditor's report.

- Statements on Auditing Standards

a. Performance audit
b. Financial Instruments and Exchange Law
c. GASB 45
d. Generally Accepted Auditing Standards

69. The _____ produces the world's de facto standard in sustainability reporting guidelines. Sustainability reporting is the action where an organization publicly communicates their economic, environmental, and social performance. The _____'s mission is to make sustainability reporting by all organizations as routine and comparable as financial reporting.

a. 529 plan
b. 4-4-5 Calendar
c. Global Reporting Initiative
d. 7-Eleven

70. A _____ is a business that functions without the intention or threat of liquidation for the foreseeable future, usually regarded as at least within 12 months.

In accounting, '_____' refers to a company's ability to continue functioning as a business entity. It is the responsibility of the directors to assess whether the _____ assumption is appropriate when preparing the financial statements.

a. Going concern
b. 529 plan
c. 4-4-5 Calendar
d. Trade credit

71. _____ is an examination of the controls within the help desk operations. The audit process collects and evaluates evidence of an organization's help desk and incident reporting practices, and operations. The audit ensures that all problems reported by users have been adequately documented and that controls exist so that only authorized staff can archive the users' entries.

a. Short positions
b. Certified Emission Reductions
c. Help desk and incident reporting auditing
d. Flow to Equity-Approach

Chapter 7. Test Preparation Part 7

72. _____ is one of the International Standards on Auditing. It serves to direct the documentation of audit working papers in order to assist the audit planning and performance; the supervision and review of the audit work; and the recording of audit evidence resulting from the audit work in order to support the auditor's opinion.

The auditor should prepare, on a timely basis, audit documentation that provides:

1. A sufficient and appropriate record of the basis for the audit report
2. Evidence that the audit was performed in accordance with ISA's and applicable legal and regulatory requirements (Paragraph 2.)

The auditor should prepare the audit documentation so as to enable an experienced auditor, having no previous connection with the audit, to understand:

1. The nature, timing, and extent of audit procedures performed to comply with ISAs and applicable legal and regulatory requirements;
2. The results of the audit procedures and the audit evidence obtained;
3. Significant matters arising during the audit and the conclusions reached thereon. (Paragraph 9)

Oral explanations by the auditor, on their own, do not represent adequate support for the work the auditor performed or conclusions the auditor reached, but may be used to clarify or explain information contained in the audit documentation.

a. ISA 400 Risk Assessments and Internal Control

b. ISA 501 Audit Evidence - Additional Considerations for Specific Items

c. ISA 505 External Confirmations

d. ISA 230 Documentation

73. _____ are formal records of a business' financial activities.

_____ provide an overview of a business' financial condition in both short and long term. There are four basic _____:

1. **Balance sheet**: also referred to as statement of financial position or condition, reports on a company's assets, liabilities, and net equity as of a given point in time.
2. **Income statement**: also referred to as Profit and Loss statement (or a 'P'L'), reports on a company's income, expenses, and profits over a period of time.
3. **Statement of retained earnings**: explains the changes in a company's retained earnings over the reporting period.
4. **Statement of cash flows**: reports on a company's cash flow activities, particularly its operating, investing and financing activities.

a. Notes to the Financial Statements

b. Financial Statements

c. Statement on Auditing Standards No. 70: Service Organizations

d. Statement of retained earnings

74. _____ is one of the International Standards on Auditing. It serves to direct all audit works are to be planned in order to perform the audit job more efficiently, timely and effectively.
   a. ISA 320 Audit Materiality
   b. ISA 310 Knowledge of the Business
   c. ISA 500 Audit Evidence
   d. ISA 300 Planning an Audit of Financial Statements

75. _____ is one of the International Standards on Auditing. It serves to expect the auditors are to have necessary knowledge of the client's business. Even before accepting the audit job, audit is to make sure if you have sufficient knowledge to perform the audit professionally.
   a. ISA 310 Knowledge of the Business
   b. ISA 320 Audit Materiality
   c. ISA 500 Audit Evidence
   d. ISA 505 External Confirmations

76. _____ is one of the International Standards on Auditing. It serves to expect the auditor is to establish an acceptable materiality level in design the audit plan.

Materiality: If the financial statements readers makes a wrong economic decision due to misstatement of the financial statements, it is called material.

   a. ISA 501 Audit Evidence - Additional Considerations for Specific Items
   b. ISA 505 External Confirmations
   c. ISA 320 Audit Materiality
   d. ISA 400 Risk Assessments and Internal Control

77. _____ is a concept or convention within auditing and accounting relating to the importance of an amount, transaction, or discrepancy. The objective of an audit of financial statements is to enable the auditor to express an opinion whether the financial statements are prepared, in all material respects, in conformity with an identified financial reporting framework such as Generally Accepted Accounting Principles (GAAP.) The assessment of what is material is a matter of professional judgment.
   a. Materiality
   b. Financial audit
   c. Trustworthy Repositories Audit ' Certification
   d. Clinical audit

78. _____ is one of the International Standards on Auditing. It serves to require the auditor is to understand the client's accounting system and internal control system and to assess control risk and inherent risk. The objective is to determine the nature, timing and extent of substantive procedures in order to reduce audit risk to an acceptable low level.
   a. ISA 400 Risk Assessments and Internal Control
   b. ISA 505 External Confirmations
   c. ISA 320 Audit Materiality
   d. ISA 500 Audit Evidence

79. In accounting and organizational theory, _____ is defined as a process effected by an organization's structure, work and authority flows, people and management information systems, designed to help the organization accomplish specific goals or objectives. It is a means by which an organization's resources are directed, monitored, and measured. It plays an important role in preventing and detecting fraud and protecting the organization's resources, both physical (e.g., machinery and property) and intangible (e.g., reputation or intellectual property such as trademarks.)
   a. OTC Bulletin Board
   b. Internal Control
   c. Interest
   d. Asian Financial Crisis

80. _____ is a step in a risk management process. _____ is the determination of quantitative or qualitative value of risk related to a concrete situation and a recognized threat (also called hazard.) Quantitative _____ requires calculations of two components of risk: R, the magnitude of the potential loss L, and the probability p that the loss will occur.

a. Risk Assessment
c. 7-Eleven
b. 4-4-5 Calendar
d. 529 plan

81. Editing _____ is one of the International Standards on Auditing. It serves to expect the auditor is to obtain audit evidence from an appropriate mix of tests of control systems and substantive tests of transaction and balances.

It requests the auditor to obtain 'sufficient' and 'appropriate' audit evidence in order to draw reasonable conclusions on which to base the audit opinion.

a. ISA 505 External Confirmations
c. ISA 500 Audit Evidence
b. ISA 310 Knowledge of the Business
d. ISA 501 Audit Evidence - Additional Considerations for Specific Items

82. _____ is one of the International Standards on Auditing. It sets out guidance additional to the ones in ISA 500 Audit Evidence to help auditor to obtain audit evidence with respect to the below certain specific financial statement account balances and discloures:

1. Physical inventory counting
2. Litigation and claims
3. Long-term investments
4. Segment information

a. ISA 320 Audit Materiality
c. ISA 501 Audit Evidence - Additional Considerations for Specific Items
b. ISA 500 Audit Evidence
d. ISA 310 Knowledge of the Business

83. _____ is one of the International Standards on Auditing. It serves to require the auditor is to obtain external sources of audit evidence. The example is bank accounts balance confirmed by client's bankers.

a. ISA 310 Knowledge of the Business
c. ISA 320 Audit Materiality
b. ISA 400 Risk Assessments and Internal Control
d. ISA 505 External Confirmations

84. ISACA is an international professional association. ISACA is an affiliates member of IFAC and IT Governance Institute. Previously known as the _____, ISACA now goes by its acronym only, to reflect the broad range of IT governance professionals it serves.

a. Information Systems Audit and Control Association
c. Accounting Principles Board
b. American Law and Economics Association
d. Accion USA

85. An _____ trail or _____ log is a chronological sequence of audit records, each of which contains data about when and by whom was a particular record changed. It can also include information about the actual changes that were made. It can enable the reconstruction and examination of the end states of data, and reconstruct the intermediate states that the data went through before the final state was established.

a. Engagement Letter
c. Audit management
b. Audit evidence
d. Information audit

86. A _____ is a manual or systematic measurable technical assessment of a system or application. Manual assessments include interviewing staff, performing security vulnerability scans, reviewing application and operating system access controls, and analyzing physical access to the systems. Automated assessments, or CAAT's, include system generated audit reports or using software to monitor and report changes to files and settings on a system.

   a. 7-Eleven
   b. 4-4-5 Calendar
   c. 529 plan
   d. Computer security audit

87. A _____ is a fungible, negotiable instrument representing financial value. They are broadly categorized into debt securities (such as banknotes, bonds and debentures), and equity securities; e.g., common stocks. The company or other entity issuing the _____ is called the issuer.

   a. Tracking stock
   b. Security
   c. Book entry
   d. Securities lending

88. _____, in auditing, is the risk that the account or section being audited is materially misstated without considering internal controls due to error; _____ does not include an assessment of the risk of material misstatement due to fraud. The assessment of _____ depends on the professional judgement of the auditor, and it is done after assessing the business environment of the entity being audited.

   _____ is typically assessed using a scale, with assessments being either low, medium, or high.

   a. AAB
   b. A Random Walk Down Wall Street
   c. Inherent risk
   d. ABN Amro

89. Established in 1941, The _____ (IIA) is internationally recognized as a trustworthy guidance-setting body. Serving members in 165 countries, The IIA is the internal audit profession's global voice, chief advocate, recognized authority, acknowledged leader, and principal educator, with global headquarters in Altamonte Springs, Fla., United States.

   The stated mission of The _____ is to provide dynamic leadership for the global profession of internal auditing.

   a. Auditing Standards Board
   b. Audit committee
   c. Institute of Internal Auditors
   d. Assurance service

90. The _____ (IFABC) was founded in 1963 in Stockholm, Sweden.

IFABC is a voluntary cooperative federation of industry-sponsored organizations established in nations throughout the world to verify and report facts about the circulations of publications and related data. (IFABC website)

A General Assembly of members is held every second year since 1963. Assemblies have been held in New York, Paris, Munich, Copenhagen, London, Chicago, Madrid, Rio de Janeiro, Stockholm, Tokyo, Toronto, Buenos Aires, Lucerne, New Delhi, Berlin, Washington, D.C., Seville, Sydney, and Kuala Lumpur.

a. Audit working paper
b. Audit evidence
c. Audit
d. International Federation of Audit Bureaux of Circulations

91. Based in London, the _____ (IRCA) was formed in 1984 as part of the UK government's enterprise initiative, designed to make industry and business more competitive through the implementation of quality principles and practices. Over 30,000 auditors have been awarded professional certification since 1984 and more than 120 countries are represented on the IRCA register.

- instill confidence in accredited certification world-wide by improving the performance of auditors
- associate the IRCA name with integrity, best practice and adding value
- promote auditing as a valued profession
- provide an excellent administration service to all our stakeholders, which sets a benchmark for others to follow
- improve the standard of auditors and auditor training
- make IRCA certification available to all relevant organizations and individuals worldwide
- promote best practice in auditing

IRCA offers five grades of certification:

- Internal auditor

This certification is designed for those who conduct internal audits of their organization's management system

- Provisional auditor

This certification is designed for entry level/trainee auditors seeking a career in auditing and experienced auditors taking a break from auditing or moving into management

- Auditor

This certification is designed for audit team members

- Lead auditor

This certification is designed for audit team leaders who typically work for certification bodies or perform supplier audits for large organizations

- Principal auditor

This certification is designed for experienced auditors who operate on their own (i.e. as a team of one, performing sole audits.) We designed this grade as an alternative to the lead auditor grade

IRCA approved training organizations offer certified training courses based on a wide range of management systems standards and industry sectors:

- Foundation courses

These certified courses are designed for students needing a basic understanding of the requirements of a specific management systems standard. Suitable for people with little or no knowledge of the relevant standard

- Internal auditor courses

These certified courses are designed for students requiring the basic skills necessary to audit areas of their own organization's management systems

- Lead auditor courses

These certified courses are designed for students requiring all knowledge and skills necessary to interpret a management systems standard in the context of a second party supplier or third party certification audit

- Conversion auditor courses

These certified courses are designed for experienced auditors wishing to audit in new contexts, against other management systems standards, by adding to their existing generic auditing skills and experience

IRCA has the following certification programs:

- Corporate Auditor (complies with ISO 17024)
- Quality (ISO 9000)
- TickIT
- Aerospace (AS 9100)
- Maritime Safety Management Systems
- Environmental (ISO 14001)
- Information Security (ISO 27001)
- Information Technology Service Management (ISO 20000)
- Business Continuity (BS 25999)
- Occupational Health ' Safety (OHSAS 18001)
- Social Systems (SA 8000)
- Sustainability Assurance Practitioner (AA 1000)

a. ABN Amro
b. A Random Walk Down Wall Street
c. International Register of Certificated Auditors
d. AAB

92. _____ are professional standards for the performance of financial audit of financial information. These standards are issued by International Federation of Accountants through the International Auditing and Assurance Standards Board.

a. Environmental audit
c. International Standards on Auditing
b. Audit regime
d. Audit evidence

93. A _____ is an audit on a legal entity (the auditee) by two or more auditors to produce a single audit report, thereby sharing responsibility for the audit. A typical _____ has audit planning performed jointly and fieldwork allocated to the auditors. The auditors are typically not individuals, but auditing firms.
   a. Generally Accepted Auditing Standards
   c. SOX 404 top-down risk assessment
   b. Chio Lim Stone Forest
   d. Joint audit

94. _____ is one of the largest professional services firms in the world. _____ employs over 123,000 people in a global network of member firms spanning over 145 countries. Composite revenues of _____ member firms in 2007 were $19.8 billion USD (17.4% growth from 2006.)
   a. KPMG
   c. Federal Deposit Insurance Corporation
   b. National Association of State Boards of Accountancy
   d. Texas ratio

95. The certified _____ designation is a professional certification for audit team leaders who typically work for certification bodies or perform supplier audits for large organizations. This certification is normally provided by the International Register of Certificated Auditors (IRCA) or by RABQSA International.

The requirements to be a certified _____ normally consist of tertiary education, audit experience (as an auditor and as a _____ in training) and at least two years of relevant working experience.

   a. Trustworthy Repositories Audit ' Certification
   c. Control environment
   b. GASB 45
   d. Lead Auditor

Chapter 8. Test Preparation Part 8

1. According to the National Association of _____ (NA_____), _____ is a litigation management practice and risk management tool, used by insurance and other consumers of legal services, to determine if hourly billing errors, abuses, and inefficiencies exist by carefully examining and indentifying unreasonable attorney fees and expenses.

   Legal auditors conduct a detailed analysis of original time records, attorney work production, expenses and hourly rate benchmarks. The purpose of a legal bill auditing is to save money for the insurance company and their clients.

   a. Legal auditing
   b. Joint audit
   c. Chio Lim Stone Forest
   d. Performance audit

2. A _____ is a comprhensive inspection of computer processes , security , and procedures ,with recommendations for improvement.

   A mainframe computer is not easy to define. Most people associate a mainframe with a large computer; but mainframes are getting smaller all the time.

   a. Chio Lim Stone Forest
   b. Financial Instruments and Exchange Law
   c. Financial audit
   d. Mainframe audit

3. In a financial audit, _____ or financial statement assertions is the set of information that the preparer of financial statements (management) is providing to another party. Financial statements represent a very complex and interrelated set of assertions. At the most aggregate level, the financial statements include broad assertions such as 'total liabilities as at 31 December are $50 million', 'total revenue for the year is $9 million' and 'net income for the year is $3 million'.

   a. Management representation
   b. Center for Audit Quality
   c. Trustworthy Repositories Audit ' Certification
   d. Management assertions

4. _____ is a letter issued by an auditor's client to the auditor in writing as one of audit evidences. The date of the document must not be later than the date of audit work completion. It is used to let the client's management acknowledge the financial statements and other presentation to the auditor are sufficient and appropriate and without omission of material facts to the financial statements.

   a. Statements on Auditing Standards
   b. Sales Tax Audit
   c. Management representation
   d. Financial Instruments and Exchange Law

5. _____ is a concept or convention within auditing and accounting relating to the importance of an amount, transaction, or discrepancy. The objective of an audit of financial statements is to enable the auditor to express an opinion whether the financial statements are prepared, in all material respects, in conformity with an identified financial reporting framework such as Generally Accepted Accounting Principles (GAAP.) The assessment of what is material is a matter of professional judgment.

   a. Clinical audit
   b. Trustworthy Repositories Audit ' Certification
   c. Financial audit
   d. Materiality

6. A _____ is type of control used in auditing to discover and prevent mistakes that may lead to uncorrected and/or unrecorded misstatements that would generally be related to control deficiencies. For example, a trader may fail to record a trade and the error may go unnoticed for several reporting periods. A _____ would be instrumental in finding and therefore, preventing such mistakes.

Chapter 8. Test Preparation Part 8

a. Rural credit cooperatives
b. National Labor Relations Act
c. Linear regression
d. Mitigating Control

7. Method used by the Certified Public Accountant to assure various parties, such as bankers and stockbrokers, that financial data under review by them is correct. _____ tells the data user that nothing has come to the CPA's attention of an adverse nature or character regarding the financial data reviewed. This type of assurance is normally given to investment bankers and the SEC when the financial data are being used for stock and bond issuance.

a. Provided by client
b. Statements on Auditing Standards
c. SOFT audit
d. Negative assurance

8. _____ refers to an examination of a program, function, operation or the management systems and procedures of a governmental or non-profit entity to assess whether the entity is achieving economy, efficiency and effectiveness in the employment of available resources. The examination is objective and systematic, generally using structured and professionally adopted methodologies.

In most countries, _____s of governmental activities are carried out by the external audit bodies at federal or state level.

a. Trustworthy Repositories Audit ' Certification
b. Generally Accepted Auditing Standards
c. Performance audit
d. Clinical audit

9. _____ is a term used by auditors. An auditor reviews documentation from multiple sources. In order to verify client data, the auditor compares documentation _____ vendors, or from sources separate from the client.

a. Performance audit
b. Management representation
c. Financial audit
d. Provided by client

10. _____ is the process of systematic examination of a quality system carried out by an internal or external quality auditor or an audit team . It is an important part of organization's quality management system and is a key element in the ISO quality system standard, ISO 9001.

_____s are typically performed at predefined time intervals and ensure that the institution has clearly-defined internal quality monitoring procedures linked to effective action.

a. 4-4-5 Calendar
b. 529 plan
c. 7-Eleven
d. Quality audit

11. Integrated _____ is an integrated audit approach that focuses on the key and material components of four differing audit approaches relevant to an auditee, based on a detailed risk assessment performed annually. This approach integrates the key aspects of:

- S - Sarbanes-Oxley Act of 2002 Compliance Audit
- O - Operational audit/Best Industry Practices
- F - Financial Substantive Audit Procedures
- T - Transactional Auditing

a. Sales Tax Audit
c. Legal auditing
b. Mainframe audit
d. SOFT audit

12. In financial auditing of public companies in the United States, _____ (TDRA) is a financial risk assessment performed to comply with Section 404 of the Sarbanes-Oxley Act of 2002 (SOX 404.) The term is used by the U.S. Public Company Accounting Oversight Board (PCAOB) and the Securities and Exchange Commission (SEC.) The TDRA is used to determine the scope and required evidence to support management's testing of its internal controls under SOX404.

a. Generally Accepted Auditing Standards
c. Clinical audit
b. SOX 404 top-down risk assessment
d. Sales Tax Audit

13. _____ is a step in a risk management process. _____ is the determination of quantitative or qualitative value of risk related to a concrete situation and a recognized threat (also called hazard.) Quantitative _____ requires calculations of two components of risk: R, the magnitude of the potential loss L, and the probability p that the loss will occur.

a. 7-Eleven
c. 4-4-5 Calendar
b. Risk assessment
d. 529 plan

14. A _____ is the examination of a company's financial documents by a U.S. state's tax agency to verify if they have collected the correct amount of sales tax from their customers.

The purpose of a _____ is to examine the business records of a vendor in order to determine if the appropriate amounts of sales tax revenue have been collected from the customer by the seller and remitted to the vendor's state. The records reviewed during an audit often include: Sales Tax Returns, Worksheets and Canceled Checks, Federal Income Tax Returns NYS Corporation Tax Returns, General Ledger, General Journal and Closing Entries, Sales Invoices, Exemption Documents Supporting Non-taxable Sales, Charts of Accounts, Fixed Asset Purchases/Sales Invoices, Expense Purchases, Merchandise Purchases, Bank Statements, Canceled Checks and Deposit Slips, Cash Receipts Journal and/or Purchase Journal, Cash Disbursement Journal and/or Purchase Journal, The Corporate Book (Minutes, Board of Directors, Articles of Incorporation),Depreciation Schedules.

a. Lead Auditor
c. Sales Tax Audit
b. Negative assurance
d. Financial Instruments and Exchange Law

15. The _____ of 2002 (Pub.L. 107-204, 116 Stat. 745, enacted July 30, 2002), also known as the Public Company Accounting Reform and Investor Protection Act of 2002 and commonly called Sarbanes-Oxley, Sarbox or SOX, is a United States federal law enacted on July 30, 2002 in response to a number of major corporate and accounting scandals including those affecting Enron, Tyco International, Adelphia, Peregrine Systems and WorldCom.

a. Foreign Corrupt Practices Act
c. Duty of loyalty
b. Blue sky law
d. Sarbanes-Oxley Act

Chapter 8. Test Preparation Part 8

16. _____, commonly abbreviated as SAS, provide guidance to external auditors on generally accepted auditing standards in regards to auditing an entity and issuing a report. They are usually issued by the certified public accountant authoritative body in the region where the standards apply, such as the American Institute of Certified Public Accountants in the United States.

- _____ (USA)
- _____ (Taiwan)

a. Mainframe audit
c. Provided by client
b. Performance audit
d. Statements on Auditing Standards

17. _____ or audit log is a chronological sequence of audit records, each of which contains evidence directly pertaining to and resulting from the execution of a business process or system function.

Audit records typically result from activities such as transactions or communications by individual people, systems, accounts or other entities.

Webopedia defines an _____ as 'a record showing who has accessed a computer system and what operations he or she has performed during a given period of time.' ()

In telecommunication, the term means a record of both completed and attempted accesses and service, or data forming a logical path linking a sequence of events, used to trace the transactions that have affected the contents of a record.

a. Audit trail
c. AAB
b. ABN Amro
d. A Random Walk Down Wall Street

18. _____ (TRAC) is a checklist that developed from work done by the OCLC/RLG Programs and National Archives and Records Administration (NARA) task force initiative.

The TRAC checklist is an Auditing tool to assess the reliability, commitment and readiness of institutions to assume long-term preservation responsibilities. Currently the repository is under the care of the Center for Research Library's (CRL) who are utilizing it in several independent projects.

a. Legal auditing
c. Provided by client
b. RSM International
d. Trustworthy Repositories Audit ' Certification

19. _____ is the abbreviated title of a government official in a number of states, including the United Kingdom, the Republic of Ireland, India, and China. The unabbreviated title in the United Kingdom is Comptroller General of the Receipt and Issue of Her Majesty's Exchequer and Auditor General of Public Accounts. Other jurisdictions use the similar titles Comptroller General or Auditor General to refer to a similar office.

a. 529 plan
c. State Auditor of Mississippi
b. Comptroller and Auditor General
d. 4-4-5 Calendar

20. An _____ is a professional designation for accountants. It requires a test and 3 years work experience. The test is based on knowledge of accounting, taxes, and business law.

    a. A Random Walk Down Wall Street   b. AAB
    c. ABN Amro   d. Accredited Business Accountant

21. The _____ (AIA) was founded in the UK in 1928 as a professional accountancy body and from conception has promoted the concept of 'international accounting' to create a global network of accountants in over 85 countries worldwide .

AIA is a Recognised Qualifying Body (RQB) for company auditors under the Companies Act 1989.

AIA merged in April 2003 with the Institute of Company Accountants (IComA.)

    a. A Random Walk Down Wall Street   b. ABN Amro
    c. Association of International Accountants   d. AAB

22. _____ are full members of those United Kingdom accountancy bodies which are themselves members of the Consultative Committee of Accountancy Bodies, a private organization or otherwise one of the six professional bodies legally recognised by Department of Trade ' Industry (DTI) of British Government under British Companies Act 1989 as Company Auditor. The UK market often refers to CCAB qualified as though it was a specific qualification rather than a group of qualifications, but this is in order to determine whether an accountant is fully qualified or not.

In addition, there are a number of historical qualifications awarded by non CCAB-qualified UK bodies whose members provide accountancy and related services and which set regulatory requirements for their members.

    a. 4-4-5 Calendar   b. Consultative Committee of Accountancy Bodies
    c. British qualified accountants   d. 529 plan

23. _____ is a designation awarded by the Association of _____s (A_____.) The A_____ is a 41,000 member-based global association dedicated to providing anti-fraud education and training.

In order to become a _____ one must meet the following requirements:

- Be an Associate Member of the A_____ in good standing
- Meet minimum academic and professional requirements
- Be of high moral character
- Agree to abide by the Bylaws and Code of Professional Ethics of the Association of _____s

Generally, applicants for _____ certification have a minimum of a bachelor's degree or equivalent from an institution of higher education. Two years of professional experience related to fraud can be substituted for each year of college.

    a. Chartered Certified Accountant   b. Chartered Accountant
    c. Certified Public Accountant   d. Certified Fraud Examiner

24. '_____' is a professional designation representing members of the _____s Association of Canada (_____-Canada), provincial and territorial _____ Associations as well as _____ Associations overseas. It was founded in 1908 and was officially established by an Act of Parliament on June 6, 1913. Having over 41,000 certified members and 23,000 students in 2006, _____ is the fastest growing and second largest professional accounting designation in Canada.
   a. Chartered Certified Accountant
   b. Chartered Accountant
   c. Certified Public Accountant
   d. Certified General Accountant

25. The title _____ is a professional designation awarded by various professional bodies around the world. The _____ designation is a post-nominal award issued to individuals who have achieved a peer-based criteria of professional competency in the field of Management Accounting. Management accounting qualifications differ from those such as the ACA or CPA 'Chartered' or 'Public' accounting qualifications in a number of ways.
   a. Commodity Pool Operator
   b. Certified Management Accountant
   c. Regulation Fair Disclosure
   d. Regulation FD

26. _____ is the statutory title of qualified accountants in the United States who have passed the Uniform _____ Examination and have met additional state education and experience requirements for certification as a _____. In most U.S. states, only _____s who are licensed are able to provide to the public attestation (including auditing) opinions on financial statements. The exceptions to this rule are Arizona, Kansas, North Carolina and Ohio where, although the '_____' designation is restricted, the practice of auditing is not.
   a. Certified General Accountant
   b. Chartered Accountant
   c. Certified Public Accountant
   d. Chartered Certified Accountant

27. _____ is the title used by members of certain professional accountancy associations in the British Commonwealth countries and Ireland. The term chartered comes from the Royal Charter granted to the world's first professional body of accountants upon their establishment in 1854.

_____s work in all fields of business and finance.

   a. Certified Public Accountant
   b. Certified General Accountant
   c. Chartered Certified Accountant
   d. Chartered Accountant

28. _____ (Designatory letters A_____ or F_____) is a British qualified accountant designation awarded by the Association of _____s (A_____)

The term _____ was introduced in 1996. Prior to that date, A_____ members were known as Certified Accountant. It is still permissible for an A_____ member to use this term. Fellow members of A_____ use the designatory letters F_____ in place of A_____.

   a. Chartered Accountant
   b. Chartered Certified Accountant
   c. Certified General Accountant
   d. Certified Public Accountant

29.

Cost accounting or cost control professional designation offered by the AAFM American Academy of Financial Management

The _____ is a Graduate Post Nominal (GPN) that is only available for accountants with an accredited degree, MBA, CPA, Chartered Accountant License, law degree, PhD or specialized executive training. The _____ is the only cost control or accounting credential at this time that has reached acceptance in North and South America as well as Asia, India, and the Middle East.

- Accountant

a. 529 plan
c. 4-4-5 Calendar
b. Hedge Accounting
d. Chartered Cost Accountant

30. In economics, business, and accounting, a _____ is the value of money that has been used up to produce something, and hence is not available for use anymore. In business, the _____ may be one of acquisition, in which case the amount of money expended to acquire it is counted as _____. In this case, money is the input that is gone in order to acquire the thing.

a. Sliding scale fees
c. Fixed costs
b. Cost
d. Marginal cost

31. The _____ (CIMA) is a UK based professional body offering training and qualification in management accountancy and related subjects, focused on accounting for business; together with ongoing support for members.

CIMA is one of a number of professional associations for accountants in the UK and Ireland. Its particular emphasis is on developing the management accounting profession within the UK and worldwide.

a. Consultative Committee of Accountancy Bodies
c. Chartered Institute of Management Accountants
b. 529 plan
d. 4-4-5 Calendar

32. _____ (or financial accounting) is the field of accountancy concerned with the preparation of financial statements for decision makers, such as stockholders, suppliers, banks, employees, government agencies, owners, and other stakeholders. The fundamental need for financial accounting is to reduce principal-agent problem by measuring and monitoring agents' performance and reporting the results to interested users.

_____ is used to prepare accounting information for people outside the organization or not involved in the day to day running of the company.

a. 4-4-5 Calendar
c. Financial accountancy
b. 529 plan
d. Working capital management

33. _____ or accounting is the system of recording, verifying, and reporting of the value of assets, liabilities, income, and expenses in the books of account (ledger) to which debit and credit entries (recognizing transactions) are chronologically posted to record changes in value Such financial information is primarily used by lenders, managers, investors, tax authorities and other decision makers to make resource allocation decisions between and within companies, organizations, and public agencies. Accounting has been defined by the AICPA as ' The art of recording, classifying, and summarizing in a significant manner and in terms of money, transactions and events which are, in part at least, of financial character, and interpreting the results thereof.'

Financial accounting is one branch of accounting and historically has involved processes by which financial information about a business is recorded, classified, summarised, interpreted, and communicated; for public companies, this information is generally publicly-accessible.

a. Accountancy
b. A Random Walk Down Wall Street
c. ABN Amro
d. AAB

34. _____ is an umbrella term which refers to the various accounting systems used by various public sector entities. In the United States, for instance, there are three levels of government which follow different accounting standards set forth by independent, private sector boards. At the federal level, the Federal Accounting Standards Advisory Board (FASAB) sets forth the accounting standards to follow.

a. Nonassurance services
b. Grenzplankostenrechnung
c. Management accounting
d. Governmental accounting

35. _____ (GPK) is a German costing methodology, developed in the late 1940's and 1950's, being designed to provide a consistent and accurate application of how managerial costs are calculated and assigned to a product or service. The term _____, often referred to as GPK, has best been translated as either Marginal Planned Cost Accounting or Flexible Analytic Cost Planning and Accounting.

The GPK methodology has become the standard for cost accounting in Germany as a 'result of the modern, strong controlling culture in German corporations'.

a. Management accounting
b. Nonassurance services
c. Governmental accounting
d. Grenzplankostenrechnung

36. _____ is concerned with the provisions and use of accounting information to managers within organizations, to provide them with the basis to make informed business decisions that will allow them to be better equipped in their management and control functions.

In contrast to financial accountancy information, _____ information is:

- usually confidential and used by management, instead of publicly reported;
- forward-looking, instead of historical;
- pragmatically computed using extensive management information systems and internal controls, instead of complying with accounting standards.

This is because of the different emphasis: _____ information is used within an organization, typically for decision-making.

According to the Chartered Institute of Management Accountants, _____ is 'the process of identification, measurement, accumulation, analysis, preparation, interpretation and communication of information used by management to plan, evaluate and control within an entity and to assure appropriate use of and accountability for its Resource (economics)resources. _____ also comprises the preparation of financial reports for non-management groups such as shareholders, creditors, regulatory agencies and tax authorities'.

a. Management accounting
b. Governmental accounting
c. Nonassurance services
d. Grenzplankostenrechnung

37. _____ provided by CPAs include accounting and bookkeeping services, tax services, and management consulting services. _____ differ from assurance services. Most accounting and bookkeeping services, tax services, and management consulting services fall outside the scope of assurance services, although there is some common area of overlap between consulting and assurance services.
a. Grenzplankostenrechnung
b. Product control
c. Governmental accounting
d. Nonassurance services

38. Within banking, _____ are a team responsible for the accounting and financial reporting of a trading desk. They are responsible for the bookkeeping of trades in the portfolios they look after, and act as a primary control function; monitoring trading activity to ensure it is within a specified remit. .
a. Management accounting
b. Nonassurance services
c. Grenzplankostenrechnung
d. Product control

39. _____ (sometimes referred to as job cost accounting) is the practice of creating financial reports specifically designed to track the financial progress of projects, which can then be used by managers to aid project management.

Standard accounting is primarily aimed at monitoring financial progress of organizational elements (geographical or functional departments, divisions and the enterprise as a whole) over defined time periods (typically weeks, months, quarters and years.)

Projects differ in that they frequently cross organizational boundaries, may last for anything from a few days or weeks to a number of years, during which time budgets may also be revised many times.

a. 7-Eleven
b. 529 plan
c. 4-4-5 Calendar
d. Project accounting

40. _____ is a fee paid on borrowed assets. It is the price paid for the use of borrowed money , or, money earned by deposited funds . Assets that are sometimes lent with _____ include money, shares, consumer goods through hire purchase, major assets such as aircraft, and even entire factories in finance lease arrangements.
a. A Random Walk Down Wall Street
b. Interest
c. AAB
d. Insolvency

41. An _____ is the price a borrower pays for the use of money they do not own, and the return a lender receives for deferring the use of funds, by lending it to the borrower. _____s are normally expressed as a percentage rate over the period of one year.

_____s targets are also a vital tool of monetary policy and are used to control variables like investment, inflation, and unemployment.

a. ABN Amro
b. A Random Walk Down Wall Street
c. Interest rate
d. AAB

42. _____ expresses an annual rate of interest taking into account the effect of compounding, usually for deposit or investment products (such as a certificate of deposit.) It is analogous to the Annual percentage rate (APR), which is used for loans. In some jurisdictions, the use and definition of _____ may be regulated by a government agency, in which case it would generally be capitalized.

   a. ABN Amro
   b. AAB
   c. A Random Walk Down Wall Street
   d. Annual Percentage Yield

43. In finance, the term _____ describes the amount in cash that returns to the owners of a security. Normally it does not include the price variations, at the difference of the total return. _____ applies to various stated rates of return on stocks (common and preferred, and convertible), fixed income instruments (bonds, notes, bills, strips, zero coupon), and some other investment type insurance products (e.g. annuities.)

   a. Macaulay duration
   b. 4-4-5 Calendar
   c. Yield to maturity
   d. Yield

44. The terms _____ , nominal _____, and effective _____ describe the interest rate for a whole year (annualized), rather than just a monthly fee/rate, as applied on a loan, mortgage, credit card, etc. Those terms have formal, legal definitions in some countries or legal jurisdictions, but in general:

- The nominal _____ is the simple-interest rate (for a year.)
- The effective _____ is the fee+compound interest rate (calculated across a year.)

The nominal _____ is calculated as: the rate, for a payment period, multiplied by the number of payment periods in a year. However, the exact legal definition of 'effective _____' can vary greatly in each jurisdiction, depending on the type of fees included, such as participation fees, loan origination fees, monthly service charges, or late fees. The effective _____ has been called the 'mathematically-true' interest rate for each year. The computation for the effective _____, as the fee+compound interest rate, can also vary depending on whether the up-front fees, such as origination or participation fees, are added to the entire amount, or treated as a short-term loan due in the first payment.

   a. AAB
   b. Annual percentage rate
   c. ABN Amro
   d. A Random Walk Down Wall Street

45. _____, also referred to as the discount rate, is the rate of interest which a central bank charges on the loans and advances that it extends to commercial banks and other financial intermediaries. Changes in the _____ are often used by central banks to control the money supply.

The term _____ is most commonly used by bankers to refer to the Federal Discount Rate of interest charged to Federally Chartered Savings Banks.

   a. Fixed interest
   b. London Interbank Offered Rate
   c. TIBOR
   d. Bank rate

46. In finance, the _____ is a mathematical model describing the evolution of interest rates. It is a type of 'one-factor model' (short rate model) as it describes interest rate movements as driven by only one source of market risk. It was the first stochastic mean and stochastic volatility model and it was introduced in 1996 by Lin Chen.

a. Random walk hypothesis
b. Rendleman-Bartter model
c. Hull-White model
d. Chen model

47. The _____ in finance is a mathematical model describing the evolution of interest rates. It is a type of 'one factor model' (Short rate model) as describes interest rate movements as driven by only one source of market risk. The model can be used in the valuation of interest rate derivatives.
    a. Rendleman-Bartter model
    b. Cox-Ingersoll-Ross model
    c. Chen model
    d. Random walk hypothesis

48. _____ is the provision of resources (such as granting a loan) by one party to another party where that second party does not reimburse the first party immediately, thereby generating a debt, and instead arranges either to repay or return those resources (or material(s) of equal value) at a later date. The first party is called a creditor, also known as a lender, while the second party is called a debtor, also known as a borrower.

Movements of financial capital are normally dependent on either _____ or equity transfers.

    a. Comparable
    b. Warrant
    c. Credit
    d. Clearing house

49. _____ is the principal way in which card issuers generate revenue. A card issuer is a bank that gives a consumer (the cardholder) a card or account number that can be used with various payees to make payments and borrow money from the bank simultaneously. The bank pays the payee and then charges the cardholder interest over the time the money remains borrowed.
    a. 7-Eleven
    b. 529 plan
    c. 4-4-5 Calendar
    d. Credit card interest

50. A '_____' is a 'Charge' that is paid to obtain the right to delay a payment. Essentially, the payer purchases the right to make a given payment in the future instead of in the Present. The '_____', or 'Charge' that must be paid to delay the payment, is simply the difference between what the payment amount would be if it were paid in the present and what the payment amount would be paid if it were paid in the future.
    a. Discount
    b. Risk aversion
    c. Value at risk
    d. Risk modeling

51. The _____ is an interest rate a central bank charges depository institutions that borrow reserves from it.

The term _____ has two meanings:

- the same as interest rate; the term 'discount' does not refer to the meaning of the word, but to the purpose of using the quantity, such as computations of present value, e.g. net present value / discounted cash flow

- the annual effective _____, which is the annual interest divided by the capital including that interest; this rate is lower than the interest rate; it corresponds to using the value after a year as the nominal value, and seeing the initial value as the nominal value minus a discount; it is used for Treasury Bills and similar financial instruments

The annual effective _____ is the annual interest divided by the capital including that interest, which is the interest rate divided by 100% plus the interest rate. It is the annual discount factor to be applied to the future cash flow, to find the discount, subtracted from a future value to find the value one year earlier.

For example, suppose there is a government bond that sells for $95 and pays $100 in a year's time.

a. Fisher equation
b. Stochastic volatility
c. Black-Scholes
d. Discount rate

52. _____ is the EURo OverNight Index Average. _____ was introduced in January 1999 by the Wholesale Markets Brokers' Association (WMBA.).
   a. International Fisher effect
   b. Official bank rate
   c. A Random Walk Down Wall Street
   d. EURONIA

53. The _____, effective annual interest rate, Annual Equivalent Rate (AER) or simply effective rate is the interest rate on a loan or financial product restated from the nominal interest rate as an interest rate with annual compound interest. It is used to compare the annual interest between loans with different compounding terms (daily, monthly, annually, or other.)

The _____ differs in two important respects from the annual percentage rate (APR):

1. the _____ generally does not incorporate one-time charges such as front-end fees;
2. the _____ is (generally) not defined by legal or regulatory authorities (as APR is in many jurisdictions.)

By contrast, the 'effective APR' is used as a legal term, where front-fees and other costs can be included, as defined by local law.

Annual Percentage Yield or effective annual yield is the analogous concept used for savings or investment products, such as a certificate of deposit.

a. Effective interest rate
b. ABN Amro
c. A Random Walk Down Wall Street
d. AAB

54. _____ (Euro OverNight Index Average) is an effective overnight rate computed as a weighted average of all overnight unsecured lending transactions in the interbank market. It has been initiated within the euro area by the contributing panel banks. It is one of the two benchmarks for the money and capital markets in the euro zone (the other one being Euribor.)
   a. Euro Interbank Offered Rate
   b. A Random Walk Down Wall Street
   c. Exchange Rate Mechanism
   d. Eonia

55. The _____ (or Euribor) is a daily reference rate based on the averaged interest rates at which banks offer to lend unsecured funds to other banks in the euro wholesale money market (or interbank market.)

Euribor rates are used as a reference rate for euro-denominated forward rate agreements, short term interest rate futures contracts and interest rate swaps, in very much the same way as LIBOR rates are commonly used for Sterling and US dollar-denominated instruments. They thus provide the basis for some of the world's most liquid and active interest rate markets.

   a. European Monetary System   b. Exchange Rate Mechanism
   c. A Random Walk Down Wall Street   d. Euro Interbank Offered Rate

56. In the United States, _____ are overnight borrowings by banks to maintain their bank reserves at the Federal Reserve. Banks keep reserves at Federal Reserve Banks to meet their reserve requirements and to clear financial transactions. Transactions in the _____ market enable depository institutions with reserve balances in excess of reserve requirements to lend reserves to institutions with reserve deficiencies.

   a. Regulation T   b. 4-4-5 Calendar
   c. Federal funds rate   d. Federal funds

57. In the United States, the _____ is the interest rate at which private depository institutions (mostly banks) lend balances (federal funds) at the Federal Reserve to other depository institutions, usually overnight. Changing the target rate is one form of open market operations that the Chairman of the Federal Reserve uses to regulate the supply of money in the U.S. economy.

U.S. banks and thrift institutions are obligated by law to maintain certain levels of reserves, either as reserves with the Fed or as vault cash.

   a. Taylor rule   b. Federal funds rate
   c. 4-4-5 Calendar   d. Regulation T

58. A _____ refers to any type debt instrument, such as a loan, bond, mortgage that does not have a fixed rate of interest over the life of the instrument. Such debt typically uses an index or other base rate for establishing the interest rate for each relevant period. One of the most common rates to use as the basis for applying interest rates is the London Inter-bank Offered Rate, or LIBOR

   a. Cost of living   b. Floating interest rate
   c. Foreign exchange hedge   d. Disposal tax effect

59. In finance, a _____ is a simultaneous purchase and sale, or vice versa, of identical amounts of one currency for another with two different value dates (normally spot to forward.)

A _____ consists of two legs:

- a spot foreign exchange transaction, and
- a forward foreign exchange transaction.

These two legs are executed simultaneously for the same quantity, and therefore offset each other.

It is also common to trade forward-forward, where both transactions are for (different) forward dates.

By far and away the most common use of FX swaps is for institutions to fund their foreign exchange balances.

    a. Foreign exchange market
    b. Forex swap
    c. Triangular arbitrage
    d. Floating exchange rate

60. In finance, a _____ is a derivative in which two counterparties agree to exchange one stream of cash flows against another stream. These streams are called the legs of the _____.

The cash flows are calculated over a notional principal amount, which is usually not exchanged between counterparties.

    a. Volatility arbitrage
    b. Volatility swap
    c. Local volatility
    d. Swap

61. In financial mathematics, the _____ is a model of future interest rates. In its most generic formulation, it belongs to the class of no-arbitrage models that are able to fit today's term structure of interest rates. It is relatively straight-forward to translate the mathematical description of the evolution of future interest rates onto a tree or lattice and so interest rate derivatives such as bermudan swaptions can be valued in the model.
    a. Put-call parity
    b. Cox-Ingersoll-Ross model
    c. Chen model
    d. Hull-White model

62. _____ is the risk (variability in value) borne by an interest-bearing asset, such as a loan or a bond, due to variability of interest rates. In general, as rates rise, the price of a fixed rate bond will fall, and vice versa. _____ is commonly measured by the bond's duration.
    a. A Random Walk Down Wall Street
    b. Interest rate risk
    c. Official bank rate
    d. International Fisher effect

63. In economics, the _____ is the proposition by Irving Fisher that the real interest rate is independent of monetary measures, especially the nominal interest rate. The Fisher equation is

$$r_r = r_n >- >\pi^e.$$

This means, the real interest rate (r_r) equals the nominal interest rate (r_n) minus expected rate of inflation ($>\pi^e$.) Here all the rates are continuously compounded.

    a. 529 plan
    b. 4-4-5 Calendar
    c. 7-Eleven
    d. Fisher hypothesis

64. The _____ is a hypothesis in international finance that says that the difference in the nominal interest rates between two countries determines the movement of the nominal exchange rate between their currencies, with the value of the currency of the country with the lower nominal interest rate increasing. This is also known as the assumption of Uncovered Interest Parity.

The Fisher hypothesis says that the real interest rate in an economy is independent of monetary variables.

a. Official bank rate
c. Interest rate risk
b. A Random Walk Down Wall Street
d. International Fisher effect

65. The _____ is a financial model of interest rates. It is used for pricing interest rate derivatives, especially exotic derivatives like Bermudan swaptions, ratchet caps and floors, target redemption notes, autocaps, zero coupon swaptions, constant maturity swaps and spread options, among many others. The quantities that are modeled, rather than the short rate or instantaneous forward rates are a set of forward rates, which have the advantage of being directly observable in the market, and whose volatilities are naturally linked to traded contracts.

a. Discount rate
c. Fisher equation
b. Treynor-Black model
d. LIBOR market model

66. The _____ (LIBID) is a bid rate; the rate bid by banks on Eurocurrency deposits (i.e., the rate at which a bank is willing to borrow from other banks.) It is 'the opposite' of the LIBOR (an offered, hence 'ask' rate.) Whilst the British Bankers' Association set LIBOR rates, there is no correspondent official LIBID fixing.

a. Shanghai Interbank Offered Rate
c. Repo rate
b. Cash accumulation equation
d. London Interbank Bid Rate

67. The _____ is a daily reference rate based on the interest rates at which banks borrow unsecured funds from banks in the London wholesale money market (or interbank market.) It is roughly comparable to the U.S. Federal funds rate.

During 1984 it became apparent that an increasing number of banks were trading actively in a variety of relatively new market instruments, notably interest rate swaps, foreign currency options and forward rate agreements.

a. London Interbank Offered Rate
c. Shanghai Interbank Offered Rate
b. Risk-free interest rate
d. Fixed interest

68. _____ is the process by which the government, or monetary authority of a country controls (i) the supply of money central bank (ii) availability of money, and (iii) cost of money or rate of interest, in order to attain a set of objectives oriented towards the growth and stability of the economy. Monetary theory provides insight into how to craft optimal _____.

_____ is referred to as either being an expansionary policy where an expansionary policy increases the total supply of money in the economy, and a contractionary policy decreases the total money supply.

a. Federal Open Market Committee
c. Tax exemption
b. Natural resources consumption tax
d. Monetary Policy

69. In finance and economics _____ refers to the rate of interest before adjustment for inflation (in contrast with the real interest rate); or, for interest balls stated' without adjustment for the full effect of compounding (also referred to as the nominal annual rate.) An interest rate is called nominal if the frequency of compounding (e.g. a month) is not identical to the basic time unit (normally a year.)

The real interest rate includes compensation for the lender's lost value due to inflation, whereas the _____ excludes inflation.

a. Shanghai Interbank Offered Rate
b. Cash accumulation equation
c. SIBOR
d. Nominal interest rate

70. The _____ (or notional principal amount or notional value) on a financial instrument is the nominal or face amount that is used to calculate payments made on that instrument. This amount generally does not change hands and is thus referred to as notional.

Contrast a bond with an interest rate swap:

- In a bond, the buyer pays the principal amount at issue (start), then receives coupons (computed off this principal) over the life of the bond, then receives the principal back at maturity (end.)
- In a swap, no principal changes hands at inception (start) or expiry (end), and in the meantime, interest payments are computed based on a _____, which acts as if it were the principal of a bond, hence the term notional principal amount, abbreviated to notional.

In simple terms the notional principal amount is essentially how much of the asset or bonds a person has. For example, if I bought a premium bond for £1 then the notional principal amount would be £1. Hence the notional principal amount is the quantity of the assets and bonds.

a. Basis trading
b. Credit derivative
c. Notional amount
d. Forward start option

71. The _____ is the interest rate paid by banks in the overnight money market in Australia and New Zealand. Through the regulated use of Exchange Settlement Accounts, a central bank is able to adjust the interest rates of a nation's economy. The _____ cannot be changed by transactions between financial institutions as this does not change the supply of money, only its location.
   a. AAB
   b. ABN Amro
   c. A Random Walk Down Wall Street
   d. Official Cash Rate

72. The _____ is the rate that the Bank of England pays Banks for money deposited with it. It is the British Government's key interest rate for enacting monetary policy.

When an announcement of the change in interest rates is made this is the rate the Bank of England is changing.

   a. Official bank rate
   b. International Fisher effect
   c. Interest rate risk
   d. A Random Walk Down Wall Street

73. The _____ is generally the rate that large banks use to borrow and lend from one another on the interbank market. In some countries (for example, Canada), the _____ may be the rate targeted by the central bank to influence monetary policy. In most countries, the central bank is also a participant on the overnight lending market, and will lend or borrow money to some group of banks.
   a. ABN Amro
   b. A Random Walk Down Wall Street
   c. AAB
   d. Overnight rate

74. _____ is a term applied in many countries to a reference interest rate used by banks. The term originally indicated the rate of interest at which banks lent to favored customers, i.e., those with high credibility, though this is no longer always the case. Some variable interest rates may be expressed as a percentage above or below _____.

   a. Time deposit
   b. Credit bureau
   c. Reserve requirement
   d. Prime rate

75. _____ is the most significant exception to the limitations imposed by § 163(h) of the Internal Revenue Code.

Sec. 163 of the IRC permits deductions for interest paid or accrued during the taxable year.

   a. Fiscal policy
   b. Monetary policy
   c. Tax compliance solution
   d. Qualified residence interest

76. The '_____' is approximately the nominal interest rate minus the inflation rate Since the inflation rate over the course of a loan is not known initially, volatility in inflation represents a risk to both the lender and the borrower.

In economics and finance, an individual who lends money for repayment at a later point in time expects to be compensated for the time value of money, or not having the use of that money while it is lent.

   a. 4-4-5 Calendar
   b. Real interest rate
   c. 7-Eleven
   d. 529 plan

77. A _____ is a rate that determines pay-offs in a financial contract and that is outside the control of the parties to the contract. It is often some form of LIBOR rate, but it can take many forms, such as a consumer price index, a house price index or an unemployment rate. Parties to the contract choose a _____ that neither party has power to manipulate.

   a. TIBOR
   b. Risk-free interest rate
   c. London Interbank Offered Rate
   d. Reference rate

78. The _____ in finance is a short rate model describing the evolution of interest rates. It is a type of 'one factor model' as describes interest rate movements as driven by only one source of market risk. It can be used in the valuation of interest rate derivatives.

   a. Cox-Ingersoll-Ross model
   b. Put-call parity
   c. Hull-White model
   d. Rendleman-Bartter model

79. The _____ is the interest rate that it is assumed can be obtained by investing in financial instruments with no default risk. However, the financial instrument can carry other types of risk, e.g. market risk (the risk of changes in market interest rates), liquidity risk (the risk of being unable to sell the instrument for cash at short notice without significant costs) etc.

Though a truly risk-free asset exists only in theory, in practice most professionals and academics use short-dated government bonds of the currency in question.

   a. London Interbank Offered Rate
   b. Cash accumulation equation
   c. Risk-free interest rate
   d. London Interbank Bid Rate

Chapter 8. Test Preparation Part 8

80. _____ stands for Singapore Interbank Offered Rate and is a daily reference rate based on the interest rates at which banks offer to lend unsecured funds to other banks in the Singapore wholesale money market (or interbank market.) It is similar to the widely used LIBOR (London Interbank Offered Rate), and Euribor (Euro Interbank Offered Rate.) Using _____ is more common in the Asian region and set by the Association of Banks in Singapore (ABS.)
   a. SIBOR
   b. Repo rate
   c. Fixed interest
   d. SONIA

81. _____ is the Sterling OverNight Index Average. Launched in 1997 by the Wholesale Markets Brokers' Association (WMBA), the weighted average is calculated using brokered unsecured overnight trades between banks listed under Section 43 of the Financial Services Act 1986.
   a. London Interbank Bid Rate
   b. Repo rate
   c. London Interbank Offered Rate
   d. SONIA

82. The _____ is a daily reference rate based on the interest rates at which banks offer to lend unsecured funds to other banks in the Shanghai wholesale (or 'interbank') money market.
   a. Nominal interest rate
   b. Repo rate
   c. SIBOR
   d. Shanghai Interbank Offered Rate

83. _____ (or STIBOR) is a daily reference rate based on the interest rates at which banks offer to lend unsecured funds to other banks in the Swedish wholesale money market (or interbank market.) STIBOR is the average (with the exception of the highest and lowest quotes) of the interest rates listed at 11 a.m.
   a. Cash accumulation equation
   b. SIBOR
   c. Risk-free interest rate
   d. Stockholm Interbank Offered Rate

84. _____ is a financial term that was popularized by the media during the 'credit crunch' of 2007 and involves financial institutions lending in ways which do not meet 'prime' standards to an extent which puts the loans into the riskiest category of consumer loans typically sold in the secondary market. These standards refer to the size of the loan, 'traditional' or 'nontraditional' structure of the loan, borrower credit rating, ratio of borrower debt to income or assets, ratio of loan to value or collateral, documentation provided on those loans which do not meet Fannie Mae or Freddie Mac underwriting guidelines for prime mortgages (are 'non-conforming'.) Although there is no single, standard definition, in the US subprime loans are usually classified as those where the borrower has a FICO score below 640.
   a. Negative equity
   b. Subprime lending
   c. Fixed rate mortgage
   d. Cash-out

85. An _____ is a derivative in which one party exchanges a stream of interest payments for another party's stream of cash flows. _____s can be used by hedgers to manage their fixed or floating assets and liabilities. They can also be used by speculators to replicate unfunded bond exposures to profit from changes in interest rates.
   a. International Swaps and Derivatives Association
   b. Implied volatility
   c. Equity swap
   d. Interest rate swap

86. The _____ is the difference between the interest rates on interbank loans and short-term U.S. government debt ('T-bills'.)

Initially, the _____ was the difference between the interest rates for three-month U.S. Treasuries contracts and the three-month Eurodollars contract as represented by the London Interbank Offered Rate (LIBOR.) However, since the Chicago Mercantile Exchange dropped T-bill futures, the _____ is now calculated as the difference between the three-month T-bill interest rate and three-month LIBOR.

a. TED spread
b. 4-4-5 Calendar
c. Gross national product
d. Purchasing power parity

87. _____ stands for the Tokyo Interbank Offered Rate and is a daily reference rate based on the interest rates at which banks offer to lend unsecured funds to other banks in the Japan wholesale money market (or interbank market.) _____ is published daily by the Japanese Bankers Association (JBA.)

_____ is calculated based on the quotes for different maturities provided by reference banks at about 11.00 a.m. each business day.

a. TIBOR
b. SONIA
c. SIBOR
d. Repo rate

88. In economics, _____ (or 'discounting') pertains to how large a premium a consumer will place on enjoyment nearer in time over more remote enjoyment.

There is no absolute distinction that separates 'high' and 'low' _____, only comparisons with others either individually or in aggregate. Someone with a high _____ is focused substantially on their well-being in the present and the immediate future compared to the average, while someone with low _____ places more emphasis than average on their well-being in the further future.

a. 7-Eleven
b. 529 plan
c. 4-4-5 Calendar
d. Time preference

89. The _____ is an economic bubble in many parts of the United States housing market including areas of California, Florida, Colorado, Michigan, the Northeast Corridor, and the Southwest markets. On a national level, housing prices peaked in early 2005, began declining in 2006 and may not yet have hit bottom. Increased foreclosure rates in 2006-2007 by U.S. homeowners led to a crisis in August 2008 for the subprime, Alt-A, Collateralized debt obligation (CDO), mortgage, credit, hedge fund, and foreign bank markets.

a. A Random Walk Down Wall Street
b. United States housing bubble
c. ABN Amro
d. AAB

90. A _____ or floating rate mortgage is a mortgage loan where the interest rate varies to reflect market conditions.

The interest rate will normally vary with changes to the base rate of the central bank and reflects changing costs on the credit markets. This method of variation directly linked to underlying costs benefits lenders by ensuring a profit by passing the interest rate risk to the borrower.

a. Credit bureau
b. Basel Accord
c. Private money
d. Variable rate mortgage

91. In finance, the _____ is a mathematical model describing the evolution of interest rates. It is a type of 'one-factor model' (short rate model) as it describes interest rate movements as driven by only one source of market risk. The model can be used in the valuation of interest rate derivatives, and has also been adapted for credit markets.
   a. The Hong Kong Securities Institute
   b. Vasicek model
   c. Double-declining-balance method
   d. Bed Bath ' Beyond Inc.

92. The _____ (WSJ Prime Rate) is defined by The Wall Street Journal (WSJ) as 'The base rate on corporate loans posted by at least 75% of the nation's 30 largest banks.' It is not the 'best' rate offered by banks. It should not be confused with the federal funds rate set by the Federal Reserve, though these two rates often move in tandem. The current rate is 4.0% (as of 2008-10-30.)
   a. Wall Street Journal prime rate
   b. Basel Accord
   c. Banking panic
   d. Prime rate

93. _____ is a term usually associated with providing venture capital in the context of humanitarian aid and development. A common component is the investment in funds that use microfinance or microcredit to provide development assistance to the poor.
   a. Adventure capital
   b. AAB
   c. A Random Walk Down Wall Street
   d. ABN Amro

94. The _____ blended adult education, co-operatives, microfinance and rural community development to help small, resource-based communities around Canada's Maritimes improve their economic and social circumstances. A group of priests and educators, including Father Jimmy Tompkins, Father Moses Coady, Rev. Hugh MacPherson and A.B. MacDonald led this movement from a base at the Extension Department at St. Francis Xavier University (St. F.X.)
   a. A Random Walk Down Wall Street
   b. Antigonish Movement
   c. AAB
   d. ABN Amro

95. In finance, a _____ is a debt security, in which the authorized issuer owes the holders a debt and, depending on the terms of the _____, is obliged to pay interest (the coupon) and/or to repay the principal at a later date, termed maturity.

Thus a _____ is a loan: the issuer is the borrower, the _____ holder is the lender, and the coupon is the interest. _____s provide the borrower with external funds to finance long-term investments, or, in the case of government _____s, to finance current expenditure.

   a. Catastrophe bonds
   b. Convertible bond
   c. Bond
   d. Puttable bond

96. The _____ or common bond is a basic building block of credit unions and co-operative banks. Common bonds substitute for collateral in the early stages of financial system development. Like solidarity lending, the common bond has since played an important role in facilitating the development of microfinance for poor people.
   a. Bond of association
   b. 4-4-5 Calendar
   c. 7-Eleven
   d. 529 plan

Chapter 8. Test Preparation Part 8

97. _____ are member-based microfinance intermediaries inspired by external technical support. Structurally they lie between informal financial market actors like moneylenders, collectors, and ROSCAs on the one hand, and formal actors like microfinance institutions and banks on the other. Other organizations in this transitional zone in financial market development include self help groups, ASCAs, rural credit co-operatives, village banks and financial service associations.
   a. Guaranteed investment contracts
   b. Doctrine of the Proper Law
   c. CODA plc
   d. CVECAs

98. The _____ was a rural development programme launched in 1959 by the Pakistan Academy for Rural Development The Academy, which is located on the outskirts of Comilla town, was founded by Akhter Hameed Khan, the cooperative pioneer who was responsible for developing and launching the programme.

While the results of the Model ultimately frustrated Khan's ambitions, it has important implications for rural community development, particularly cooperative microfinance and microcredit

The _____ was Khan's reply to the failure of Village Agricultural and Industrial Development (V-AID) programme, launched in 1953 in East and West Pakistan with technical assistance from the US government.

   a. 529 plan
   b. 4-4-5 Calendar
   c. CVECAs
   d. Comilla Model

99. _____ is the delivery of banking services at affordable costs to vast sections of disadvantaged and low income groups. Unrestrained access to public goods and services is the sine qua non of an open and efficient society. It is argued that as banking services are in the nature of public good, it is essential that availability of banking and payment services to the entire population without discrimination is the prime objective of public policy.
   a. Solidarity lending
   b. Microcredit Summit Campaign
   c. Microgrant
   d. Financial inclusion

100. _____ loans are often used by traditional moneylenders in the informal economy of developing countries. They are also used by many microfinance institutions. One reason for their popularity is their ease of use.
   a. Rural credit cooperatives
   b. Naked call
   c. Controlled foreign corporations
   d. Flat interest rate

101. The _____ is a private foundation incorporated in Michigan and based in New York City created to fund programs that were chartered in 1936 by Edsel Ford and Henry Ford.

The foundation makes grants through its New York headquarters and through twelve international field offices. In fiscal year 2007, it reported assets of $13.7 billion and approved $530 million in grants for projects that focused on strengthening democratic values, community and economic development, education, media, arts and culture, and human rights.

   a. Texas ratio
   b. PKF
   c. Ford Foundation
   d. Foreign direct investment

102. _____ refers to the provision of financial services to poor or low-income clients, including consumers and the self-employed. The term also refers to the practice of sustainably delivering those services. Microcredit (or loans to poor microenterprises) should not be confused with _____, which addresses a full range of banking needs for poor people.

a. Depository Trust Company
b. Corporation
c. MicroFinance
d. Foreign direct investment

103. _____, founded in 2006, is a broker-dealer registered with the SEC and a member of FINRA (formerly NASD), _____ is currently the only broker-dealer specializing in microfinance securities for retail investors. Started by Tracey Pettengill Turner, _____ was bought by eBay Inc. in 2006.
 a. National Association of State Boards of Accountancy
 b. Public company
 c. National Bureau of Economic Research
 d. MicroPlace

104. The _____ (MABS) Program is an initiative designed to accelerate national economic transformation by encouraging the Philippine rural banking industry to significantly expand microenterprise access to microfinance services. To do so, the MABS Program assists client rural banks in the Philippines to increase the financial services they provide to the microenterprise sector by providing microfinance technical assistance and training to rural banks. Trained banks in turn offer microfinance loan and deposit services specially tailored to microenterprise clients.
 a. 4-4-5 Calendar
 b. 7-Eleven
 c. 529 plan
 d. Microenterprise Access to Banking Services

105. A _____ is a small sum of money distributed to an individual living on less than $1/day, extreme poverty, for the purpose of creating a sustainable livelihood or microenterprise. While microfinance and other financial services are intended to serve the poor, many of the poorest are either too risk-averse to seek out a loan, or do not qualify for a microloan or other form of microcredit. Organizations such as the Trickle Up Program, started by Glenn Leet and Mildred Robbins Leet in 1979, offer _____s in order to reach the poorest of the poor.
 a. Solidarity lending
 b. Microcredit Summit Campaign
 c. Village Banking
 d. Microgrant

106. Micro-insurance is a term increasingly used to refer to insurance characterized by low premium and low caps or low coverage limits, sold as part of atypical risk-pooling and marketing arrangements, and designed to service low-income people and businesses not served by typical social or commercial insurance schemes.

The institutions or set of institutions implementing micro-insurance are commonly referred to as a _____ scheme.

1. Micro-insurance is insurance with low premiums and low caps / coverage. In this definition, 'micro' refers to the small financial transaction that each insurance policy generates. The Micro-insurance Regulations, issued in 2005 by the Indian Insurance Regulatory and Development Authority (IRDA), for example, adopted this definition in explaining 'micro-insurance products' as those within defined (low) minimum and maximum caps. The IRDA's characterization of micro-insurance by the product features is further complemented by their definition for micro-insurance agents, those appointed by and acting for an insurer, for distribution of micro-insurance products (and only those products.)
2. Micro-insurance is a financial arrangement to protect low-income people against specific perils in exchange for regular premium payments proportionate to the likelihood and cost of the risk involved. The author of this definition adds that micro-insurance does not refer to: (i) the size of the risk-carrier (some are small and even informal, others very large companies); (ii) the scope of the risk (the risks themselves are by no means 'micro' to the households that experience them); (iii) the delivery channel: it can be delivered through a variety of different channels, including small community-based schemes, credit unions or other types of microfinance institutions, but also by enormous multinational insurance companies, etc.
3. Micro-insurance is synonymous to community-based financing arrangements, including community health funds, mutual health organizations, rural health insurance, revolving drugs funds, and community involvement in user-fee management. Most community financing schemes have evolved in the context of severe economic constraints, political instability, and lack of good governance. The common feature within all, is the active involvement of the community in revenue collection, pooling, resource allocation and, frequently, service provision.
4. Micro-insurance is the use of insurance as an economic instrument at the 'micro' (i.e. smaller than national) level of society. This definition integrates the above approaches into one comprehensive conceptual framework. It was first published in 1999, pre-dating the other three approaches, and has been noted to be the first recorded use of the term 'micro-insurance'. Under this definition, decisions in micro-insurance are made within each unit, (rather than far away, at the level of governments, companies, NGOs that offer support in operations, etc.).

Insurance functions on the concept of risk pooling, and likewise, regardless of its small unit size and its activities at the level of single communities, so does micro-insurance. Micro-insurance links multiple small units into larger structures, creating networks that enhance both insurance functions (through broader risk pools) and support structures for improved governance (i.e. training, data banks, research facilities, access to reinsurance etc.).

a. 4-4-5 Calendar
c. Title insurance
b. Microinsurance
d. 529 plan

Chapter 9. Test Preparation Part 9

1. _____ is the provision of resources (such as granting a loan) by one party to another party where that second party does not reimburse the first party immediately, thereby generating a debt, and instead arranges either to repay or return those resources (or material(s) of equal value) at a later date. The first party is called a creditor, also known as a lender, while the second party is called a debtor, also known as a borrower.

Movements of financial capital are normally dependent on either _____ or equity transfers.

   a. Comparable
   c. Warrant

   b. Credit
   d. Clearing house

2. A _____ is a cooperative financial institution that is owned and controlled by its members, and operated for the purpose of promoting thrift, providing credit at reasonable rates, and providing other financial services to its members. Many _____s exist to further community development or sustainable international development on a local level. Worldwide, _____ systems vary significantly in terms of total system assets and average institution asset size since _____s exist in a wide range of sizes, ranging from volunteer operations with a handful of members to institutions with several billion dollars in assets and hundreds of thousands of members.

   a. Corporate credit union
   c. Credit Union Service Organization

   b. Fi-linx
   d. Credit Union

3. _____, a federally chartered credit union headquartered in Las Vegas, Nevada, is one of the largest credit unions in the state with locations in Las Vegas, Henderson, Reno, Sparks, North Las Vegas and Pahrump. It operates several Credit Union Service Organizations (CUSOs) including: Community Realty Services of Nevada, LLC; Community Insurance Services of Nevada, LLC; Community Title Services of Nevada; Nevada Federal Investment Group and others.

As of August, 2008, Nevada Federal has 23 branch locations, 82,108 members, and has USD 819 million in assets.

   a. 7-Eleven
   c. 529 plan

   b. 4-4-5 Calendar
   d. Nevada Federal Credit Union

4. A profit for social purpose business model, _____ was delivered by Terry Hallman as a volunteer for the Clinton re-election campaign committee in 1996. Though itself returning 100% of profit to social purpose, it made the case for a wider interpretation, 'at least 50%' of profit being rendered to social purpose in the P-CED paradigm.

P-CED directs profit into international advocacy for peace and social enterprise and was first delivered to Russia in 2000 in the Tomsk Regional Initiative.

   a. 529 plan
   c. People-Centered Economic Development

   b. 7-Eleven
   d. 4-4-5 Calendar

5. _____ is an international non profit organization, which aims to alleviate poverty by contributing to the development of the microfinance sector. By providing access to financial services to the poorest populations, the financial intermediaries, including banks, cooperatives, Non Governmental Organizations (NGO), and the Microfinance Institutions, have showed for thirty years that microfinance is one of the most efficient tool to create economic opportunities for the poor. _____ was founded by Jacques Attali on October 13th, 1998.

a. National Bureau of Economic Research
b. Privately held company
c. MRU Holdings
d. PlaNet Finance

6. A _____ or ROSCA is a group of individuals who agree to meet for a defined period of time in order to save and borrow together. 'ROSCAs are the poor man's bank, where money is not idle for long but changes hands rapidly, satisfying both consumption and production needs.'

Meetings can be regular or tied to seasonal cash flow cycles in rural communities. Each member contributes the same amount at each meeting, and one member takes the whole sum once.

a. Solidarity lending
b. Microcredit Summit Campaign
c. Village Banking
d. Rotating Savings and Credit Association

7. _____ is an American community development bank and green bank. It was founded in 1973 in Chicago. A pioneer in profitably lending to underserved urban and rural communities, _____ has grown to $2.1 billion in assets and has affiliates across the United States and international consulting projects.

a. Certified Public Accountant
b. ShoreBank
c. Holding company
d. MicroPlace

8. _____ is an important building block of microfinance.

_____ takes place through 'solidarity groups'. These groups are a distinctive banking distribution channel used primarily to deliver microcredit to poor people.

a. Solidarity lending
b. Microcredit Summit Campaign
c. Microgrant
d. Village Banking

9. _____, in bookkeeping, refers to assets, liabilities, income, and expenses recorded on individual pages of the so called book of final entry or ledger. Changes in _____ value are made by chronologically posting debit (DR) and credit (CR) entries to its page. Examples of _____s are cash, _____s receivable, mortgages, loans, land and buildings, common stock, sales, services provided, wages, and payroll overhead.

a. Alpha
b. Accretion
c. Option
d. Account

10. _____ is a microcredit methodology developed by FINCA International founder John Hatch. Among US-based non-profit agencies there are at least 31 microfinance institutions (MFIs) that have collectively created over 400 _____ programs in at least 90 countries. And in many of these countries there are host-country MFIs--sometimes dozens--that are _____ practitioners as well.

a. Microgrant
b. Microcredit Summit Campaign
c. Solidarity lending
d. Village Banking

11. The _____ refers to the police investigation and subsequent court case in Norway in early 1998 where four members of AUF (Arbeidernes Ungdomsfylking, or Workers' Youth League) stood accused of deliberately inflating membership numbers of their organization in order to receive increased government funding .

They were eventually found guilty of fraud and handed jail sentences. The unlawful practice of submitting higher membership numbers to city council offices had at the time become an accepted culture in various political youth organizations, and it is believed that the leadership of the parties involved were aware of this practice.

a. ABN Amro
b. AAB
c. A Random Walk Down Wall Street
d. AUF membership scandal

12. _____ includes investment frauds that prey upon members of identifiable groups, such as religious or ethnic communities, the elderly, or professional groups. The fraudsters who promote affinity scams frequently are - or pretend to be - members of the group. They often enlist respected community or religious leaders from within the group to spread the word about the scheme, by convincing those people that a fraudulent investment is legitimate and worthwhile.

a. A Random Walk Down Wall Street
b. AAB
c. ABN Amro
d. Affinity fraud

13. _____ is the use of fraudulent means to obtain money, assets, or other property owned or held by a financial institution. In many instances, _____ is a criminal offense. While the specific elements of a particular banking fraud law vary between jurisdictions, the term _____ applies to actions that employ a scheme or artifice, as opposed to bank robbery or theft.

a. Tobashi scheme
b. Bank fraud
c. Guinness share-trading fraud
d. Demand draft

14. _____ is a brokerage firm that 'books' (i.e., takes the opposite side of) retail customer orders without actually having them executed on an exchange. These brokerages are also often called boiler rooms. The term is a defined term under the criminal law of many states in the United States which make it a crime to operate a _____.

a. Procter ' Gamble
b. Clearing
c. Comparable
d. Bucket shop

15. A _____ is a private or public market for the trading of company stock and derivatives of company stock at an agreed price; these are securities listed on a stock exchange as well as those only traded privately.

The size of the world _____ is estimated at about $36.6 trillion US at the beginning of October 2008 . The world derivatives market has been estimated at about $480 trillion face or nominal value, 12 times the size of the entire world economy.

a. Anton Gelonkin
b. Stock market
c. Adolph Coors
d. Andrew Tobias

16. A _____ is a check created by a seller with a buyer's checking account number on it, but without the buyer's signature. Instead of the signature, the check has verbiage such as 'authorized by depositor, lack of endorsement guaranteed by XYZ Bank'. The seller deposits the check into his or her bank account, and the check then clears out of the buyer's account.

a. Guinness share-trading fraud
b. Tobashi scheme
c. Demand draft
d. Get-rich-quick scheme

17. A _____ can require immediate payment by the second party to the third upon presentation of the _____. This is called a sight _____. A Cheques is a sight _____. An importer might write a _____ promising payment to an exporter for delivery of goods with payment to occur 60 days after the goods are delivered. Such a _____ is called a time _____.

   a. Cashflow matching
   b. Gross profit margin
   c. Draft
   d. Second lien loan

18. The _____, an incidence of securities fraud, was a false 2000-08-24 press release claiming to be from Emulex Corporation. The release falsely claimed that the company's CEO was stepping down, that previously stated quarterly earnings were being revised downward, and that the company was under investigation by the U.S. Securities and Exchange Commission.

The next morning, on 2000-08-25, the false release was picked up by Bloomberg Television and other news outlets.

   a. AAB
   b. A Random Walk Down Wall Street
   c. ABN Amro
   d. Emulex hoax

19. _____ is a fraudulent act of invoicing or otherwise requesting funds from an individual or firm without showing obligation to pay. Such notices are often sent to owners of domain names, purporting to be legitimate renewal notices, although not originating from the owner's own registrar.

   a. False billing
   b. Volatility clustering
   c. Package loan
   d. Conglomerate merger

20. A _____ is any trading scheme used to defraud individual traders by convincing them that they can expect to gain a high profit by trading in the foreign exchange market. Currency trading 'has become the fraud du jour' as of early 2008, according to Michael Dunn of the U.S. Commodity Futures Trading Commission. But 'the market has long been plagued by swindlers preying on the gullible,' according to the New York Times.

   a. Forex swap
   b. Currency future
   c. Floating exchange rate
   d. Forex scam

21. _____ was a Russian bank chief who was disgraced in the 1995 collapse of the Moscow City Bank and later convicted of running an international organised internet based fraud in 2006.

Anton Dolgov was the chairman of the Moskovsky Gorodskoi Bank, or Moscow City Bank, and in late August 1995 disappeared after taking an unknown amount of money. The bank later collapsed with debts of 120 million US dollars.

   a. Andrew Tobias
   b. Adolph Coors
   c. Arthur Betz Laffer
   d. Anton Gelonkin

22. A _____ is a plan to acquire high rates of return for a small investment. Most such schemes promise that participants can obtain this high rate of return with little risk.

Most _____s also promise that little skill, effort, or time is required.

a. Tobashi scheme
c. Guinness share-trading fraud
b. Demand draft
d. Get-rich-quick scheme

23. The _____ was a famous British business scandal of the 1980s. It involved an attempt to manipulate the stock market on a massive scale to inflate the price of Guinness shares and thereby assist a £2.7 billion take-over bid for the Scottish drinks company Distillers. The scandal was discovered after testimony as part of a plea bargain by the US stock trader Ivan Boesky.
   a. Tobashi scheme
   c. Demand draft
   b. Get-rich-quick scheme
   d. Guinness share-trading fraud

24. _____ is any act committed with the intent to fraudulently obtain payment from an insurer.

_____ has existed ever since the beginning of insurance as a commercial enterprise. Fraudulent claims account for a significant portion of all claims received by insurers, and cost billions of dollars annually.

   a. A Random Walk Down Wall Street
   c. ABN Amro
   b. AAB
   d. Insurance fraud

25. _____ is a limited company that was listed on the Alternative Investment Market of the London Stock Exchange as Crown Corporation Limited in 2003 and is subject of the biggest share fraud on the Exchange to date. It is presently being investigated by the Serious Fraud Office, the City of London Police, the Accountancy Investigation and Disciplinary Board and the subject of many civil legal actions in the High Court.

Crown Corporation, which changed its name to _____ Limited in 2005, was a pump and dump fraud, in that the company did not possess the assets that it declared at listing.

   a. 529 plan
   c. 7-Eleven
   b. 4-4-5 Calendar
   d. Langbar International

26. The _____ (DoM) is a micronation known largely for facilitating large scale banking fraud in many parts of the world.

The DoM was created in 1986 by Evan David Pedley and his son, Mark Logan Pedley. The latter also uses a number of pseudonyms, including 'Tzemach Ben David Netzer Korem' and 'Branch Vinedresser'.

   a. 7-Eleven
   c. Dominion of Melchizedek
   b. 4-4-5 Calendar
   d. 529 plan

27. _____ is a form of securities fraud involving stocks of 'microcap' companies, generally defined in the United States as those with a market capitalization of under $250 million. Its prevalence has been estimated to run into the billions of dollars a year. Many microcap stocks are penny stocks, which trade at below $5 a share.
   a. 7-Eleven
   c. 529 plan
   b. 4-4-5 Calendar
   d. Microcap stock fraud

28. The Principality of _____ is a micronation project established and operated by Lazarus Long (a.k.a. Howard Turney.)

The project was publicised by various media outlets in Europe and the United Statescom called '_____' a 'fake nation scam'.

   a. New Utopia
   c. 7-Eleven
   b. 4-4-5 Calendar
   d. 529 plan

29. The multi-year investigation into what officials call the _____ is being handled from SEC headquarters in Washington, D.C.

The U.S. Securities and Exchange Commission has sent out subpoenas, to more than 100 people and companies, and corporate records show that many of those companies tie back to a common group of Dallas-area business people.

Investors bought into an Illinois roofing business, an Oklahoma company advertising a cancer-treating nose spray and an Addison producer of a video series, Racetrack Girls Go Nutz.

   a. Guaranteed investment contracts
   c. Naked call
   b. Securitization
   d. Shell Creation Group

30. A _____ is a financial fraud where a clients losses are hidden by an investment firm by shifting them between the portfolios of other (genuine or fake) clients. Any real client with portfolio losses can therefore have their accounts flattered by this process. This cycling cannot continue indefinitely and so the investment firm itself ends up picking up the cost.
   a. Guinness share-trading fraud
   c. Get-rich-quick scheme
   b. Demand draft
   d. Tobashi scheme

31. _____ is the nickname given to a scandal involving Italian real estate developer Raffaello Follieri, who is accused of misappropriating a $50 million investment from billionaire Ronald Burkle meant to buy up Roman Catholic churches in the United States Following disclosure of the bishop's involvement in _____, the Council of Parishes of Southern New Jersey demanded 'a complete halt to the Bishop's planned church closure program.'

On July 24, 2008, the New York Daily News reported that in a second raid of Follieri's apartment in New York City, the FBI had confiscated the private journals of Follieri's former girlfriend, actress Anne Hathaway, as part of their ongoing investigation into the scandal.

   a. Certified Emission Reductions
   c. Selling short
   b. National Labor Relations Act
   d. Vati-Con

32. The _____ is a Government of Canada program, administered through Human Resources and Skills Development Canada, to assist with savings for Canadian children's higher education. Under the _____ program, the government will contribute an amount to a Registered Education Savings Plan (RESP) according to a formula which is dependent on the amount contributed and the income level of the family in which the contributions are made.

The grant payment is at least 20% of the total annual contributions up to $2500 per child.

a. Canada Student Loans Program
b. 529 plan
c. 4-4-5 Calendar
d. Canada Education Savings Grant

33. In finance, a _____ is a debt security, in which the authorized issuer owes the holders a debt and, depending on the terms of the _____, is obliged to pay interest (the coupon) and/or to repay the principal at a later date, termed maturity.

Thus a _____ is a loan: the issuer is the borrower, the _____ holder is the lender, and the coupon is the interest. _____s provide the borrower with external funds to finance long-term investments, or, in the case of government _____s, to finance current expenditure.

a. Puttable bond
b. Catastrophe bonds
c. Convertible bond
d. Bond

34. Student loans in Canada help post-secondary students pay for their education in Canada. The federal government funds the Canada Student Loan Program and the provinces may fund their own programs or run in parallel with the _____. In addition, Canadian banks offer commercial loans targeted for students in professional programs.

a. 4-4-5 Calendar
b. Dominion-Provincial Student Loan Program
c. 529 plan
d. Canada Student Loans Program

35. The _____ was the first federally funded student loan program accessible to university students in Canada. Originally only 5 provinces joined the initiative, but by 1944 all nine provinces were participating. Newfoundland joined the scheme in 1950, a short while after joining confederation in 1949.

a. 529 plan
b. Canada Student Loans Program
c. Dominion-Provincial Student Loan Program
d. 4-4-5 Calendar

36. The Academic Competitiveness Grant, more commonly known by its acronym _____, is a federal assistance grant reserved for college students with the greatest need for financial aid to attend school. To be eligible for this grant you must meet all of the following criteria:

1. You must be a United States citizen or eligible non-citizen
2. You must be Federal Pell Grant eligible
3. You must be enrolled full-time in a degree program
4. You must be in your first or second year of study at a two-year or four-year degree granting institution
5. If you are a first year student, you may not have been previously enrolled in an Undergraduate program
6. If you are a second year student, you must have at least a cumulative 3.0 GPA on a 4.0 scale your first year.

The _____ provides up to $750 for your first year and $1300 for your second year of study.

a. AAB
b. Expected Family Contribution
c. ACG Grant
d. A Random Walk Down Wall Street

37. The _____ is a refundable tax credit proposed by President-elect Barack Obama to help students and families pay for post-secondary education. While details remain vague, the proposal calls for a $4000 credit in exchange for community service.

a. A Random Walk Down Wall Street
b. AAB
c. ABN Amro
d. American opportunity tax credit

38. The term _____ describes two different concepts:

- The first is a recognition of partial payment already made towards taxes due.
- The second is a state benefit paid to workers through the tax system, which has the effect of increasing (rather than reducing) net income.

Within the Australian, Canadian, United Kingdom, and United States tax systems, a _____ is a recognition of partial payment already made towards taxes due. A similar concept exists (fr:Avoir fiscal) in the French tax system. This situation arises, for example, when standard rate tax has been deducted at source , but the tax-payer is subject to further taxation at a higher rate. It also applies in dividend imputation systems.

a. 4-4-5 Calendar
b. 529 plan
c. 7-Eleven
d. Tax credit

39. The _____ (formerly Summerbridge National) is a collaboration of programs across the United States and in Hong Kong - all functioning independently from one another - that aims to effect positive change in urban schools. It attempts to attain this goal by offering high-potential, under-served middle school students the opportunity to participate in its rigorous academic enrichment programs throughout the summer and school year. Students make a commitment to participate in the program for multiple years and in turn, Breakthrough provides many services to students and their families ranging from academic enrichment to one-on-one tutoring to high school and college preparation.

a. 529 plan
b. Breakthrough Collaborative
c. 4-4-5 Calendar
d. 7-Eleven

40. _____ is a Missouri merit-based scholarship in the amount of $2000 per annum to Missouri's qualifying graduating high school seniors who enroll in a Missouri accredited college or university. From June 2004 to July 2005, 8390 students were enrolled in the _____ program, which totaled over $15 million in state expenditures.

- To qualify for _____, a student must be in the top 3% of his or her state-wide high school class as determined by normalized tests, the ACT and SAT composite scores. To date, a score of 31 or above on the ACT or an SAT-equivalent score qualifies. A score of 31 will be needed to qualify for the 2008-2009 school year.
- Students must maintain at least a 2.5 GPA in college and full-time student status to renew the scholarship, which can be renewed for up to five years for a maximum compensation of $10,000.
- Students must not be pursuing a degree in theology or divinity.
- _____ students must attend school continuously, that is, they cannot cease attending school unless they worked for a non-profit organization or held a government job/served for the armed services. Academic interruption must not exceed 20 months.

Appropriated by the Missouri General Assembly in 1986, students have not seen an increase in awarded monies since _____'s introduction. Again, _____ has never been increased.

a. Federal Perkins Loan
b. CSS Profile
c. Federal Supplemental Educational Opportunity Grant
d. Bright Flight

41. _____ is the name of a scholarship program in the state of Florida. It is funded by the Florida Lottery and was first started in 1997.

The _____ program allows Florida high school seniors with academic merit to earn a scholarship to any public college in the state.

a. 7-Eleven
c. Bright Futures
b. 4-4-5 Calendar
d. 529 plan

42. In finance, a _____ is a standardized contract, to buy or sell a specified commodity of standardized quality at a certain date in the future, at a market determined price (the futures price.)

The price is determined by the instantaneous equilibrium between the forces of supply and demand among competing buy and sell orders on the exchange at the time of the purchase or sale of the contract.

In many cases, the items may be such non-traditional 'commodities' as foreign currencies, commercial or government paper [e.g., bonds], or 'baskets' of corporate equity ['stock indices'] or other financial instruments.

a. Financial future
c. Futures contract
b. Repurchase agreement
d. Heston model

43. The CSS/Financial Aid PROFILE (often written as _____), short for the College Scholarship Service Profile, is an application distributed by the College Board in the United States allowing college students to apply for financial aid. It is primarily designed to give private member institutions of the College Board a closer look into the finances of a student and family, it is much more detailed than the FAFSA.

The _____ asks questions about the financial status of the student and the student's parents.

a. 4-4-5 Calendar
c. CSS Profile
b. Federal Perkins Loan
d. FAFSA

44. The _____ awards are the most prestigious scholarships for entering college students in Canada.

The _____ grants Loran Awards to 30 students each year. Loran Awards are tenable at only twenty-five universities throughout Canada; however, the lower level awards (provincial awards and finalist awards) can be used at any public Canadian university or college.

a. Canadian Merit Scholarship Foundation
c. The Security Industry Association
b. Moving average
d. BootStrap Method

45. The _____ is a private, independent organization created by an act of the Parliament of Canada in 1998. It received an initial endowment of $2.5 billion from the federal government to provide awards annually for ten years. The foundation distributes $325 million in the form of bursaries and scholarships each year throughout Canada in support of post-secondary education.

a. 4-4-5 Calendar
b. 7-Eleven
c. 529 plan
d. Canada Millennium Scholarship Foundation

46. A _____ is an association of two or more individuals, companies, organizations or governments (or any combination of these entities) with the objective of participating in a common activity or pooling their resources for achieving a common goal.
   a. 7-Eleven
   b. 4-4-5 Calendar
   c. Consortium
   d. 529 plan

47. _____ or financing is to provide capital (funds), which means money for a project, a person, a business or any other private or public institutions.

Those funds can be allocated for either short term or long term purposes. The health fund is a new way of _____ private healthcare centers.

   a. Product life cycle
   b. Funding
   c. Proxy fight
   d. Synthetic CDO

48. The _____ programme is part of a scheme implemented for education in Singapore by the Ministry of Education for Singapore. Its stated aim is to maximise opportunities for all Singaporean children. The scheme aims to reward students who perform well or who make good progress in their academic and non-academic work, and provides students and schools who qualify with funds to pay for enrichment programmes or to purchase additional resources.
   a. AAB
   b. ABN Amro
   c. Edusave
   d. A Random Walk Down Wall Street

49. _____ (EOP'S) is designed and funded by the State of California and Community College districts to recruit and assist college students who show academic and financial need, considered educationally disadvantaged and/or academically underprepared. Created in January 1969, introduced by Senator Al Alquist, its purpose is to encourage enrollment, retention and transfer of students disadvantaged by various factors, such as language, social, economic and education. EOP'S promotes student academic success with enrollment assistance, educational planning, tutoring/educational services, and limited financial assistance when available.
   a. Expected Family Contribution
   b. Extended Opportunity Programs and Services
   c. A Random Walk Down Wall Street
   d. AAB

50. The _____, more commonly known by its acronym _____, is a federal assistance grant reserved for college students with the greatest need for financial aid to attend school. To be eligible for this grant you must meet all of the following criteria:

   1. You must be a United States citizen or eligible non-citizen
   2. You must not already have a bachelors degree
   3. You must not be in default of any federal student loan
   4. You must not have a Federal Pell Grant overpayment
   5. You must file your FAFSA

The maximum _____ is $4,000 a year and the amount you are eligible for is at the discretion of your college.

a. Federal Supplemental Educational Opportunity Grant   b. FAFSA
c. 4-4-5 Calendar   d. Federal Perkins Loan

51. The _____, FWS, is a United States federally funded program that assists students with the costs of postsecondary education. The _____ helps students earn financial funding through a part-time work program. The funds can be used at one of approximately 3,400 institutions across the country that participates in the program.
a. Garnishment   b. The Security Industry Association
c. Federal Work Study program   d. Stock or scrip dividends

52. _____, or The Knowledge Capital Project is a global non-profit venture that enables qualified adults to obtain discounted loans to use towards vocational re-training programs. Qualified graduates of _____'s training programs are guaranteed jobs from corporate sponsors, thus almost ensuring that the loans will be repaid. _____ offers a range of training programs, from healthcare receivables management training to film production training.
a. 4-4-5 Calendar   b. 7-Eleven
c. K-Capital   d. 529 plan

53. _____ is the standard framework of guidelines for financial accounting used in the United States of America. It includes the standards, conventions, and rules accountants follow in recording and summarizing transactions, and in the preparation of financial statements. _____ are now issued by the Financial Accounting Standards Board (FASB).
a. Net income   b. Depreciation
c. Revenue   d. Generally Accepted Accounting Principles

54. _____ or accounting is the system of recording, verifying, and reporting of the value of assets, liabilities, income, and expenses in the books of account (ledger) to which debit and credit entries (recognizing transactions) are chronologically posted to record changes in value Such financial information is primarily used by lenders, managers, investors, tax authorities and other decision makers to make resource allocation decisions between and within companies, organizations, and public agencies. Accounting has been defined by the AICPA as ' The art of recording, classifying, and summarizing in a significant manner and in terms of money, transactions and events which are, in part at least, of financial character, and interpreting the results thereof.'

Financial accounting is one branch of accounting and historically has involved processes by which financial information about a business is recorded, classified, summarised, interpreted, and communicated; for public companies, this information is generally publicly-accessible.

a. ABN Amro   b. A Random Walk Down Wall Street
c. AAB   d. Accountancy

55. The basic _____ is the foundation for the double-entry bookkeeping system. It shows how assets were financed: either by borrowing money from someone (liability) or by paying your own money (shareholders' equity.)

Assets = Liabilities + (Shareholders or Owners equity)

a. Annual report
b. Accounting methods
c. Earnings before interest, taxes, depreciation and amortization
d. Accounting equation

56. In finance and economics, an _____ is an equality that must be true regardless of the value of its variables, or a statement that by definition (or construction) must be true. The term is also used in economics to refer to equalities that are by definition or construction true, such as the balance of payments. Where an _____ applies, any deviation from the identity signifies an error in formulation, calculation or measurement.

a. Invoice processing
b. Earnings before interest, taxes, depreciation and amortization
c. Accounting equation
d. Accounting identity

57. _____ is a measure of the ability of a debtor to pay their debts as and when they fall due. It is usually expressed as a ratio or a percentage of current liabilities.

For a corporation with a published balance sheet there are various ratios used to calculate a measure of liquidity.

a. Operating leverage
b. Accounting liquidity
c. Operating profit margin
d. Invested capital

58. Two primary _____, cash and accrual basis, and their combination, called modified cash basis, are used in recognizing income (revenues) and expenses in bookkeeping in order to measure net income for a specified time interval (accounting period.) Both methods differ on such recognition leading to varying income recordings, which may be subject to error or - manipulation. Many financial scandals involved accounting manipulations.

a. Accounting equation
b. Accounting methods
c. Asset
d. Outstanding balance

59. _____ is a file or account that contains money that a person or company owes to suppliers, but hasn't paid yet (a form of debt.) When you receive an invoice you add it to the file, and then you remove it when you pay. Thus, the A/P is a form of credit that suppliers offer to their purchasers by allowing them to pay for a product or service after it has already been received.

a. Earnings before interest, taxes, depreciation and amortization
b. Accrual
c. Outstanding balance
d. Accounts payable

60. _____ is one of a series of accounting transactions dealing with the billing of customers who owe money to a person, company or organization for goods and services that have been provided to the customer. In most business entities this is typically done by generating an invoice and mailing or electronically delivering it to the customer, who in turn must pay it within an established timeframe called credit or payment terms.

An example of a common payment term is Net 30, meaning payment is due in the amount of the invoice 30 days from the date of invoice.

Chapter 9. Test Preparation Part 9

a. Accounting methods
c. Income

b. Accounts receivable
d. Impaired asset

61. Accrual, in accounting, describes the accounting method known as _____, whereby revenues and expenses are recognized when they are accrued, i.e. accumulated (earned or incurred), regardless when the actual cash is received or paid out.

E.g. a company delivers a product to a customer who will pay for it 30 days later in the next fiscal year starting a week after the delivery. The company recognizes the proceeds as a revenue in its current income statement still for the fiscal year of the delivery, even though it will get paid in cash during the following accounting period.

a. ABN Amro
c. AAB

b. Accrual basis
d. A Random Walk Down Wall Street

62. _____ are liabilities which have occurred, but have not been paid or logged under accounts payable during an accounting period; in other words, obligations for goods and services provided to a company for which invoices have not yet been received. Examples would include accrued wages payable, accrued sales tax payable, and accrued rent payable.

There are two general types of _____:

- Routine and recurring
- Infrequent or non-routine

a. Adjusting entries
c. Accrued liabilities

b. Outstanding balance
d. Accounting methods

63. In tax accounting, _____ is the net cost of an asset after adjusting for various tax-related items.

_____ is one of two variables in the formula used to compute gains and losses when determining gross income for tax purposes. The Amount Realized - _____ tells the amount of Realized Gain (if positive) or Realized Loss (if negative.)

a. Invoice processing
c. Accounts payable

b. Accounting methods
d. Adjusted basis

64. In accounting/accountancy, _____ are journal entries usually made at the end of an accounting period to allocate income and expenditure to the period in which they actually occurred. The revenue recognition principle is the basis of making _____ that pertain to unearned and accrued revenues under accrual-basis accounting. They are sometimes called Balance Day adjustments because they are made on balance day.

a. Accounts receivable
c. Adjusting entries

b. Adjusted basis
d. OIBDA

65. An _____ is a document a company presents at an annual general meeting for approval by its shareholders, or a charitable organization presents its trustees. The report is made up of reports, which may include the following:

- Chairman's report
- CEO's report
- Auditor's report on corporate governance
- Mission statement
- Corporate governance statement of compliance
- Statement of directors' responsibilities
- Invitation to the company's AGM

as well as financial statements including:

- Auditor's report on the financial statements
- Balance sheet
- Statement of retained earnings
- Income statement
- Cash flow statement
- Notes to the financial statements
- Accounting policies

Other information deemed relevant to stakeholders may be included, such as a report on operations for manufacturing firms. In the case of larger companies, it is usually a sleek, colorful, high gloss publication.

The details provided in the report are of use to investors to understand the company's financial position and future direction.

a. Amortization schedule
b. Accrued liabilities
c. Outstanding balance
d. Annual report

66. _____ is a term used in accounting relating to the increase in value of an asset. In this sense it is the reverse of depreciation, which measures the fall in value of assets over their normal life-time.

_____ is a rise of a currency in a floating exchange rate.

a. A Random Walk Down Wall Street
b. Appreciation
c. Other Comprehensive Basis of Accounting
d. Operating cash flow

67. In business and accounting, _____s are everything of value that is owned by a person or company. The balance sheet of a firm records the monetary value of the _____s owned by the firm. The two major _____ classes are tangible _____s and intangible _____s.

a. Income
b. Accounts payable
c. EBITDA
d. Asset

68. _____ is a financial ratio that measures the efficiency of a company's use of its assets in generating sales revenue or sales income to the company.

$$Asset\ Turnover = \frac{Sales}{Average\ Total\ Assets}$$

- 'Sales' is the value of 'Net Sales' or 'Sales' from the company's income statement
- 'Average Total Assets' is the value of 'Total assets' from the company's balance sheet in the beginning and the end of the fiscal period divided by 2.

- Assets turnover

a. Average accounting return
c. Asset turnover

b. Earnings yield
d. Inventory turnover

1. In business and accounting, _____s are everything of value that is owned by a person or company. The balance sheet of a firm records the monetary value of the _____s owned by the firm. The two major _____ classes are tangible _____s and intangible _____s.

   a. Asset
   c. Accounts payable
   b. Income
   d. EBITDA

2. _____ is a business term and may be used as a broad measure of asset efficiency and is calculated by dividing sales revenue by the total assets.

It's also used in the Du Pont Identity:

$$\frac{Net\ Earnings}{Shareholders\ Eq.} = \frac{Net\ Earnings}{Sales(Income)} * \frac{Sales(Income)}{Total\ Assets} * \frac{Total\ Assets}{Shareholders\ Eq.}$$

In which,

$$Net\ Margin = \frac{Net\ Earnings}{Sales(Income)}$$

$$Total\ Asset\ Turnover = \frac{Sales(Income)}{Total\ Assets}$$

$$Financial\ Leverage = \frac{Average\ Total\ Assets}{Average\ Total\ Equity}$$

The net margin is a summary indicator of an income statement, Asset turnover is an indicator of the left side of the balance sheet (total assets' side) and Leverage is an indicator of the right side of the Balance Sheet (liabilities and shareholders' equity' side.)

The Du Pont Identity helps many companies or individuals, visualize and comprehend the analysis of a financial statement or annual report of a company, in return on assets and return on investments.

   a. Earnings yield
   c. Invested capital
   b. Operating profit margin
   d. Assets turnover

3. In accounting and finance, _____ is the portion of receivables that can no longer be collected, typically from accounts receivable or loans. _____ in accounting is considered an expense.

There are two methods to account for _____:

1. Direct write off method (Non - GAAP)

A receivable which is not considered collectible is charged directly to the income statement.

1. Allowance method (GAAP)

An estimate is made at the end of each fiscal year of the amount of _____. This is then accumulated in a provision which is then used to reduce specific receivable accounts as and when necessary.

Chapter 10. Test Preparation Part 10

a. 529 plan
c. 4-4-5 Calendar
b. Bad debt
d. Tax expense

4. _____ is that which is owed; usually referencing assets owed, but the term can cover other obligations. In the case of assets, _____ is a means of using future purchasing power in the present before a summation has been earned. Some companies and corporations use _____ as a part of their overall corporate finance strategy.
   a. Partial Payment
   c. Cross-collateralization
   b. Credit cycle
   d. Debt

5. In financial accounting, a _____ or statement of financial position is a summary of a person's or organization's balances. Assets, liabilities and ownership equity are listed as of a specific date, such as the end of its financial year. A _____ is often described as a snapshot of a company's financial condition.
   a. Balance sheet
   c. Statement on Auditing Standards No. 70: Service Organizations
   b. Statement of retained earnings
   d. Financial statements

6. In accounting, _____ or *Carrying value* is the value of an asset according to its balance sheet account balance. For assets, the value is based on the original cost of the asset less any depreciation, amortization or impairment costs made against the asset. A company's _____ is its total assets minus intangible assets and liabilities.
   a. Pro forma
   c. Current liabilities
   b. Retained earnings
   d. Book value

7. The term _____ has three unrelated technical definitions, and is also used in a variety of non-technical ways.

   - In financial economics, it refers to any asset used to make money, as opposed to assets used for personal enjoyment or consumption. This is an important distinction because two people can disagree sharply about the value of personal assets, one person might think a sports car is more valuable than a pickup truck, another person might have the opposite taste. But if an asset is held for the purpose of making money, taste has nothing to do with it, only differences of opinion about how much money the asset will produce. With the further assumption that people agree on the probability distribution of future cash flows, it is possible to have an objective _____ pricing model. Even without the assumption of agreement, it is possible to set rational limits on _____ value.
   - In governmental accounting, it is defined as any asset used in operations with an initial useful life extending beyond one reporting period. Generally, government managers have a 'stewardship' duty to maintain _____ s under their control. See International Public Sector Accounting Standards for details.
   - In US tax accounting, it is defined as any property other than a list of exceptions. The main exceptions are anything held for sale, and any real estate or depreciable property used in business. Almost everything you own and use for personal purposes, pleasure or investment is a _____. If something is a _____ for tax purposes, gains or losses on sale or disposition are capital gains or capital losses. For individuals, however, capital losses on property held for personal use are generally not deductible. See the IRS publication Tax Facts about Capital Gains and Losses for details.

A well-known financial accounting textbook advises that the term be avoided except in tax accounting because it is used in so many different senses, not all of them well-defined. For example it is often used as a synonym for fixed assets or for investments in securities.

A common non-technical usage occurs when people ask that employees or the environment or something else be treated as a _____.

   a. Settlement date
   c. Political risk
   b. Capital asset
   d. Solvency

8. _____ is an accounting term which frequently appears as a balance sheet item as a component of shareholders' equity. _____ is used to account for any funds the issuing firm has received over and above the par value of the common stock. It may also be used to account for any gains the firm may derive from selling treasury stock, although this is less commonly seen.

   a. Capital surplus
   c. Stock market index option
   b. Flight-to-quality
   d. Commercial finance

9. _____ is the balance of the amounts of cash being received and paid by a business during a defined period of time, sometimes tied to a specific project. Measurement of _____ can be used

- to evaluate the state or performance of a business or project.
- to determine problems with liquidity. Being profitable does not necessarily mean being liquid. A company can fail because of a shortage of cash, even while profitable.
- to generate project rate of returns. The time of _____s into and out of projects are used as inputs to financial models such as internal rate of return, and net present value.
- to examine income or growth of a business when it is believed that accrual accounting concepts do not represent economic realities. Alternately, _____ can be used to 'validate' the net income generated by accrual accounting.

_____ as a generic term may be used differently depending on context, and certain _____ definitions may be adapted by analysts and users for their own uses. Common terms include operating _____ and free _____.

_____s can be classified into:

1. Operational _____s: Cash received or expended as a result of the company's core business activities.
2. Investment _____s: Cash received or expended through capital expenditure, investments or acquisitions.
3. Financing _____s: Cash received or expended as a result of financial activities, such as interests and dividends.

All three together - the net _____ - are necessary to reconcile the beginning cash balance to the ending cash balance. Loan draw downs or equity injections, that is just shifting of capital but no expenditure as such, are not considered in the net _____.

   a. Real option
   c. Corporate finance
   b. Shareholder value
   d. Cash flow

10. In financial accounting, a _____ or statement of cash flows is a financial statement that shows a company's flow of cash. The money coming into the business is called cash inflow, and money going out from the business is called cash outflow. The statement shows how changes in balance sheet and income accounts affect cash and cash equivalents, and breaks the analysis down to operating, investing, and financing activities.
   a. 529 plan
   b. Cash flow statement
   c. 4-4-5 Calendar
   d. 7-Eleven

11. _____ is a list of all accounts including a unique number identifying each. A _____ can track a specific financial information. Each account in the chart has assigned a unique identifier, typically an account number.
   a. Chart of accounts
   b. General journal
   c. General ledger
   d. Journal entry

12. _____, in bookkeeping, refers to assets, liabilities, income, and expenses recorded on individual pages of the so called book of final entry or ledger. Changes in _____ value are made by chronologically posting debit (DR) and credit (CR) entries to its page. Examples of _____s are cash, _____s receivable, mortgages, loans, land and buildings, common stock, sales, services provided, wages, and payroll overhead.
   a. Alpha
   b. Accretion
   c. Option
   d. Account

13. _____ are journal entries made at the end of an accounting period to transfer temporary accounts to permanent accounts. An 'income summary' account may be used to show the balance between revenue and expenses, or they could be directly closed against retained earnings where dividend payments will be deducted from. This process is used to reset the balance of these temporary accounts to zero for the next accounting period.
   a. Closing entries
   b. Generally Accepted Accounting Principles
   c. Historical cost
   d. Net profit

14. _____ are financial statements that factor the holding company's subsidiaries into its aggregated accounting figure. It is a representation of how the holding company is doing as a group. The consolidated accounts should provide a true and fair view of the financial and operating conditions of the group.
   a. Consolidated financial statements
   b. Fund Accounting
   c. Net operating profit after tax
   d. Treynor ratio

15. _____ are formal records of a business' financial activities.

   _____ provide an overview of a business' financial condition in both short and long term. There are four basic _____:

   1. **Balance sheet**: also referred to as statement of financial position or condition, reports on a company's assets, liabilities, and net equity as of a given point in time.
   2. **Income statement**: also referred to as Profit and Loss statement (or a 'P'L'), reports on a company's income, expenses, and profits over a period of time.
   3. **Statement of retained earnings**: explains the changes in a company's retained earnings over the reporting period.
   4. **Statement of cash flows**: reports on a company's cash flow activities, particularly its operating, investing and financing activities.

a. Statement on Auditing Standards No. 70: Service Organizations
b. Statement of retained earnings
c. Financial statements
d. Notes to the Financial Statements

16. _____ or amalgamation is the act of merging many things into one. In business, it often refers to the mergers or acquisitions of many smaller companies into much larger ones. The financial accounting term of _____ refers to the aggregated financial statements of a group company as consolidated account.
   a. Write-off
   b. Cost of goods sold
   c. Consolidation
   d. Retained earnings

17. An accountancy term, _____ asset entry records the cost of construction work, which is not yet completed (typically, applied to capital budget items.) A _____ item is not depreciated until the asset is placed in service. Normally, upon completion, a _____ item is reclassified, and the reclassified asset is capitalized and depreciated.
   a. Fixed asset
   b. Percentage of Completion
   c. Construction in Progress
   d. Credit memo

18. In accounting, the _____ is an account in the general ledger to which a corresponding subsidiary ledger has been created. The subsidiary ledger allows for tracking transactions within the _____ in more detail. Individual transactions are posted both to the _____ and the corresponding subsidiary ledger, and the totals for both are compared when preparing a trial balance to ensure accuracy.
   a. Controlling account
   b. Non Performing Asset
   c. Creative accounting
   d. Momentum Accounting and Triple-Entry Bookkeeping

19. In economics, business, and accounting, a _____ is the value of money that has been used up to produce something, and hence is not available for use anymore. In business, the _____ may be one of acquisition, in which case the amount of money expended to acquire it is counted as _____. In this case, money is the input that is gone in order to acquire the thing.
   a. Marginal cost
   b. Sliding scale fees
   c. Fixed costs
   d. Cost

20. _____, _____ includes the direct costs attributable to the production of the goods sold by a company. This amount includes the materials cost used in creating the goods along with the direct labor costs used to produce the good. It excludes indirect expenses such as distribution costs and sales force costs.
   a. Net profit
   b. Deferred financing costs
   c. Cost of goods sold
   d. Goodwill

21. In accounting, a _____ is an asset on the balance sheet which is expected to be sold or otherwise used up in the near future, usually within one year, or one business cycle - whichever is longer. Typical _____s include cash, cash equivalents, accounts receivable, inventory, the portion of prepaid accounts which will be used within a year, and short-term investments.

On the balance sheet, assets will typically be classified into _____s and long-term assets.

a. Long-term liabilities
b. Historical cost
c. Current asset
d. Write-off

22. In accounting, _____ are considered liabilities of the business that are to be settled in cash within the fiscal year or the operating cycle, whichever period is longer.

For example accounts payable for goods, services or supplies that were purchased for use in the operation of the business and payable within a normal period of time would be _____.

Bonds, mortgages and loans that are payable over a term exceeding one year would be fixed liabilities.

a. Current liabilities
b. Gross sales
c. Closing entries
d. Net income

23. In the most general sense, a _____ is anything that is a hindrance, or puts individuals at a disadvantage.

Before we discuss the financial terms, we should note that a _____ can also have a much more important slang meaning.

This is best described in an example.

a. Covenant
b. McFadden Act
c. Limited liability
d. Liability

24. _____, in accrual accounting, is any account where the asset or liability is not realized until a future date, e.g. annuities, charges, taxes, income, etc. The _____ item may be carried, dependent on type of deferral, as either an asset or liability. See also: accrual

_____ is also used in the university admissions process. It is the action by which a school rejects a student for early admission but still opts to review that student in the general admissions pool.

a. Revenue
b. Net profit
c. Deferred
d. Current asset

25. _____ (e.g. cash received from a client), in accrual accounting, is a not yet earned revenue according to revenue recognition or billed and, until then, it will have been owed to the payer, hence it remains a liability.

For example, a customer pays an annual software license fee upfront on the January 1. However the company's fiscal year ends on May 31.

a. Trial balance
b. Pro forma
c. Deferred income
d. Current asset

Chapter 10. Test Preparation Part 10

26. _____, refers to consumption opportunity gained by an entity within a specified time frame, which is generally expressed in monetary terms. However, for households and individuals, '_____ is the sum of all the wages, salaries, profits, interests payments, rents and other forms of earnings received... in a given period of time.' For firms, _____ generally refers to net-profit: what remains of revenue after expenses have been subtracted.

   a. Accrual
   b. Income
   c. Annual report
   d. OIBDA

27. _____ is a term used in accounting, economics and finance to spread the cost of an asset over the span of several years.

In simple words we can say that _____ is the reduction in the value of an asset due to usage, passage of time, wear and tear, technological outdating or obsolescence, depletion or other such factors.

In accounting, _____ is a term used to describe any method of attributing the historical or purchase cost of an asset across its useful life, roughly corresponding to normal wear and tear.

   a. Matching principle
   b. Deferred financing costs
   c. Depreciation
   d. Bottom line

28. A '_____' is a 'Charge' that is paid to obtain the right to delay a payment. Essentially, the payer purchases the right to make a given payment in the future instead of in the Present. The '_____', or 'Charge' that must be paid to delay the payment, is simply the difference between what the payment amount would be if it were paid in the present and what the payment amount would be paid if it were paid in the future.

   a. Value at risk
   b. Risk modeling
   c. Risk aversion
   d. Discount

29. _____ are reductions to a basic price of goods or services. They can occur anywhere in the distribution channel, modifying either the manufacturer's list price (determined by the manufacturer and often printed on the package), the retail price (set by the retailer and often attached to the product with a sticker), or the list price (which is quoted to a potential buyer, usually in written form.) The market price (also called effective price) is the amount actually paid.

   a. Price index
   b. Price discrimination
   c. Transfer pricing
   d. Discounts and allowances

30. In financial and business accounting, _____ is a measure of a firm's profitability that excludes interest and income tax expenses.

EBIT = Operating Revenue - Operating Expenses (OPEX) + Non-operating Income

Operating Income = Operating Revenue - Operating Expenses

Operating income is the difference between operating revenues and operating expenses, but it is also sometimes used as a synonym for EBIT and operating profit. This is true if the firm has no non-operating income.

   a. AAB
   b. A Random Walk Down Wall Street
   c. ABN Amro
   d. Earnings before interest and taxes

31. _____ is a fee paid on borrowed assets. It is the price paid for the use of borrowed money, or, money earned by deposited funds. Assets that are sometimes lent with _____ include money, shares, consumer goods through hire purchase, major assets such as aircraft, and even entire factories in finance lease arrangements.
   a. AAB
   b. A Random Walk Down Wall Street
   c. Insolvency
   d. Interest

32. _____ (EBITDA) is a non-GAAP metric that can be used to evaluate a company's profitability.

$$EBITDA = Operating\ Revenue - Operating\ Expenses + Other\ Revenue$$

Its name comes from the fact that Operating Expenses do not include interest, taxes, or amortization. EBITDA is not a defined measure according to Generally Accepted Accounting Principles (GAAP), and thus can be calculated however a company wishes.

   a. Accounting methods
   b. Annual report
   c. Accrued liabilities
   d. Earnings before interest, taxes, depreciation and amortization

33. _____ is the process of decreasing an amount over a period of time. The word comes from Middle English amortisen to kill, alienate in mortmain, from Anglo-French amorteser, alteration of amortir, from Vulgar Latin admortire to kill, from Latin ad- + mort-, mors death. Particular instances of the term include:

   - _____ (business), the allocation of a lump sum amount to different time periods, particularly for loans and other forms of finance, including related interest or other finance charges.
     - _____ schedule, a table detailing each periodic payment on a loan (typically a mortgage), as generated by an _____ calculator.
     - Negative _____, an _____ schedule where the loan amount actually increases through not paying the full interest
   - Amortized analysis, analyzing the execution cost of algorithms over a sequence of operations.
   - _____ of capital expenditures of certain assets under accounting rules, particularly intangible assets, in a manner analogous to depreciation.
   - _____ (tax law)

_____ is also used in the context of zoning regulations and describes the time in which a property owner has to relocate when the property's use constitutes a preexisting nonconforming use under zoning regulations.

   - Depreciation

   a. Option
   b. Intrinsic value
   c. AT'T Inc.
   d. Amortization

34. In accounting, an _____ is one of the assumptions made in generally accepted accounting principles. Basically, any organization or unit in society can be an _____.

Examples of economic entities are hospitals, companies, municipalities, and federal agencies.

a. Economic entity
b. Interest rate option
c. Eurobond
d. Education production function

35. _____ or First In, First Out, is an abstraction in ways of organizing and manipulation of data relative to time and prioritization. This expression describes the principle of a queue processing technique or servicing conflicting demands by ordering process by first-come, first-served (FCFS) behaviour: what comes in first is handled first, what comes in next waits until the first is finished, etc.

Thus it is analogous to the behaviour of persons queueing (or 'standing in line', in common American parlance), where the persons leave the queue in the order they arrive, or waiting one's turn at a traffic control signal.

a. 4-4-5 Calendar
b. Penny stock
c. FIFO
d. Risk management

36. _____ methods are means of managing inventory and financial matters involving the money a company ties up within inventory of produced goods, raw materials, parts, components, or feed stocks.

In LIFO accounting, a historical method of recording the value of inventory, a firm records the last units purchased as the first units sold. LIFO is an acronym for 'last in, first out.' Sometimes the term FILO ('first in, last out') is used synonymously.

a. General journal
b. FIFO and LIFO accounting
c. Net sales
d. Payroll

37. _____ is an acronym which stands for last in, first out. In computer science and queueing theory this refers to the way items stored in some types of data structures are processed. By definition, in a _____ structured linear list, elements can be added or taken off from only one end, called the 'top'.

a. 7-Eleven
b. 4-4-5 Calendar
c. LIFO
d. 529 plan

38. A _____ (or financial year, or sometimes budget year) is a period used for calculating annual ('yearly') financial statements in businesses and other organizations. In many jurisdictions, regulatory laws regarding accounting and taxation require such reports once per twelve months, but do not require that the period reported on constitutes a calendar year (i.e., January through December.) _____s vary between businesses and countries.

a. Special journals
b. Purchase ledger
c. Matching principle
d. Fiscal year

39. _____ plant, and equipment, is a term used in accountancy for assets and property which cannot easily be converted into cash. This can be compared with current assets such as cash or bank accounts, which are described as liquid assets. In most cases, only tangible assets are referred to as fixed.

a. Fixed asset
b. Petty cash
c. Remittance advice
d. Percentage of Completion

40. _____ in economics refers to investment in fixed capital, i.e. tangible capital goods (real means of production or residential buildings), or to the replacement of depreciated capital goods.

Thus, _____ is investment in physical assets such as machinery, land, buildings, installations, vehicles, or technology. Normally, a company balance sheet will state both the amount of expenditure on fixed assets during the quarter or year, and the total value of the stock of fixed assets owned.

a. Pro forma
b. Net profit
c. Generally Accepted Accounting Principles
d. Fixed investment

41. _____ (or FF'E) is an accounting term used in valuing, selling, or liquidating a company or a building.

FF'E are movable furniture, fixtures or other equipment that have no permanent connection to the structure of a building or utilities. These items depreciate substantially but definitely are important costs to consider when valuing a company, especially in liquidation.

a. Salvage value
b. Furniture, Fixtures and Equipment
c. Depreciation
d. Deferred income

42. The _____ is where double entry bookkeeping entries are recorded by debiting one account and crediting another account with the same amount. The amount debited and the amount credited should always be equal, thereby ensuring the accounting equation is maintained.

Depending on the business's accounting information system, specialized journals may be used in conjunction with the _____ for record-keeping.

a. Ledger
b. General journal
c. Journal entry
d. General ledger

43. The _____, sometimes known as the nominal ledger, is the main accounting record of a business which uses double-entry bookkeeping. It will usually include accounts for such items as current assets, fixed assets, liabilities, revenue and expense items, gains and losses.

The _____ is a collection of the group of accounts that supports the items shown in the major financial statements.

a. Journal entry
b. General journal
c. Ledger
d. General ledger

44. A _____ is the principal book for recording transactions. Originally, the term referred to a large volume of Scripture/service book kept in one place in church and accessible.

According to Charles Wriothesley's Chronicle (1538):

> the curates should provide a booke of the bible in Englishe, of the largest volume, to be a lidger in the same church for the parishioners to read on.

It is an application of this original meaning that is found in the commercial usage of the term for the principal book of account in a business house, the general _____ or nominal _____ and also in the terms purchase _____ and sales _____.

    a. General journal
    c. Journal entry
    b. Ledger
    d. General ledger

45. _____ is an accounting term used to reflect the portion of the book value of a business entity not directly attributable to its assets and liabilities; it normally arises only in case of an acquisition. It reflects the ability of the entity to make a higher profit than would be derived from selling the tangible assets. _____ is also known as an intangible asset.
    a. Cost of goods sold
    c. Consolidation
    b. Goodwill
    d. Net profit

46. _____ is commonly defined as the amount of a company's or a person's income before all deductions or any taxpayer's income, except that which is specifically excluded by the Internal Revenue Code, before taking deductions or taxes into account. For a business, this amount is pre-tax net sales less cost of sales. Section 61 of the Internal Revenue Code (Code) defines '_____' as 'all income from whatever source derived.' Section 61(a) of the Code lists fifteen examples of items included in _____; however, the list is not exhaustive.
    a. Second lien loan
    c. Shareholder value
    b. Gross income
    d. Financial distress

47. In accounting, _____ or sales profit is the difference between revenue and the cost of making a product or providing a service, before deducting overhead, payroll, taxation, and interest payments. Note that this is different than operating profit.

Net sales are calculated:

    Net sales = Sales - Sales returns and allowances

_____ is found by deducting the cost of goods sold:

    _____ = Net sales - Cost of goods sold

_____ should not be confused with net income:

    Net income = _____ - Total operating expenses

Cost of goods sold is calculated differently for merchandising business than for a manufacturer.

    a. Real option
    c. Gross profit
    b. Cash flow
    d. Gross income

48. _____ is the difference between price and the costs of bringing to market whatever it is that is accounted as an enterprise (whether by harvest, extraction, manufacture, or purchase) in terms of the component costs of delivered goods and/or services and any operating or other expenses.

A key difficulty in measuring profit is in defining costs. Pure economic monetary profits can be zero or negative even in competitive equilibrium when accounted monetized costs exceed monetized price.

a. Economic profit
b. AAB
c. A Random Walk Down Wall Street
d. Accounting profit

49. _____ is a financial ratio used to assess the profitability of a firm's core activities, excluding fixed costs.

The general calculation is

$$\text{Gross profit margin} = \frac{\text{Revenue} - \text{Cost of Sales}}{\text{Revenue}}$$

The _____ is related to the net profit margin, which assesses the profitability of an organization after including fixed costs.

Indicates the relationship between net sales revenue and the cost of goods sold.

a. Gross profit
b. Gross profit margin
c. Tender offer
d. Second lien loan

50. In finance, a _____ is collateral that the holder of a position in securities, options, or futures contracts has to deposit to cover the credit risk of his counterparty (most often his broker.) This risk can arise if the holder has done any of the following:

- borrowed cash from the counterparty to buy securities or options,
- sold securities or options short, or
- entered into a futures contract.

The collateral can be in the form of cash or securities, and it is deposited in a _____ account. On U.S. futures exchanges, '_____' was formally called performance bond.

_____ buying is buying securities with cash borrowed from a broker, using other securities as collateral.

a. Procter ' Gamble
b. Share
c. Credit
d. Margin

51. _____, Net Margin, Net _____ or Net Profit Ratio all refer to a measure of profitability. It is calculated using a formula and written as a percentage or a number.

$$\text{Net profit margin} = \frac{\text{Net profit after taxes}}{\text{Net Sales}}$$

The _____ is mostly used for internal comparison.

a. Net profit margin
c. 4-4-5 Calendar

b. Profit maximization
d. Profit margin

52. _____ is defined to be the total invoice value of sales, before deducting customers' discounts, returns, or allowances.

$$\text{Net Sales} = \text{Gross Sales} - (\text{Customer Discounts, Returns, Allowances})$$

a. Write-off
c. Gross sales

b. Long-term liabilities
d. Trial balance

53. In accounting, _____ is the original monetary value of an economic item. In some circumstances, assets and liabilities may be shown at their _____, as if there had been no change in value since the date of acquisition. The balance sheet value of the item may therefore differ from the 'true' value.

a. Historical cost
c. Deferred income

b. Pro forma
d. Treasury stock

54. An _____ is a condition in which an asset's market value falls below its carrying amount and is not expected to recover. This means that an asset's market valuation is less than the book value of the asset and the future cash flows to be generated from the asset are less than the net difference of the market value and the book value of the asset. At this point it becomes necessary to write down the value of the asset in the books by debiting a loss account (which will show up as an expense in the income statement) and crediting the respective asset account.

a. Impaired asset
c. OIBDA

b. Accrual
d. Adjusting entries

55. An _____ is a financial statement for companies that indicates how Revenue is transformed into net income The purpose of the _____ is to show managers and investors whether the company made or lost money during the period being reported.

The important thing to remember about an _____ is that it represents a period of time.

a. A Random Walk Down Wall Street
c. Income statement

b. ABN Amro
d. AAB

56. An _____ or bill is a commercial document issued by a seller to the buyer, indicating the products, quantities, and agreed prices for products or services the seller has provided the buyer. An _____ indicates the buyer must pay the seller, according to the payment terms.

In the rental industry, an _____ must include a specific reference to the duration of the time being billed, so rather than quantity, price and discount the invoicing amount is based on quantity, price, discount and duration.

a. A Random Walk Down Wall Street
b. ABN Amro
c. Invoice
d. AAB

57. _____ involves the handling of incoming invoices from arrival to post. Invoices have many variations and types. In general, invoices are grouped into two types: 1.
a. Income
b. Accounting equation
c. OIBDA
d. Invoice processing

58. A _____, in accounting, is a logging of transcriptions into items accounting journal. The _____ can consist of several items, each of which is either a debit or a credit. The total of the debits must equal the total of the credits, or the _____ is said to be 'unbalanced.' Journal entries can record unique items or recurring items such as depreciation or bond amortization.
a. Ledger
b. General ledger
c. General journal
d. Journal entry

59. In economic models, the _____ time frame assumes no fixed factors of production. Firms can enter or leave the marketplace, and the cost (and availability) of land, labor, raw materials, and capital goods can be assumed to vary. In contrast, in the short-run time frame, certain factors are assumed to be fixed, because there is not sufficient time for them to change.
a. Long-run
b. Short-run
c. 529 plan
d. 4-4-5 Calendar

60. _____ are liabilities with a future benefit over one year, such as notes payable that mature greater than one year.

In accounting, the _____ are shown on the right wing of the balance-sheet representing the sources of funds, which are generally bounded in form of capital assets.

Examples of _____ are debentures, mortgage loans and other bank loans (note: not all bank loans are long term as not all are paid over a period greater than a year, the example is bridging loan.)

a. Matching principle
b. Deferred income
c. Bottom line
d. Long-term liabilities

61. _____ is a cornerstone of accrual accounting together with revenue recognition. They both determine the point, at which expenses and revenues are recognized. According to the principle, expenses are recognized when they are (1) incurred and (2) offset against recognized revenues, which were generated from those expenses (related on the cause-and-effect basis), no matter when cash is paid out.
a. Pro forma
b. Matching principle
c. Retained earnings
d. Gross sales

62. _____ in business is an accounting concept that refers to ownership of a company (subsidiary) that is less than 50% of outstanding shares. _____ belongs to other investors and is reported on the consolidated balance sheet of the owning company to reflect the claim on assets belonging to other, non-controlling shareholders. Also, _____ is reported on the consolidated income statement as a share of profit belonging to minority shareholders.
- a. Credit memo
- b. Fixed asset
- c. Construction in Progress
- d. Minority interest

63. _____ is equal to the income that a firm has after subtracting costs and expenses from the total revenue. _____ can be distributed among holders of common stock as a dividend or held by the firm as retained earnings. _____ is an accounting term; in some countries (such as the UK) profit is the usual term.
- a. Write-off
- b. Furniture, Fixtures and Equipment
- c. Historical cost
- d. Net income

64. In business and finance accounting, _____ is equal to the gross profit minus overheads minus interest payable plus/minus one off items for a given time period (usually: accounting period.)

A common synonym for '_____' when discussing financial statements (which include a balance sheet and an income statement) is the bottom line. This term results from the traditional appearance of an income statement which shows all allocated revenues and expenses over a specified time period with the resulting summation on the bottom line of the report.

- a. Deferred
- b. Gross sales
- c. Salvage value
- d. Net profit

65. _____ means an asset or account of borrower, which has been classified by a bank or financial institution as substandard, doubtful or loss asset, in accordance with the directions or guidelines relating to asset classification issued by The Reserve Bank of India.

An amount due under any credit facility is treated as 'past due' when it has not been paid within 30 days from the due date. Due to the improvement in the payment and settlement systems, recovery climate, upgradation of technology in the banking system, etc., it was decided to dispense with 'past due' concept, with effect from March 31, 2001.

- a. Non Performing Asset
- b. Money measurement concept
- c. Creative accounting
- d. Double-entry bookkeeping

66. _____ are additional notes and information added to the end of the financial statements to supplement the reader with more information. Notes to Financial Statements help explain the computation of specific items in the financial statements as well as provide a more comprehensive assessment of a company's financial condition. Notes to Financial Statements can include information on debt, going concern, accounts, contingent liabilities, or contextual information explaining the financial numbers (e.g. to indicate a lawsuit.)
- a. Statement of retained earnings
- b. Financial statements
- c. Statement on Auditing Standards No. 70: Service Organizations
- d. Notes to the Financial Statements

Chapter 10. Test Preparation Part 10

67. In financial accounting, _____, cash flow provided by operations or cash flow from operating activities, refers to the amount of cash a company generates from the revenues it brings in, excluding costs associated with long-term investment on capital items or investment in securities.

_____ = Cash generated from operations less taxation and interest paid, investment income received and less dividends paid gives rise to _____s per International Financial Reporting Standards.

To calculate cash generated from operations, one must calculate cash generated from customers and cash paid to suppliers.

a. Operating cash flow
b. A Random Walk Down Wall Street
c. Other Comprehensive Basis of Accounting
d. Appreciation

68. In accounting terms, after all liabilities are paid, _____ is the remaining interest in assets. If valuations placed on assets do not exceed liabilities, negative equity exists.

Shareholders' equity (or stockholders' equity, shareholders' funds, shareholders' capital employed) is this interest in remaining assets, spread among individual shareholders of common or preferred stock.

a. Amortising swap
b. Intelligent investor
c. Ownership equity
d. Asset-backed commercial paper

69. In a company, _____ is the sum of all financial records of salaries, wages, bonuses and deductions.

A paycheck, is traditionally a paper document issued by an employer to pay an employee for services rendered. While most commonly used in the United States, recently the physical paycheck has been increasingly replaced by electronic direct deposit to bank accounts.

a. 529 plan
b. Tax expense
c. 4-4-5 Calendar
d. Payroll

70. _____ (PoC) is an accounting method of work-in-progress evaluation, for recording long-term contracts. For such tasks, this is the only method authorised by the International Financial Reporting Standards (IFRS.)

Revenues and gross profit are recognized each period based on the construction progress-in other words, the _____.

a. Percentage of Completion
b. Fixed asset
c. Remittance advice
d. Suspense account

71. Businesses often need small amounts of discretionary funds in the form of cash known as _____ for expenditures where it is not practical to make the disbursement by Cheque.

The most common way of accounting expenditures is to use the imprest system. The initial fund would be created by issuing a check for the desired amount.

a. Petty cash
b. Percentage of Completion
c. Construction in Progress
d. Credit memo

72. The term _____ is a term applied to practices that are perfunctory, or seek to satisfy the minimum requirements or to conform to a convention or doctrine. It has different meanings in different fields.

In accounting, _____ earnings are those earnings of companies in addition to actual earnings calculated under the Generally Accepted Accounting Principles (GAAP) in their quarterly and yearly financial reports.

a. Long-term liabilities
b. Deferred financing costs
c. Deferred income
d. Pro forma

73. In financial accounting, _____s are precautions for which the amount or probability of occurrence are not known. Typical examples are _____s for warranty costs and _____ for taxes the term reserve is used instead of term _____; such a use, however, is inconsistent with the terminology suggested by International Accounting Standards Board.

a. Provision
b. Money measurement concept
c. Petty cash
d. Momentum Accounting and Triple-Entry Bookkeeping

74. A _____ in accountancy contains the personal accounts of suppliers from whom the business has bought on credit. (The creditors.) It records information such as invoices received, credit notes received and payments sent.

a. Reserve
b. Purchase ledger
c. Consolidation
d. Goodwill

75. In financial accounting, the term _____ is most commonly used to describe any part of shareholders' equity, except for basic share capital. Sometimes, the term is used instead of the term provision; such a use, however, is inconsistent with the terminology suggested by International Accounting Standards Board. For more information about provisions, see provision (accounting.)

a. Treasury stock
b. Reserve
c. FIFO and LIFO accounting
d. Closing entries

76. In accounting, _____ refers to the portion of net income which is retained by the corporation rather than distributed to its owners as dividends. Similarly, if the corporation makes a loss, then that loss is retained and called variously retained losses, accumulated losses or accumulated deficit. _____ and losses are cumulative from year to year with losses offsetting earnings.

a. Generally Accepted Accounting Principles
b. Matching principle
c. Historical cost
d. Retained earnings

77. In business, _____ is income that a company receives from its normal business activities, usually from the sale of goods and services to customers. Some companies also receive _____ from interest, dividends or royalties paid to them by other companies. _____ may refer to business income in general, or it may refer to the amount, in a monetary unit, received during a period of time, as in 'Last year, Company X had _____ of $32 million.'

In many countries, including the UK, _____ is referred to as turnover.

Chapter 10. Test Preparation Part 10

a. Revenue
c. Furniture, Fixtures and Equipment
b. Matching principle
d. Bottom line

78. _____ are designed to facilitate the process of journalizing and posting transactions. _____ are used for the most frequent transactions in a business. For example, in merchandising businesses, companies acquire merchandise from vendors, and then in turn sell the merchandise to individuals or other businesses.
   a. Floor broker
   c. Special journals
   b. Certified Emission Reductions
   d. Voluntary Emissions Reductions

79. The _____ is one of the basic financial statements as per Generally Accepted Accounting Principles, and it explains the changes in a company's retained earnings over the reporting period. It breaks down changes affecting the account, such as profits or losses from operations, dividends paid, and any other items charged or credited to retained earnings. A retained earnings statement is required by Generally Accepted Accounting Principles (GAAP) whenever comparative balance sheets and income statements are presented.
   a. Notes to the Financial Statements
   c. Statement on Auditing Standards No. 70: Service Organizations
   b. Financial statements
   d. Statement of retained earnings

80. In accountancy, a _____ is an account used temporarily to carry doubtful receipts and disbursements or discrepancies pending their analysis and permanent classification.

It can be a repository for monetary transactions (cash receipts, cash disbursements ' journal entries) entered with invalid account numbers. The account specified may not exist, or it may be deleted/frozen.

   a. Construction in Progress
   c. Petty cash
   b. Remittance advice
   d. Suspense account

81. At its simplest, a company's _____ as it sometimes called, is computed in by multiplying the income before tax number, as reported to shareholders, by the appropriate tax rate. In reality, the computation is typically considerably more complex due to things such as expenses considered not deductible by taxing authorities ('add backs'), the range of tax rates applicable to various levels of income, different tax rates in different jurisdictions, multiple layers of tax on income, and other issues.

Historically, in many places, a revenue-expense method was used, in which the income statement was seen as primary, and the balance sheet as secondary.

   a. Tax expense
   c. Payroll
   b. 529 plan
   d. 4-4-5 Calendar

82. A _____ or reacquired stock is stock which is bought back by the issuing company, reducing the amount of outstanding stock on the open market ('open market' including insiders' holdings.)

Stock repurchases are often used as a tax-efficient method to put cash into shareholders' hands, rather than pay dividends. Sometimes, companies do this when they feel that their stock is undervalued on the open market.

a. Current asset
b. Trial balance
c. Treasury stock
d. Generally Accepted Accounting Principles

83. In accounting, the _____ is a worksheet listing the balance at a certain date, of each ledger account in two columns, namely debit and credit. Under the double-entry system, in any transaction the total of any debits must equal the total of any credits, so in a _____ the total of the debit side should always be equal to the total of the credit side. The _____ thus serves as a tool to detect errors, which can result in the totals not being equal.

a. Long-term liabilities
b. Deferred income
c. Fixed investment
d. Trial balance

84. _____ was developed in the late 1960s and shepherded by the United States Government Accountability Office, (the chief audit arm of the US federal government.) _____ has since spread to most state governments and many closely managed local governments.

Some progressively managed local governments have also begun to employ continuous municipal performance audits, e.g. Baltimore CitiStat, consisting of weekly accountability sessions where senior politicians question staff closely on performance questions.

a. Government performance auditing
b. 7-Eleven
c. 529 plan
d. 4-4-5 Calendar

85. The _____ is a public corporation in the United Kingdom, established under the Local Government Finance Act 1982, to appoint auditors to all local authorities in England and Wales. The National Health Service and Community Care Act 1990 extended the remit of the Commission to cover health service bodies. Legislation covering the Commission's activities was consolidated into the _____ Act 1998.

a. AAB
b. A Random Walk Down Wall Street
c. ABN Amro
d. Audit Commission

86. The role of the _____ is to aid accountability by conducting independent audits of federal government operations. The Auditor General reports to the House of Commons, not to the government. These audits provide members of Parliament with objective information to help them examine the government's activities and hold it to account.

a. Auditor General of Canada
b. A Random Walk Down Wall Street
c. ABN Amro
d. AAB

87. The _____ is the national auditor for the Parliament of Australia and Government of Australia. It reports directly to Parliament but is administratively located in the Portfolio of Prime Minister and Cabinet.

The _____ supports the Auditor-General of Australia, who is an independent officer of the Parliament of Australia.

a. A Random Walk Down Wall Street
b. ABN Amro
c. AAB
d. Australian National Audit Office

88. The _____ is an independent Parliamentary body in the United Kingdom which is responsible for auditing central government departments, government agencies and non-departmental public bodies. The _____ also carries out Value for Money (VFM) audit into the administration of public policy, although not into the merits of policy objectives themselves.

Chapter 10. Test Preparation Part 10

The _____ reports to the Comptroller and Auditor General who is an officer of the House of Commons of the Parliament of the United Kingdom and in turn reports to the Public Accounts Committee, a select committee of the House of Commons.

a. National Audit Office
c. 4-4-5 Calendar
b. 7-Eleven
d. 529 plan

89. The _____ reviews government expenditures and submits an annual report to the Diet. The 1947 _____ Law gives this body substantial independence from both cabinet and Diet control. .
a. Gordon growth model
c. Naked call
b. Selling short
d. Board of Audit

90. The _____ (Federal Court of Auditors; also Federal Audit Office) is the supreme federal authority for federal audit matters in Germany. There are equivalent bodies at state level. The status of the _____, its members and its essential functions are guaranteed by the German Constitution , and regulated by other legislation (i.e. _____ Act, Federal Budget Code.)
a. Joint venture
c. Family and Medical Leave Act
b. Limited liability
d. Bundesrechnungshof

91. The _____ is an independent auditing institution established in Egypt in 1942 as an instrument of public finance control. Originally created as the Divan of Accounting, its name was changed to Divan of Auditing in 1960, before acquiring its current designation in 1964. It supervises the management of public-sector companies and government departments.
a. 7-Eleven
c. 4-4-5 Calendar
b. 529 plan
d. Central Auditing Organization

92. In the UK the _____ , conducted by the Audit Commission, aims to assess the performance of every local authority and the services that they provide for local people. This will be replaced by the Comprehensive Area Assessment in April 2009.

The Audit Commission conducts the _____ to help councils to focus on improvement, comprising evidence from other external review bodies plus the Audit Commission's judgements.

a. Variable Interest Entity
c. 4-4-5 Calendar
b. 529 plan
d. Comprehensive Performance Assessment

93. A _____ (more commonly, _____) is a government financial statement, which goes beyond the minimums established for public sector companies by NCGA statement 1. Public sector companies will not have a statistical section in their Annual Financial Report (AFR) A _____ has three major sections : Introductory, financial, and statistical. The _____ is created with a showing offund accounting and Enterprise Authority accounting.
a. Comprehensive Performance Assessment
c. 529 plan
b. 4-4-5 Calendar
d. Comprehensive annual financial report

94. In management accounting, _____ is that part of management accounting which establishes budget and actual cost of operations, processes, departments or product and the analysis of variances, profitability or social use of funds. Managers use _____ to support decision making to reduce a company's costs and improve its profitability. As a form of management accounting, _____ need not follow standards such as GAAP, because its primary use is for internal managers, rather than external users, and what to compute is instead decided pragmatically.

    a. Cost Accounting   b. Variable costs
    c. Sliding scale fees   d. Marginal cost

95. _____ are a set of 19 standards and rules promulgated by the United States Government for use in determining costs on negotiated procurements. _____ differs from the Federal Acquisition Regulation (FAR) in that FAR applies to substantially all contractors, whereas _____ applies primarily to the larger ones.

In 1970, Congress established the original _____ Board (_____B) to 1) promulgate _____ designed to achieve uniformity and consistency in the cost accounting principles followed by defense contractors and subcontractors under Federal contracts in excess of $100,000 and 2) establish regulations to require defense contractors and subcontractors, as a condition of contracting, to disclose in writing their cost accounting practices, to follow the disclosed practices consistently and to comply with promulgated _____.

    a. Cost Accounting Standards   b. State Auditor of Mississippi
    c. 529 plan   d. 4-4-5 Calendar

96. The _____ is a French government quasi-judicial body charged with conducting audits of most public institutions and some private institutions, including the central government, national public corporations, social security bodies (since 1950) and public services (since 1976.)

The three missions of the court are the verification of the compliance of accounts; verification of management; and provision of assistance to Parliament and the government. The court checks whether accounting is in good form, and whether public funds have been well-employed.

    a. 4-4-5 Calendar   b. 7-Eleven
    c. Cour des Comptes   d. 529 plan

97. The _____ is a Belgian governmental institution established by article 180 of the Belgian Constitution. The Court of Audit is a collateral body of the Belgian Federal Parliament and exerts external control on the budgetary, accounting and financial operations of the Federal State, the Communities, the Regions, the public service institutions and the provinces. The task of the Court of Audit is defined in its organic law of 29 October 1846.

    a. Court of Audit of Belgium   b. Business valuation
    c. Bundesrechnungshof   d. Law of one price

98. A _____ is an exchange of promises between two or more parties to do an act which is enforceable in a court of law. It is where an unqualified offer meets a qualified acceptance and the parties reach Consensus ad Idem. The parties must have the necessary capacity to _____ and the _____ must not be either trifling, indeterminate, impossible or illegal.

    a. 7-Eleven   b. Contract
    c. 4-4-5 Calendar   d. 529 plan

Chapter 10. Test Preparation Part 10

99. The _____, under the authority, direction, and control of the United States Under Secretary of Defense (Comptroller), is responsible for performing all contract audits for the United States Department of Defense (DoD) (and, to a lesser extent, to other agencies outside DoD), and providing accounting and financial advisory services regarding contracts and subcontracts to all DoD Components responsible for procurement and contract administration. These services are provided in connection with negotiation, administration, and settlement of contracts and subcontracts.

Audits of military contracts can be traced back 60 years or more.

   a. Defense Contract Audit Agency   b. 4-4-5 Calendar
   c. 7-Eleven   d. 529 plan

100. The role of the _____ is to ensure the financial order of the Hong Kong Government and heads the Audit Commission. This role is similar to that of auditor generals or auditors in other jurisdictions. The director reports directly to the Chief Executive of Hong Kong.

   a. 529 plan   b. 4-4-5 Calendar
   c. 7-Eleven   d. Director of Audit

101. The _____ is the fifth institution of the European Union (EU.) It was established in 1975 in Luxembourg to audit the accounts of EU institutions. The Court is composed of one member from each EU member state and its current president (as of 2008) is Vítor Manuel da Silva Caldeira.

   a. AAB   b. A Random Walk Down Wall Street
   c. European Court of Auditors   d. ABN Amro

102. The phrase _____ refers to the aspect of corporate strategy, corporate finance and management dealing with the buying, selling and combining of different companies that can aid, finance, or help a growing company in a given industry grow rapidly without having to create another business entity.

An acquisition, also known as a takeover, is the buying of one company (the 'target') by another. An acquisition may be friendly or hostile.

   a. 4-4-5 Calendar   b. 529 plan
   c. 7-Eleven   d. Mergers and acquisitions

103. The _____ is the principal set of rules in the _____ System. That system consists of sets of regulations issued by agencies of the Federal government of the United States to govern what is called the 'acquisition process,' which is the process through which the government purchases ('acquires') goods and services. That process consists of three phases: (1) need recognition and acquisition planning, (2) contract formation, and (3) contract administration. The _____ System regulates the activities of government personnel in carrying out that process.

   a. Legal tender   b. Federal Acquisition Regulations
   c. Loan agreement   d. Bond indenture

104. A _____ an audit of financial statements, is the review of the financial statements of a company or any other legal entity (including governments), resulting in the publication of an independent opinion on whether or not those financial statements are relevant, accurate, complete, and fairly presented.

_____s are typically performed by firms of practicing accountants due to the specialist financial reporting knowledge they require. The _____ is one of many assurance or attestation functions provided by accounting and auditing firms, whereby the firm provides an independent opinion on published information.

a. Provided by client
b. Lead Auditor
c. Joint audit
d. Financial Audit

105. In the United States, a _____ is one of the five fund types established by GAAP classified as a government fund, put simply a _____ may be used to generate and disperse money to those entitled to receive payments by qualification or agreement, as in the case of Alaska citizens or residents that satisfy the rules for payment from their permanet fund from State oil revenues. It was first introduced through GASB Statement 34. The name of the fund comes from the purpose of the fund: a sum of equity used to permanently generate payments to maintain some financial obligation.

a. 529 plan
b. 7-Eleven
c. 4-4-5 Calendar
d. Permanent fund

106. In the United States, the _____ is a rigorous, organization-wide audit or examination of an entity that expends $500,000 or more of Federal assistance received for its operations. Usually performed annually, the _____'s objective is to provide assurance to the US federal government as to the management and use of such funds by different recipients, such as States, cities, universities, and non-profit organizations, among others. The audit is typically performed by an independent certified public accountant and encompasses both financial and compliance components.

a. Single Audit
b. 7-Eleven
c. 4-4-5 Calendar
d. 529 plan

107. _____ is an Israel Defense Forces unit which supervises and oversees the fitness, preparedness, and legality of the Israeli Security Forces' activities, in all its parts. It reports to the Minister of Defense, Director-general of the Ministry of Defense, and the Chief of Staff on these issues.

The body was established in 1976 and was originally subordinate to what then the Operations Directorate (the most senior branch in the IDF.)

a. 7-Eleven
b. 4-4-5 Calendar
c. 529 plan
d. Defense Establishment Comptroller Unit

108. The _____ is an amalgamation of The Society of Public Accountants which was founded in 1989, and the _____ which was formed in 1991. The Association represents wholly and exclusively the interests of the practising Certified Public Accountant in the United Kingdom.

The Associations headquarters are in Wigan, England.

a. Audit Command Language
b. International Federation of Accountants
c. Association of Certified Public Accountants
d. Institute of Financial Accountants

109. _____ is the statutory title of qualified accountants in the United States who have passed the Uniform _____ Examination and have met additional state education and experience requirements for certification as a _____. In most U.S. states, only _____s who are licensed are able to provide to the public attestation (including auditing) opinions on financial statements. The exceptions to this rule are Arizona, Kansas, North Carolina and Ohio where, although the '_____' designation is restricted, the practice of auditing is not.
   a. Chartered Accountant
   b. Chartered Certified Accountant
   c. Certified Public Accountant
   d. Certified General Accountant

110. A _____ is when an entity displays its financial statements or other financial information in a currency that is different from either its functional currency or its presentation currency simply by translating all amounts at end-of-period exchange rates. A result of making a _____ is that the resulting financial information does not comply with all Generally Accepted Accounting Principles.
   a. Consumer lending
   b. Clientele effect
   c. Carrying charge
   d. Convenience translation

111. A _____ is a type of business entity in which partners (owners) share with each other the profits or losses of the business undertaking in which all have invested. _____s are often favored over corporations for taxation purposes, as the _____ structure does not generally incur a tax on profits before it is distributed to the partners (i.e. there is no dividend tax levied.) However, depending on the _____ structure and the jurisdiction in which it operates, owners of a _____ may be exposed to greater personal liability than they would as shareholders of a corporation.
   a. Fiduciary
   b. Partnership
   c. National Securities Markets Improvement Act of 1996
   d. Clayton Antitrust Act

112. _____ is the provision of resources (such as granting a loan) by one party to another party where that second party does not reimburse the first party immediately, thereby generating a debt, and instead arranges either to repay or return those resources (or material(s) of equal value) at a later date. The first party is called a creditor, also known as a lender, while the second party is called a debtor, also known as a borrower.

Movements of financial capital are normally dependent on either _____ or equity transfers.

   a. Clearing house
   b. Comparable
   c. Credit
   d. Warrant

113. A _____ is a cooperative financial institution that is owned and controlled by its members, and operated for the purpose of promoting thrift, providing credit at reasonable rates, and providing other financial services to its members. Many _____s exist to further community development or sustainable international development on a local level. Worldwide, _____ systems vary significantly in terms of total system assets and average institution asset size since _____s exist in a wide range of sizes, ranging from volunteer operations with a handful of members to institutions with several billion dollars in assets and hundreds of thousands of members.
   a. Credit Union Service Organization
   b. Fi-linx
   c. Corporate credit union
   d. Credit union

114. The _____ is a method of evaluating the health of credit unions by the National Credit Union Administration. The rating is based upon five critical elements of a credit union's operations: capital adequacy, asset quality, management, earnings and asset/liability management. This rating system is designed to take into account and reflect all significant financial and operational factors examiners assess in their evaluation of a credit union's performance.

a. Corporate credit union
c. Credit Union Service Organization
b. Credit union
d. CAMEL rating system

Chapter 11. Test Preparation Part 11

1. A _____ provides services to natural person credit unions. In the credit union industry, they are sometimes referred to as 'the credit union's credit union'. _____s may either be chartered by the National Credit Union Administration, or under state authority if permitted under that state's financial services laws.
   a. Credit union
   b. Corporate credit union
   c. Fi-linx
   d. Credit Union Service Organization

2. _____ is the provision of resources (such as granting a loan) by one party to another party where that second party does not reimburse the first party immediately, thereby generating a debt, and instead arranges either to repay or return those resources (or material(s) of equal value) at a later date. The first party is called a creditor, also known as a lender, while the second party is called a debtor, also known as a borrower.

   Movements of financial capital are normally dependent on either _____ or equity transfers.

   a. Credit
   b. Warrant
   c. Comparable
   d. Clearing house

3. A _____ is a cooperative financial institution that is owned and controlled by its members, and operated for the purpose of promoting thrift, providing credit at reasonable rates, and providing other financial services to its members. Many _____s exist to further community development or sustainable international development on a local level. Worldwide, _____ systems vary significantly in terms of total system assets and average institution asset size since _____s exist in a wide range of sizes, ranging from volunteer operations with a handful of members to institutions with several billion dollars in assets and hundreds of thousands of members.
   a. Credit Union Service Organization
   b. Credit union
   c. Fi-linx
   d. Corporate credit union

4. In United States federal law, a _____ allows a credit union the ability to conduct business that they would otherwise be restricted from due to regulatory constraints. Most _____s are limited liability companies (LLC) which also provide a measure of protection to the credit union from the actions of their _____. _____s are usually wholly-owned subsidiaries of their corresponding credit union, and most if not all of the profits generated by a _____ are returned to the credit union.
   a. Credit union
   b. Fi-linx
   c. Corporate credit union
   d. Credit Union Service Organization

5. _____ (intentionally lower-case) is a Credit Union Service Organization owned by MaPS Service Agency, a subsidiary of MaPS Credit Union, and headquartered in Salem, Oregon. A financial software development company, _____ products are specifically marketed to credit unions. The company has been featured in credit industry related publications such as the Credit Union Times and the Credit Union Journal and their services are offered both directly and through the Credit Union Executives Society (CUES.)
   a. Corporate credit union
   b. Credit union
   c. Credit Union Service Organization
   d. Fi-linx

6. The _____ is a credit union and consumer finance think tank, committed to research and innovation to further the credit union movement. The Institute was founded in 1989 and is named for Boston-based United States credit union pioneer, Edward Filene. The _____ is headquartered in Madison, Wisconsin.
   a. 7-Eleven
   b. 4-4-5 Calendar
   c. 529 plan
   d. Filene Research Institute

7. _____ are a state-sanctioned means of providing credit in rural areas in the People's Republic of China.

In the 1950s, a network of _____ was created. At this time, they were not commercial enterprises similar to banks, but rather channeled credit between the state and the people's communes in rural areas.

- a. Reputational risk
- b. Rural credit cooperatives
- c. Time-based currency
- d. Foreign Language and Area Studies

8. The _____ is the audit, evaluation, and investigative arm of the United States Congress. It is located in the Legislative branch of the United States government.

The _____ was established as the General Accounting Office by the Budget and Accounting Act of 1921 (Pub.L.

- a. 7-Eleven
- b. 4-4-5 Calendar
- c. 529 plan
- d. Government Accountability Office

9. The _____ of 2004 (Pub.L. 108-271, 118 Stat. 811) is a United States federal law designed to provide new human capital flexibilities with respect to the Government Accountability Office, and for other purposes.
- a. 4-4-5 Calendar
- b. GAO Human Capital Reform Act
- c. Public Utility Holding Company Act
- d. 529 plan

10. _____ refers to the stock of skills and knowledge embodied in the ability to perform labor so as to produce economic value. Many early economic theories refer to it simply as labor, one of three factors of production, and consider it to be a fungible resource -- homogeneous and easily interchangeable. Other conceptions of labor dispense with these assumptions.
- a. Behavioral finance
- b. Mercantilism
- c. Market structure
- d. Human Capital

11. _____ are typically audits in which the Government Accountability Office (GAO), the United States Congress' investigative arm, studies how the Department of Defense spends taxpayer dollars. Since the GAO is accountable only to the legislative branch, it is in a unique position to investigate the military; no other agency can audit Federal departments with the same degree of independence from the President. However, the GAO is still subject to influence from powerful members of Congress.
- a. 529 plan
- b. 4-4-5 Calendar
- c. 7-Eleven
- d. Government Accountability Office investigations of the Department of Defense

ANSWER KEY

Chapter 1

1. c	2. d	3. d	4. d	5. c	6. b	7. a	8. d	9. b	10. c
11. a	12. d	13. c	14. b	15. b	16. d	17. d	18. d	19. d	20. a
21. c	22. d	23. a	24. d	25. d	26. b	27. d	28. d	29. b	30. a
31. c	32. d	33. c	34. d	35. c	36. d	37. d	38. b	39. c	40. a
41. d	42. b	43. d	44. d	45. d	46. d	47. d	48. c	49. d	50. a
51. d	52. c	53. c	54. c	55. d	56. c	57. d	58. d	59. c	60. d
61. c	62. d	63. d	64. c	65. d	66. a	67. c	68. c	69. c	70. a
71. d	72. d	73. d	74. b	75. c	76. d	77. d	78. b	79. b	80. d
81. c	82. a	83. a	84. d	85. a	86. b	87. a	88. d	89. d	90. d
91. a	92. d	93. c	94. d	95. d	96. a	97. d	98. d	99. a	100. c
101. d	102. a	103. b	104. c	105. a	106. d	107. d	108. d	109. c	110. d
111. d	112. c	113. d	114. a	115. a	116. d	117. b	118. d	119. d	120. b
121. a	122. d	123. c	124. b	125. b	126. a	127. c	128. b	129. c	

Chapter 2

1. d	2. d	3. d	4. b	5. d	6. d	7. a	8. c	9. b	10. d
11. c	12. d	13. d	14. a	15. d	16. d	17. a	18. d	19. b	20. a
21. c	22. d	23. d	24. a	25. a	26. a	27. c	28. d	29. a	30. d
31. b	32. b	33. c	34. d	35. d	36. d	37. c	38. b	39. d	40. a
41. c	42. d	43. a	44. d	45. a	46. d	47. b	48. a	49. a	50. a
51. a	52. c	53. b	54. d	55. a	56. d	57. d	58. d	59. b	60. a
61. c	62. c	63. d	64. d	65. b	66. d	67. c	68. a	69. d	70. b
71. b	72. d	73. b	74. c	75. d	76. d	77. b	78. d	79. d	80. b
81. d	82. b	83. a	84. a	85. c	86. d	87. d	88. d	89. a	90. a
91. a	92. d	93. d	94. c	95. d	96. b	97. d	98. c	99. b	100. d
101. d	102. d	103. c	104. a	105. b	106. d	107. d	108. d	109. a	110. d
111. a	112. c	113. a	114. d	115. c	116. d	117. b	118. c	119. c	120. d
121. d	122. d	123. d	124. d	125. c	126. d	127. d	128. d	129. d	130. d
131. d	132. c	133. b	134. d	135. c					

Chapter 3

1. c	2. d	3. d	4. b	5. d	6. b	7. d	8. b	9. b	10. d
11. b	12. d	13. a	14. b	15. a	16. a	17. b	18. c	19. b	20. d
21. a	22. d	23. d	24. c	25. d	26. d	27. d	28. c	29. d	30. d
31. b	32. b	33. d	34. d	35. d	36. b	37. c	38. d	39. a	40. b
41. d	42. b	43. b	44. d	45. a	46. d	47. d	48. d	49. d	50. d
51. a	52. a	53. d	54. d	55. d	56. c	57. d	58. c	59. b	60. c
61. b	62. b	63. d	64. b	65. d	66. d	67. a	68. c	69. d	70. d
71. d	72. d	73. d	74. d	75. d	76. c	77. d	78. d	79. d	80. c
81. c	82. c	83. a	84. d	85. d	86. b	87. d	88. a	89. c	90. d
91. b	92. d	93. d	94. c	95. a	96. b	97. d			

Chapter 4

1. a	2. c	3. d	4. d	5. c	6. d	7. d	8. a	9. a	10. a
11. d	12. b	13. b	14. a	15. d	16. d	17. a	18. a	19. b	20. b
21. a	22. d	23. c	24. b	25. d	26. a	27. c	28. a	29. d	30. d
31. d	32. d	33. d	34. c	35. c	36. a	37. d	38. d	39. c	40. d
41. d	42. d	43. a	44. d	45. d	46. d	47. a	48. d	49. c	50. d
51. d	52. b	53. b	54. a	55. a	56. d	57. d	58. b	59. b	60. d
61. c	62. d	63. d	64. d	65. d	66. b	67. d	68. b	69. d	70. b
71. c	72. d	73. d	74. d	75. d	76. d	77. c	78. d	79. c	80. c
81. d	82. d	83. a	84. c	85. a	86. d	87. c	88. d	89. d	90. d
91. d	92. d	93. d	94. a	95. b	96. c	97. d	98. b	99. d	100. a
101. a									

Chapter 5

1. d	2. a	3. c	4. c	5. a	6. d	7. d	8. d	9. a	10. d
11. d	12. a	13. d	14. b	15. d	16. a	17. d	18. a	19. a	20. a
21. a	22. d	23. d	24. b	25. c	26. d	27. d	28. d	29. a	30. b
31. a	32. d	33. d	34. a	35. a	36. d	37. b	38. c	39. d	40. d
41. a	42. c								

Chapter 6

1. c	2. d	3. b	4. a	5. d	6. b	7. c	8. d	9. c	10. a
11. c	12. b	13. d	14. b	15. c	16. b	17. d	18. a	19. d	20. c
21. b	22. a	23. a	24. a	25. b	26. c	27. d	28. a	29. d	30. c
31. c	32. d	33. b	34. c	35. c	36. d	37. a	38. c	39. c	40. d
41. c	42. d	43. b	44. b	45. c	46. a	47. d	48. c	49. d	50. d
51. d	52. d	53. c	54. d	55. d	56. d				

Chapter 7

1. d	2. d	3. c	4. c	5. d	6. a	7. d	8. a	9. a	10. d
11. a	12. a	13. d	14. b	15. b	16. c	17. d	18. d	19. c	20. d
21. d	22. a	23. d	24. c	25. d	26. d	27. d	28. d	29. d	30. d
31. d	32. d	33. a	34. d	35. d	36. d	37. d	38. a	39. d	40. a
41. b	42. d	43. c	44. b	45. d	46. b	47. b	48. d	49. d	50. b
51. d	52. d	53. d	54. a	55. d	56. d	57. d	58. d	59. b	60. d
61. d	62. d	63. d	64. d	65. b	66. c	67. b	68. d	69. c	70. a
71. c	72. d	73. b	74. d	75. a	76. c	77. a	78. a	79. b	80. a
81. c	82. c	83. d	84. a	85. d	86. d	87. b	88. c	89. c	90. d
91. c	92. c	93. d	94. a	95. d					

ANSWER KEY

Chapter 8

1. a	2. d	3. d	4. c	5. d	6. d	7. d	8. c	9. d	10. d
11. d	12. b	13. b	14. c	15. d	16. d	17. a	18. d	19. b	20. d
21. c	22. c	23. d	24. d	25. b	26. c	27. d	28. b	29. d	30. b
31. c	32. c	33. a	34. d	35. d	36. a	37. d	38. d	39. d	40. b
41. c	42. d	43. d	44. b	45. d	46. d	47. b	48. c	49. d	50. a
51. d	52. d	53. a	54. d	55. d	56. d	57. b	58. b	59. b	60. d
61. d	62. b	63. d	64. d	65. d	66. d	67. a	68. d	69. d	70. c
71. d	72. a	73. d	74. d	75. d	76. b	77. d	78. d	79. c	80. a
81. d	82. d	83. d	84. b	85. d	86. a	87. a	88. d	89. b	90. d
91. b	92. a	93. a	94. b	95. c	96. a	97. d	98. d	99. d	100. d
101. c	102. c	103. d	104. d	105. d	106. b				

Chapter 9

1. b	2. d	3. d	4. c	5. d	6. d	7. b	8. a	9. d	10. d
11. d	12. d	13. b	14. d	15. b	16. c	17. c	18. d	19. a	20. d
21. d	22. d	23. d	24. d	25. d	26. c	27. d	28. a	29. d	30. d
31. d	32. d	33. d	34. d	35. c	36. c	37. d	38. d	39. b	40. d
41. c	42. c	43. c	44. a	45. d	46. c	47. b	48. c	49. b	50. a
51. c	52. c	53. d	54. d	55. d	56. d	57. b	58. b	59. d	60. b
61. b	62. c	63. d	64. c	65. d	66. b	67. d	68. c		

Chapter 10

1. a	2. d	3. b	4. d	5. a	6. d	7. b	8. a	9. d	10. b
11. a	12. d	13. a	14. a	15. c	16. c	17. c	18. a	19. d	20. c
21. c	22. a	23. d	24. c	25. c	26. b	27. c	28. d	29. d	30. d
31. d	32. d	33. d	34. a	35. c	36. b	37. c	38. d	39. a	40. d
41. b	42. b	43. d	44. b	45. b	46. b	47. c	48. d	49. b	50. d
51. d	52. c	53. a	54. a	55. c	56. c	57. d	58. d	59. a	60. d
61. b	62. d	63. d	64. d	65. a	66. d	67. a	68. c	69. d	70. a
71. a	72. d	73. a	74. b	75. b	76. d	77. a	78. c	79. d	80. d
81. a	82. c	83. d	84. a	85. d	86. a	87. d	88. a	89. d	90. d
91. d	92. d	93. d	94. a	95. a	96. c	97. a	98. b	99. a	100. d
101. c	102. d	103. b	104. d	105. d	106. a	107. d	108. c	109. c	110. d
111. b	112. c	113. d	114. d						

Chapter 11

1. b	2. a	3. b	4. d	5. d	6. d	7. b	8. d	9. b	10. d
11. d									

www.ingramcontent.com/pod-product-compliance
Lightning Source LLC
Chambersburg PA
CBHW081351230426
43667CB00017B/2799